MADMAN'S JHOLI

In Dialogue with a God-Intoxicated Soul

SRI SRI SITARAMDAS OMKARNATH

Translated into English by Dr. Nirmal Kumar Panigrahi.
Edited by Vikas Shukla.

CELESTIAL
BOOKS

ISBN 978-93-82473-68-8
© Omkarnath Mission, the International Welfare Unit of Akhil
Bharat Jai Guru Sampradaya, 2013

Cover Design   Aniruddha Mukherjee
Layouts   Ajay Shah
Printing   Jasmine Art Printers Pvt. Ltd.   .

Published in India 2013 by
CELESTIAL BOOKS
An imprint of
LEADSTART PUBLISHING PVT LTD
Trade Centre Level 1, Bandra Kurla Complex,
Bandra (E) Mumbai 400 051, INDIA
T + 91 22 40700804   **F** +91 22 40700800
E info@leadstartcorp.com **W** www.leadstartcorp.com
US Office Axis Corp, 7845 E Oakbrook Circle,
Madison, WI 53717, USA

CONTENTS

FOREWORD

Two years ago, when Dr. Nirmal Kumar Panigrahi (M.A., LLB., P.R.S., Ph. D., Sankhya-Vedantatirtha, F.R.A.S.) handed over the manuscript of this book (a product of an old typewriter) to me, I was mad with joy. Here was a chronicle of a saint and mystic that people had been looking for. Dr. Panigrahi had rendered it in English with remarkable elegance and it was time for it to reach the seekers.

The title of this book Madman's Jholi is an amusing one. It raises the obvious questions: who is the madman? What's in his Jholi (bag)?

Sri Sri Sitaramdas Omkarnath used to carry a Jholi (bag). On one occasion around 1923, when he visited Ramdayal Majumdar, a notable disciple of Lahiri Mahasaya, the latter said: "Tomar khepar jhuli te ja achhe amai dao" (give me whatever is there in that madman's bag of yours). A bouquet of most wonderful essays on spirituality was the result of that request. While Khepar Jhuli got published in Bengali only on Janmashthami, in August 1951, some of the essays started getting published as early as 1923 in a magazine called 'Utsav'. Around 1961, Prof. S. C. Sarkar translated some of these pieces and published them in the pages of the magazine The Mother (now revived online at www.themotherdivine.com), but the complete translation was to be inspired by Dr. Panigrahi.

Coming back to madness, the following passages from this book will acquaint us with the nature of madness of the madman in this book.

'Sitaram Sitaram. Not only am I mad, but my father and mother are also mad. The Father has gone mad and sings the name of Rama from his five mouths. He plays the damaru and dances. Father had been very calm but went mad only because of the Mother. She too has become mad and dances wildly on the Father's chest. She feels no shame and has no time to put on her clothes. When will the one who has to give birth to millions of worlds every moment, get time to wear clothes?'

"It is not easy to be mad. A madman, who is rational, cannot find the Mother. You will never find the Mother if you do not go mad for good. A 'sane' madman by cunning will never find the real 'Ma'. Do you not know, this world around is a pure imagined thing? It is the core of Shri Nath's tale. Open your eyes and see. With detachment at your side set out to seek the Truth chanting the name of 'Kali'. Go mad in love and·dance in defense of accusation you are completely mad!"

Having understood the true nature of this madness, we can hardly dismiss the madman's dialogues as the raving of a madcap. We have, in fact, a great saint discoursing in the guise of a madman. Sri Sri Sitaramdas Omkarnath's wisdom finds expression in the utterances of a 'Madman', who is mad in love of the Divine. Madman's replies to visitors' queries spring spontaneously from the deep state of enlightenment of Sitaramdas and his vast knowledge of scriptures. This text brings unaccountable grace of God and embodies profound truth.

As we know, there are varieties of *jivanmuktas*, the liberated souls. They are all curious persons. One does not behave in the same way as the other. Jadabharata was like an idiot. He would not talk to anybody; he sat there like a stone. Shuka did not even know that he had a body. He would walk like a raving mad man, and children would pelt stones at him, thinking that he was crazy. Bauls are mad. In Sufi philosophy, a *mast* (pronounced "must") is a person who is overcome with love for God, with concomitant external disorientation resembling intoxication. Ramakrishna Paramhamsa was mad from God-intoxication and so were so many others. This is a happy madness— something one can pray for!

The specialty of these 'mad' essays is that they are essentially discussions in dialogue forms entailing conversations between *khepa* (Sri Sri Sitaramdas Omkarnath Himself) and various seekers. The style is dramatic yet simple on topics of high profundity such as *Kundalini, Omkar, Atma,* and other such subjects, no aspect of spiritual life is left untouched.

Madman argues with the modern man, one unfamiliar with Shastras and unwilling to subscribe to blind faith. He tells us how to approach the Guru, how the mantra is fulfilled, what are the pitfalls in the journey, what is true realization. He proves existence of the soul, maps out the stages of spiritual path and its perfection. He conducts the seeker to the innermost recesses of the heart. He teaches how to meditate on God in the form of the pure Omkara, steady as a lamp. The devotee goes straight into the world of eternal joy, overflowing with waves of light and nectar. Madman makes the truth manifest in the Brahma-conscious heart lotus of the reader. As we read, there is only glorious effulgence on all sides; we almost feel that light of Brahma that is blazing in the higher worlds. He throws open the doors of the subtle Sushumna, light begins to play outside and inside and a tear-filled Samadhi is imminent. Served between the covers of the book, is an ocean of knowledge and spiritual nectar. How much one imbibes is limited only by the size of one's thirst.

I would like to express my heartfelt gratitude to Kinkar Vitthal Ramanuj Maharaj for always igniting the words of Sri Sri Sitaramdas Omkarnath in his writings and discourses; his inspiration has been the motivation for publication of so many important texts.

Vikas Shukla edited this book diligently, Aniruddha Mukherjee designed the beautiful cover, Urvi Dutt set the canvas for the text, Lopamudra Roy Dasgupta swiftly went through the proofs and Swarup Nanda made sure this book is published – to all of them, we owe sincere thanks.

Tears stream from the madman's eyes, he bathes his Guru's feet with his tears, he becomes overwhelmed, his body shivers with ecstasy, he begins to dance with abandon and he floats in the sea of joy as he discourses. In this madhouse of the world, one learns from this book what only a super madman can teach!

Raj Supe (Kinkar Vishwashreyananda)
Hanuman Jayanti, 2013- Rishikesh.

ॐ ॐ ॐ

1. The Soul's Self-evidence

In the twilight on the lonely banks of the Ganga, the madman finished his evening prayers. In a trance-like state, he sang long to himself:

'Ram Krishna Ram Krishna Ram Krishna Hare Hare'

As he sang, he cried, then laughed and after a while became silent.

Something made him turn around. There sat a Brahmin youth behind him.

The youth bowed and said, 'I have been looking for you these last few days.'

The Madman said, 'Me! Why?'

The Brahmin said, 'Ever since I heard what you had said the other day, I wanted to ask you a few questions.'

Madman   : What have you to ask?

Brahmin   : See, I have neither read the Shastras nor interacted with Sadhus. I have received modern education. I have no blind faith. Please make me understand why one should admit the existence of the soul.

Madman   : Son, you want to pour ten litres of milk
             in a pot that can take just one ounce. The
             knowledge of the nature of the soul is almost
             completely beyond one's grasp. I myself have
             not been able to understand it, then how can
             I explain it to you? Besides, you will neither
             listen to the Shastras nor believe in what the
             Sadhus have to say.

Brahmin   : I know nothing. Please explain in a simple
             language that there is a soul separate from
             the body.

Madman   : Do you admit that there are these two things;
             matter and consciousness?

Brahmin   : How is consciousness different? Everything
             is matter.

Madman   : If everything is matter, whose power enables
             you to see, move and hear? How is it that
             you are alive?

Brahmin   : Combinations of different types of matter
             spontaneously give rise to the vibration of
             life. Then why should we admit the existence
             of the soul? As lime and turmeric when
             mixed together turn red, life is created when
             blood, flesh, fat, marrow and bone are mixed
             together. Where do you find the soul in this?

Madman   : If it is so, then why doesn't a living being last
             the same way as does the colour of the lime
             and turmeric mixture? Why are happiness,
             sorrow, disease and grief of different kinds?

And why does it happen that someone is blind, another is disabled, someone is rich while someone else is penniless? If the same mix of blood, flesh and bones creates life in all the creatures, then why does death come upon them in different ways? Why does someone die in boyhood, some in youth and the others in old age?

Brahmin : All this is due to differences in the proportion of the constituents.

Madman : Why do these materials get combined in differing proportions? Moreover, if you look at a dead body, all the materials or ingredients of that body are there but why is it not alive? The analogy of lime and turmeric advanced by you does not at all hold well, because lime and turmeric when mixed together lose their original appearance and form a different substance. But blood, flesh and bones, collected together, undergo no transformation and yet a spark of life is created. What is this? Where is the similarity between these two things you compared?

Brahmin : Pray do not use the mechanics of logic or complex terms to convince me. Could you please explain in simple language?

Madman : Well, if life is a mixture of matter, why does any mixture of flesh and blood not come alive when put together? Why can't you give life to it?

Brahmin : Don't say that, because science has not yet reached its full development. Why must I admit the existence of the soul only because today I cannot make such mixture come alive? This is not fair. In future, someone may be able to do this.

Madman : How can I ignore a self-evident fact today on the basis that someone may or may not be able to confirm it at some point in time in the future? Well, if I speak of your house do you understand that you and your house are two different things?

Brahmin : Yes, Sir.

Madman : Your hands, legs, eyes, nose, blood, flesh, body all are yours. Then are 'you' separate from your body? Just as you are not these also, that self of yours that is beyond your body and other things is a soul.

Brahmin : You are again trying to convince me by logical reasoning!

Madman : Look, when you are not able to argue, you protest about 'the trap of logical reasoning'! Well, son, why is your body unconscious when you sleep? If life is a compound of matter, then why does it assume different states in waking, dreaming and dreamless sleep? Who takes it to the dreaming state from the waking state? Who passes on from the dreaming to the dreamless sleeping state? Can you say who again brings it to the waking state?

Brahmin : That is Swabhava (own state). Dream is nothing. Activities and thoughts of the day remain as impressions in the brain and are expressed in dreams.

Madman : But sometimes we dream of things that have not been thought of or experienced at all. Sometimes there are no dreams. Had it been Swabhava, dreams would have happened consistently. Sometimes it occurs and other times it does not. What sort of Swabhava is it? What does Swabhava mean?

Brahmin : Swabhava means Prakriti (nature).

Madman : Well, well, that which experiences the Prakriti is the soul.

Brahmin : Who can be the experiencer of Prakriti? It is everything.

Madman : No-no, Prakriti is not everything. Prakriti consisting of twenty four constituents (Tattvas) is an object of experience and the soul is its user. A bed made of quilt, sheet and pillow suggests that, there is someone to sleep on it. Similarly, Prakriti implies there is a soul (Purusha) experiencing it.

Brahmin : Are you speaking of the scriptural doctrines?

Madman : Son, how can I say anything 'un-scriptural'?

Brahmin   : I could not understand your words properly.

Madman   : Suppose, the river Ganga in front of you is the object, the eyes are the instruments and he who sees with their help is the soul. The scent of a flower is the object. He who smells it with the nose is the soul. Ganga makes a rushing sound as it flows towards the sea. This sound is the object, the ears are the instruments. He who hears the sound with his ears is the soul.

Brahmin   : What is it that you say? Please point out and make the soul apparent to me.

Madman   : What do you mean by apparent?

Brahmin   : What is seen with the eyes is apparent. No intelligent person can believe without seeing with one's eyes. What is not directly seen does not exist.

Madman   : Well, you intelligent person, you are blind, so how will you see?

Brahmin   : Well, here are my eyes.

Madman   : Who says that these are eyes? Can you directly see your own eyes?

Brahman   : Sir, Sir......

Madman   : Do not say, Sir, Sir. If you do not directly see your own eyes then as per your own reasoning you must admit that you are blind.

14

You did not see your grandfather, does that mean that your grandfather did not exist? You do not see your wife and son now. Then have you no wife and son? You cannot see your hunger and thirst. Then have you no hunger and thirst?

Brahmin : Well, Sir, I can see my eyes when I place a mirror in front of me. By simple inference, my grandfather existed because I exist. I can see my wife and son if I go home. Then how my eyes, grandfather, wife and son are not apparent?

Madman : Good, good, so you admit use of inference. If you use the mirror of intelligence that is lit up by the light of Shastras, you can see the soul. As one can infer the existence of your grandfather from your own existence, similarly existence of the soul as the rider can be inferred from the existence of the chariot (the body), the horses (the senses) and the charioteer (the discriminative thought). As you can see your wife and children when you go near them, so you can see the soul when you come near it.

Brahmin : Sir, I have been defeated by you in argument but I still cannot understand the soul.

Madman : Sir, you cannot understand what the soul is. I made the mistake of beginning a discussion about the soul with you. If a blind man is told, 'Look, there rises the Sun!' he cannot see the Sun, though the Sun is self-evident. Similarly, you lack the means of seeing the soul though it is self-evident. You will not be able to grasp the idea of soul even if given a thousand explanations based on Shrutis, logic and realization. This life of yours is that of a creature of little intellect. You will not be able to experience the nature of the soul unless you are born again.

Brahmin : Why do you call me a beast?

Madman : The scriptures say 'Eating, sleeping, fear, copulation are common to beasts and men. The beasts eat, sleep, fear and copulate as you do'. Then where is the difference between you and the beasts?

Brahmin : Then is every man a beast?

Madman : No, the one who is virtuous is not a beast.

Brahmin : I am twice-born, then why should I be regarded a beast?

Madman : You are certainly a Brahmin. But because you do not pray and worship you are still impure and not yet been born again. You could have been called twice-born had you prayed and worshipped and eaten pure food. You are still the creature that you had been born as. You have no faith and reverence for your preceptor and you have only grave doubts about the teachings of the Vedanta.

Brahmin : Well, do I not have recourse to any remedy?
I have never prayed or engaged in worship
and have never made sure that the food I eat
is pure. I never have observed the prescribed
practices. I have eaten according to my
wishes and have never prayed to God. Is
there not a remedy for a state such as mine?
Is there no scope for salvation for me? I have
no devotion, respect or faith; will my life
then pass in vain? I throw myself at your
feet, show me the way.

Thus the Brahmin catches hold of the feet of the Madman.

Madman : Let go my feet, let go my feet. You can have
recourse to the Name of God; why then
should you fear?

Brahmin : Ah, will the Name of the Lord save me?

Madman : Surely, it will save you. Seek refuge with the
Name that delivered Ratnakar and Ajamil,
and surely you will find peace.

Brahmin : See, I know nothing. I have not been initiated
into any mantra. Please tell me what am I to
do?

Madman : Wake up at 4 in the morning and perform
ablution. Next, meditate on the two-petaled
white-complexioned Guru, on top of your
head. The time from twenty-four minutes
before sunrise up to twenty-four minutes
after sunrise is the suitable time for the

morning prayers. Prayers must be said within that time. Specially, you ought to chant the Gayatri, read the Gita and worship Shiva and Vishnu. Begin all these practices and you will certainly receive the grace of God. Pure food is essential. Utter the Name, my son, utter the Name. In this, Kaliyuga peace will come only if you utter the Name.

'The Name of Hari (3) is the only way. In Kali Yuga there is no other way (3)'

The Madman claps his hands and sings:
'Hare Rama, Hare Rama, Rama, Rama, Hare, Hare
Hare Krishna, Hare Krishna, Krishna Krishna, Hare Hare.'

The waters of Ganga dance and sportingly join his song.

ಇ ಓಂ ಜು

2. The Touchstone

Part A

How sweet is your touch! It has transformed me! I am no longer someone overwhelmed with happiness or sorrow. Everything is sweet, everything has become sweet! This world is a cause of sorrow; relationships built on expectations are causes of sorrow. The emptiness inside is a cause of sorrow. Lust for objects is a cause of sorrow. Thinking of all this sorrow, and undergoing suffering, I was chanting the Name of Rama. Whence you appeared like this pleasant sensation? When you touched me, where did everything else go? Sheer delight! Ah, keep me immersed. Keep me immersed in your presence. Do not leave me; please do not take away this sensation.

At your touch everything is transformed. When you touch me, the feeling of sorrow within me, is no longer to be found. And if I do find it, I see your kind hand in it. When I imagine that I am sitting on your lap and you are holding me firmly, how do I feel? Feels good; it does. I know that you do have many things to do, but why do you touch me and then run away? Once you come, why do you not stay? No, no, why would you fly? It is my mind that flies. Well, you naughty mind! Why do you flee? Nobody speaks! The mind does not speak, you too do not speak. Listen, listen!

19

As soon as you touch me, I am transformed into another being. The objects of happiness and sorrow do change, but my suffering ceases. There remains only joy and more joy. Up to the moment you touched me, how much anxiety had I had; how many resolutions and reiterations I had made, how much had I laughed and cried, but all was gone with your touch. Even if I deliberately try to think of sorrow, it is not to be found. Truly, you are a great magician. As soon as you touch me, nothing remains. The noise returns only when you are not around. You want that everybody should cling to you. Do you not? Very well, what objection can I have? Do I ask you to go away or want to live without you? Keep on holding me in this way for all eternity. I will remain immersed in you. If you say that I want something else instead, I will not agree. I want only you. In how many guises I have been seeking you! I liked my relations and wealth, only to find happiness. But true joy is only in you. It is joy that I have been seeking. But instead of searching for the real jewel, I have been feeling elated on holding a piece of ordinary glass. This is it! Would you still say that I do not want you? It is fine if the others say this but it does not become of you. You are omniscient. You understand the feeling of the soul. I have been wrong in chasing objects but you are the embodiment of joy. It is you that I want.

- Hey madman, what are you scribbling?

- What else can I write? I write about your qualities.

- What will you do by writing?

- I will spread the message in the world.

- What profit will you get from it?

- When nobody will want you, you will have to remain alone. You will get the rewards of your mischief.

- I am indeed alone.

- Then, what are these men and women, worms and insects, trees and creepers, I see?

- They are nothing. I am alone. All these are illusions.

- Very nice! I can see them and you say they are nothing!

- No, there is nothing. It is only I. Look properly. Ask the trees and creepers, the worms and the insects if I am everything or not. Ask the earth, water, fire, air and ether if I am everything or not. Why are you silent? Ask the six senses, the mind, intellect, spirit and pride, whether I am everything or not.

- Well, I admit that you are everything. Even then you are not alone. I also exist.

- Who are you?

- You are funny person. You want to wipe out even my existence! Here I am.

- Who are you?

- You are God and I am yours.

- Say what you are to me.

- I... I am your... you are very naughty, you do not allow me to say, you have suppressed my tongue, how can I say?

- Do, you understand then? It is I who exists. Now try to dive in me.

- That is why I shout, 'Rama Rama'.

- See, he who is far away is to be called aloud. He, who is near, need not be called aloud. I have said this through the mouths of the *sadhus*. Now, call for me, within yourself.

- When I forget that you are near me, there remains no way other than calling you aloud.

- This is alright. When you come to realise that I am near you, there will be no need to even call out to me. This too, I have said through the mouths of the *sadhus*. For the present, keep your mind engaged in either the worldly play of the Name or my appearance. Otherwise, your mind will create a world, become involved in it and wail.

- It is true that when I forget you, my mind does wail!

- That is why I say: never forget me. Even if you forget me mentally, don't let your tongue forget to chant my Name. Call! Call! Call insistently!

- Well, let me call

'Rama, Rama, Sitaram, Jai Jai Rama, Sitaram!'

Part B

- Touchstone, you are very naughty.

- Why do you call me naughty?

- Why shan't I call you naughty? How many things I was doing for you, by surrendering to you. But when I turned around, you were gone. Why do you have a mind that flits? Now I will keep you tied.

- What will you bind me with?

- Why, I will bind you with a rope.

- Where will you find the rope?

- You will give it to me.

- So, I give you a rope and will you tie me? Nicely said!

- Look, there is no way of getting this rope if you do not give it. I thought that this rope could be had by listening and chanting. Now I well understand that it cannot be obtained in that way. Nothing can be done without your grace. I am guilty of many offences, forgive me. I seek your shelter. Make me yours.

- Here, here. Don't cry. Don't look at people. Keep looking at me. Your eyes should not see anything apart from me. Begin to see me in all things. Hear me in all the sounds, feel me in all the sensations and taste me in all the juices. Smell me in all the scents. Look, I love you dearly. I have put you in my lap. Just turn and see.

- Then, why do you go away?

- Where will I go? Say who I am.

- You are everything for me; you are the life-force of my existence.

- If you were alive, then how did I leave you? Had I left, you would have died. I am here. Tell me who am I?

- You are my revered deity.

- Is your revered deity very small?

- Why?

- Everyone's revered deity is the same Being. Isn't He your object of desire as well?

- He is the object of my desire also.

- If it be so, then there is nothing in the world except me. Where could I go? Nothing else exists outside me. There is nothing else. Ignore all external appearances, ignore everything. Cover this life with me. I am in front of you, behind you, above you, below you, within you, outside you, in your mind, in your senses, in your enemies and friends, in your disease and grief, in your want and fulfillment. I am all. I am in all. Don't be afraid. Don't be afraid. Accept everything as same, and always utter the Name of Rama.

Part C

- Touchstone, where are you?

- Are you calling me?

- Yes, I am calling you. Gradually, everything is getting mixed up.

- Don't worry, I am everything. I make up all your experiences. I am your singing of prayers; in your mental repetition of mantras. There is no reason to worry. Utter my Name without worries and see me in all living and nonliving things. Don't look at the creatures with your physical eyes. Try to peer into their inner being. Don't be deceived by varied guises and garments. See the real person who is wearing the garments. That bird is singing. Who gave him the voice? I am that.

- What is the matter? You have suddenly appeared in the guise of a dog. What kind of game is this? What mistake did I commit that you disrupted my chanting?

- Why? You were not able to catch me. Why did you say, 'Stay, Stay?' Let it be, don't worry. Don't give up calling me. Call me. Keep calling me.

- I like to call you only if you come. Otherwise, I keep calling and then go silent.

- I do come! Are you not able to sense my presence?

- I cannot always make out. How am I to know whether it is indeed you or a creation of the mind?

- The state in which you forget everything, your body is thrilled, tears flow profusely, the soul is overwhelmed; is my presence. Do you hear me?

- I have heard much. I will know only when you keep everything aside and accept me.

- You are already mine. Tell me what part of you are you.

- Everything. My body, house, wife, son, family all are mine and I belong to them. Then how am I, yours?

- Only when one has control over something, it can be called one's own. Do you have any right to any of these; the body, house, relations, kinsmen, wife or son? Can you move them according to your will or can they move you as per their will? Think clearly and reply.

- No, I cannot make anybody move according to my will nor can anybody make me move according to his will. My relations and kinsman are not within my control.

- Is your body, senses and mind within your control?

- No, they are also not within my control.

- How can those who are not within your control be called yours? All those belong to me. It is I who makes your body, house, relations and kinsmen, wife and son, move according to my will. Then how are you not mine?

- Yes, that is also true.

- Then you have nothing. Everything belongs to me. Do you understand now? Don't worry. You are in my lap; so what is there to fear? Only I am present as your relations and kinsmen on the stage of this world and I assume different forms to engage with you. I alone am present in your disease and grief, sorrow and poverty, honour and insult, enemies and friends, above you, below you, before you, behind you, on your left and right, in your wife and son, body and house, senses, mind, intellect, spirit and pride. Only I am in everything and everywhere.

Part D

- Are you calling me?

- Why no, I did not call you.

- Are you not telling the rosary beads?

- What happens if I tell the beads? I was telling the beads and also thinking of this body. I did not call you. I do not have the concentration needed to call you. Yet you have come! Come, come, and see. Please accept my worship. Please accept this flower and this sandal paste. Please accept all this.

- You need not worship any more.

- No, no, why should I not worship? I won't listen if

you speak to me while being hidden from my eyes. If you have anything to say, assume your own form and come and speak.

- O Conscious Being, Be Awake! Do not identify with your body and forget. You are neither the body; nor the mind; you are eternal, pure, conscious, free and true. O Conscious Being, Be Awake!

- Who is speaking and to whom? Who are you? Who has fallen asleep? Whom are you waking?

- O Conscious Being, Be Awake!

- What is this! Who are you? Whom are you calling? Why is my body filled with sensations? Why are tears coming into my eyes? O, dear! Whom are you calling and where does he live?

- In the inner heart.

- What is his name?

- Atmarama.

- What does he look like?

- Smaller than the atom; larger than the greatest object.

- How long has he been asleep?

- Long. He has covered himself with three coverings and has been sleeping. How long I have been calling! Remaining unaware, he discards the external clothes, acquires new ones and goes back to sleep again. In this sleep state, how many dreams has he seen and cried! He sometimes imagines himself a beast, a bird, a tree, a creeper, different types of people, a man, a woman, a divine being, and cries. Alas! His crying moves me to great pity, so I go on following him; calling out to him.

- Well, what are the names of the three cloths?

- The outermost is called Gross; the middle one is called Subtle and the third, Causal.

- What is the Gross covering made up of?

- Of the elements. It is made of five elements of earth, water, fire, air and ether. The middle one is made of five pranas, the mind, the intellect and the ten senses. The first one is made of the three attributes; *sattva*, *rajas* and *tama*. This time round, the Gross body is called a Brahmin. This Gross body is wholly immersed in a dream. He is dreaming of many things; houses, gods, and deities, relations and kinsmen. Sometimes he laughs; sometimes he cries, sometimes puts on the guise of a *sadhu* and utters the name of Rama. Sometimes as a householder he wields a pickaxe and at other times he sits on the bank of the Ganges and watches the river. Sometimes he runs after money. Whatever he does, because he utters the name of Rama, I keep calling, 'Rise O Conscious Being. You are not a separate individual mind; you are not the Gross-Subtle-Causal body. You are eternally conscious and free of bondage. You are a being, immersed in bliss and beyond words. Awake! Awake! Hari Om!'

- Ah, your call is very sweet Hari Om, Hari Om. Ah! Ah! Hari Om, Hari Om. Tell me, how his sleep will break?

- By always repeating Hari Om, Hari Om.

- What will happen by repeating Hari Om, Hari Om at a gross level?

- Atmaram's identification with the gross body will go. When he will repeat 'Hari Om, Hari Om' at the subtle level, the identification with the subtle body will go. Then he will say, 'Hari Om, Hari Om' at the causal level. After the ego at causal level will be removed, what will remain will be the kingdom of joy. Hari Om, Hari Om.

- Shall I say?

- Go on, say Hari Om.

- Hari Om, Hari Om, Ah! Ah! Hari Om, Hari Om, Ah! Ah! Om Om Om Om Om Om Om Om Om Om Om Om Om Om Om Om Om Om Om.

Part E

- Touchstone, do I call you naughty without any reason?

- Why, what naughtiness have you seen?

- Everything is naughtiness. How many kinds of waves you are creating! I do not know what is happening. Feels as though I have lost myself in these waves. How great is your Maya! You are great.

- Is it my fault if you cry from believing this playacting to be the truth? Whose fault is it, if you become a king in your dreams and dance like a madman?

- Why do you put on this show? Why do you create a belief by calling the dream, the truth? Can't you will this show to stop? Can't you break the intoxication of the dream? You don't do any of these but come out from time to time to watch the fun.

- I have said, 'These are not things different from me. Only I alone exist. I am the Sun, the Moon, the planets and the stars. I am earth, water, fire, air and ether. I am the trees and creepers, beasts and birds, worms and insects, man and woman, and the sinful and the virtuous. I am the honest and the dishonest. I am happiness and sorrow, sin and suffering, and disease and grief. I am the laughter and the crying, the rebuke and the praise. I am effort and laziness, the beautiful and the ugly. I am all.' See how beautiful is my appearance?

- Beautiful! Beautiful! You are very beautiful. This is a new guise of yours. Very beautiful! Very beautiful! My power of speech is dwindling and seems to exist no more. With your touch everything seems to be turning into nothingness. I seem to be changing. I can no more tell my beads. Why are you taking everything away? See, I had a heart full of joy. Why can't I feel that joy now? I feel like remaining silent. I have no desire to think of anything. I am sitting still. Do what you like.

31

- Do self-study; repeat the mantra that you have received. Understand my true nature with the help of the Shrutis and meditate on it. Know the world as illusion and take refuge in me.

- You have just said that you are everything. Again you are saying that the world is illusion. Then where shall I take shelter?

- Omit the name and form from the world. It is correct that I am everything but I am not its name and form. I am that which remains when the name and form is removed. I am that which cannot be seen, heard, touched, consumed or tasted. Speech cannot express me; I am the power behind the speech.

- See, I wish that you assume a shape and come to me. I cannot hold that attributeless, changeless, shapeless beauty of yours in this little container of mine.

- I am a better judge of what you are eligible for. It is up to me to assess your capacity.

- And what shall I do?

- You shall repeat Hari Om, Hari Om, Hari Om.

- Then let me say Hari Om, Hari Om, Hari Om. What will you do?

- I will wake up the sleeping Purusha. 'O Conscious Being, Arise and Be Awake!'

- See, I do not know what power lies hidden in that call of yours but my body is tingling.

- Conscious Being, Be Awake.

- Feels as if there is a covering in between. Tell me how this covering can be removed.

- By reciting Hari Om, Hari Om, Hari Om, Om Om Om Om Om Om Om Om Om Om Om Om Om Om Om Om Om Om.

Part F

- Why does such a thing happen?

- So long as attachment and identification with the physical self will exist, this agony must be endured. Give up everything. Man cannot gain peace without sacrifice. Only by sacrifice can man gain emancipation. Hence give up everything. Nobody can gain the truth without giving up the false. This world is false just as a dream is false. Both these things are to be ignored.

- Oh! I am not able to sacrifice. What shall I do? By what means can fitness for sacrifice be acquired?

- By uttering the Name. Repeat the Name incessantly. Neither pay heed to anyone else nor say anything to anybody. Only repeat the name of Rama. I will take care of everything. What you think to be sorrow is a dream. You are not an actor in the play that is going on; you are only a spectator. I am the raging fire of your unrest; I am the gentle breeze of your peace. Ignore the Gross-Subtle-Causal and look at me, the Great Cause. I am everything and you are the spectator. Do not laugh or cry on watching the drama. Do not wail, taking the dream as the truth. Do not forget even for a moment that you are the spectator. Let this be your firm belief that you are not the actor. What is to fear? He who seeks refuge in me, I keep in my heart. That, which makes you restless, is nothing but my auspicious presence. This universe is made of good; there is not even an iota of evil in this universe. Repeat the Name.

- Rama…Rama…Rama. Ah, I feel calm within.

- Yes, why will he who is sheltered by me, look at enjoyment? My devotee cannot be a worm in the cesspool of enjoyment. Money and attachments are objects of enjoyment. Your accumulated wealth will not be able to deliver you from the world of death. Money will bring only trouble. Ignore money. Every human body perishes one day; is it something to lust after? Fie, fie! That is Hell. Do not look at it in that way. Come back, come back. This body of yours is the home to diseases, is the cause of pain and sorrow and is continuously rotting. Although this body can die any moment, you are carefree! You tremble with fear on watching certain acts in this drama. Fie, fie! Get ready. Get ready for death. Leave all that you are doing.

- Can all be given up?

- Certainly, all can be given up. I am everything. I am assuming various forms to destroy the fruit of your work. I am your worldly relations, I am your preceptor. I am your disciple and devotee. It is I who destroys your evil deeds by decrying you. It is I who destroy your good deeds by praising you. Whom will you be angry with? Me, me, me. Whom will you love? Me, me, me. Come away. Leave the realm of the Gross and come to the Subtle. Close your eyes and fix your sight on the first level. Shake and rouse the mad girl that is sleeping on the level below. Accompanied by her, observe the rooms in the six storeys of this structure. And just above the last level is the abode of the Pranava. That is my favourite name; Pranava. Call me as you observe all this. That is the Bindu; that is the Nada. Go up and sit silently on the sixth level. Do you not like to stay there? There are sunrays in the Sahasrara. Go there. Follow those rays and go to the region of the Sun. If you can keep your attention fixed on the sunrays in the Sahasrara, you shall have control over your death. You would be able to penetrate the Brahmarandhra and leave the mortal coil at will.

- You are saying many things but I find neither the shore nor the brink.

- I am the shore; I am the brink. Emancipation comes from repeating Om Om Om Om Om Om Om Om.

- I say, Om Om Om Om Om Om Om Om.

- Say, Om Om Om Om Om Om mmmmm.

- I say, Om Om Om Om Om Om Om m m.

- Om Om Om Om Om Om Om m m.

- Om Om Om Om Om Om Om m m.

- Shantih Shantih Shantih.

Part G

- I love you very much.

- Why do you love me?

- There is no reason for my love. I love without any reason.

- I do not do any such thing that you can love me.

- Yet I love you very much.

- Do you love only me?

- No, I love all.

- If you love all why do they suffer so much?

- That too is my way of loving.

- Oh, how unique is your love! I cannot understand what kind of love this is.

- See, I want to keep everyone near me. When they go mad being deluded by worldly things and cannot remember me anymore, I snatch away the false enjoyment conceived by their minds and make them remember me and thus keep them near me. Isn't this love?

- Is the enjoyment conceived by the mind?

- Why only enjoyment? This world also is conceived by the mind. The world has no reality. This world is untrue.

- How can I call what I see, as false?

- Seeing is a mistake.

- Are the two eyes seeing erroneously?

- Well, can't the eyes see erroneously? Do you not remember the rising of the Sun in the West in Azimganj? How did these eyes that had seen the Sun rise in the East all through life, see the Sun rise that day in the West?

- That was due to mistaken directions.

- With the eyes closed did you not reason within yourself that the Sun does not rise in the West and just as you opened your eyes the Sun rose in the West, was it not so?

- Still the illusion had not gone!

- You could not make out what happened to the illusion as soon as you started seeing with your mind. Similarly, this world is an illusion like mistaken directions. Like the Sun rising in the West. The world exists in Brahma. This illusion of the world will not go till the mind's eye becomes active. Till the vision of the world goes, you will not become calm.

- How will there be direct mental vision?

- Immerse your mind in my name, beauty, quality

and true nature, and then there will be direct mental vision.

- How shall I immerse the mind?

- You can immerse it by uttering the Name.

- What of the wailing coming from all directions, which wants to create disturbance in uttering the Name?

- There is no disturbance in the world that can dislodge my devotee from his path. If Yama hears the roar of the name of Rama, his hold on the scepter becomes slackened. You think that you have many weakness, many defects in you. Let there be weaknesses and defects; utter the Name. All weakness and defects will vanish. They are sure to vanish. Whenever you feel distant from me, say 'Rama, Rama, Sitaram' aloud. The six enemies living in the body will freeze in fear. Don't be frightened on any account. Just look behind and see that I am holding you close. Just as your body is present all around the organisms living in your blood, you exist completely engulfed by my body because I am the whole universe. I alone am above, beneath, in front of and behind you. I...I...I.

- I have been listening to you speak of 'I...I...I' for many days now. How much longer will these talks of 'I...I...I' go on?

- Till your 'I' merges with my 'I'.

- Do whatever you like.

- Don't sit idle, do meditative repetition.

- With what shall I tell my beads?

- My favourite Name!

ॐ

3. Pursuit of Reality

'Jai Rama, Sitaram, Jai Jai Rama, Sitaram, Jai Jai Rama, Sitaram'

The cottage of the madman was resonant with this song. He was absorbed in chanting the Name when Niranjan Bhattacharya came and said, 'O, madman saint! What is the use of merely chanting the name of Rama? Enquire into the nature of Reality.'

Madman : I shall reach by chanting the name of Rama the same destination that you will reach by enquiring into the nature of Reality.

Niranjan : Emancipation cannot be achieved without enquiring into the nature of Reality.

Madman : It can surely be achieved, my son. The name of Rama itself is the highest principle. If you chant the name of Rama, knowledge comes automatically.

Niranjan : Ha! Ha! Ha!

Madman : Are you laughing? Do you believe in the Shruti?

Niranjan : Surely.

40

Madman : Listen to what the Shruti says! It is said in Sriramarahasyopanishad, 'Rama is the supreme Brahma, Rama is the supreme penance, Rama is the supreme Reality and Sri Rama is the supreme deliverer.'

Sriramapurvatapani says, 'Like riches are pursued through the worship of fortune, the path of dharma is pursued through the strength of character and the path of wisdom through chanting of the Name and detachment from the world through meditation.'

So, my son, the path of wisdom can be attained by chanting the Name.

Niranjan : That is not exactly an original Shruti.

Madman : Because it does not fit your opinion? Jai Rama, Sitaram.

Niranjan : The Shastra says, 'Emancipation comes from knowledge.'

Madman : Just as it says that Moksha comes from knowledge, it also speaks of one who is eligible for Moksha. It is proper to speak of knowledge only after the mind attains concentration by worship, and the Prana is stabilized in the Sahasrara and becomes single-pointed. Otherwise the talk of wisdom to a person of impure mind, who is allured by lust and wealth, is nothing but

41

the ravings of a mad man. That knowledge is of no benefit to a man of hollow intellect. Distressed and running like a man whose hair is on fire, when a person renounces the world and seeks shelter under an adept teacher, only then he receives instructions about Reality. Then with the aid of listening, meditating on what is heard and letting knowledge settle down to the intuitive level, the seeker attains direct perception of the Reality and is emancipated. Is it not so?

Niranjan : Yes.

Madman : Have you had such intense craving for salvation? You are a householder; you have wife and sons. Do you meditate on 'I am He' or 'I am Brahma' while being surrounded by your wife and sons?

Niranjan : Yes. Should I feel shackled because I am householder? Have I no right to the attainment of learning?

Madman : Jai Rama, Sitaram. Have I said that? Everything is eligibility. All right, what does learning mean?

Niranjan : The realisation that 'I am not the body but a conscious soul' is wisdom and knowledge.

Madman : Now, my son, the 'conscious soul', if you are not the body, to whom does these house and wife and sons belong? Why do all these exist?

Niranjan : I have not yet been able to ascertain it, I am practicing this enquiry.

Madman : What is practice?

Niranjan : Doing the same thing again and again is called practice.

Madman : By remaining at home, you are only practicing 'I am the body.'

Niranjan : How?

Madman : Your wife and sons, your house, your relations, honour and dignity are making you realise that you are the body only. Do you understand it, my son?

Niranjan : Then do you mean to say that the pursuit of knowledge bears no fruits.

Madman : God forbid. Can I say that? A knowledgeable man, who is devoid of devotion, can strike terror into the hearts of the innocent and simple devotees by demolishing their belief.

Niranjan : Devotion is surely necessary.

Madman : Just a sprinkling of devotion, my son, will not do. If the deluge of your devotion can wash away the world, emancipation herself will come running and embrace you.

Niranjan : Lord Shankaracharya has said, 'Moksha comes from knowledge.'

Madman	:	Who is Lord Shankaracharya?
Niranjan	:	O madman, do you not know Shankaracharya, the incarnation of Shiva Himself?
Madman	:	Did he come from Shiva?
Niranjan	:	Yes.
Madman	:	My Mahavira also came from Shiva. To this day he is chanting the name of Rama and he has said that everything can be achieved by the name of Rama.
Niranjan	:	Ha! Ha! Ha!
Madman	:	You did not believe in Him because he is a monkey? Well, listen to what is said by Shankara, whose incarnation is Shankaracharya and who is the source of incarnations; is merciful; full of grace; a lover of devotees; the deliverer of those who have no chance of deliverance; the refuge of the poor; the friend of the poor; Parvati's husband. 'I, fulfilled by the chanting of your name, live in Kashi with Bhavani and administer your name of Rama into the ears of those dying for deliverance.'

Will I not be able to fulfill the mission of my life by chanting the same name that fulfilled my Shankara?

Niranjan	:	All those things are stories of the Puranas.

Madman	: You do believe in history. You have no hesitation in believing your Lord Shankaracharya as the incarnation of Shiva, but you cannot accept the Adhyatma Ramayana? Praised be your belief! Shankaracharya has said the very thing Lord Shankara said about Reality in the Adhyatma Ramayana. First acquire the eligibility, only then will you get the essence of the scriptures. Otherwise, you will only break the heads of others with the stick of philosophy and carrying it around will create calluses on your shoulders. Listen to what my Shankara says. 'First you have to cleanse your mind by the performing the duties of the Ashrama you belong to and then you have to renounce the world and go to a Guru for shelter. Only then can you practice knowledge.' Do you understand, my son? What is needed are devotion and the vow of worshipping the Lord. Then the mind will be purified. After that you have to renounce the world and the practice of knowledge will follow.
Niranjan	: You are talking of devotion, father. Say where the Shruti has said that the knowledge of the Reality comes from devotion.
Madman	: Have you read the Chhandogya Upanishad? There, worship of Pranava and Gayatri, is called devotion.
Niranjan	: Please tell me which Upanishad says

definitely that the knowledge of the Reality comes from devotion.

Madman : It certainly does. My Lord makes the garland of the Reality and puts it round the neck of the devotee.

Niranjan : Then do you mean to say that only with *bhakti* can a man attain *moksha*?

Madman : Not only I, but the Shruti too says this.

Niranjan : There is no necessity for a householder to read the Mokshashastra?

Madman : There is a great necessity.

Niranjan : What is the good of doing that?

Madman : Running a business by calling oneself a scholar of philosophy and earning money, and on top of that if one manages to sit in meditation one or two hours, thinking that he has become King Janaka! Rama, Rama, Sitaram. The scriptures must be appropriate to the path. Else sorrow is not removed by those scriptures. If a householder reads the scriptures of a *sannyasi*, it does not do him any good and increases his pride instead.

Niranjan : Somebody has passed the Matriculation Examination. If he is not informed of the M.A. Examination, how will he know the goal?

Madman : He is to be told of the M.A. Examination and he is to be encouraged. But what good would it be to him if he is directly given the books of M.A. to read? Suppose initiation is the passing of the Matriculation Examination. The preceptor gives the initiation, shows the path of *sadhana* and studies begin for the I.A. class. Its syllabus is as follows. First: to work for God's love without any desire for the fruit. Second: With the belief that 'There is a merciful God', listening, singing hymns, thinking of Him, serving at His feet, making offerings, praying, acting as His servant, being a companion and surrendering oneself. This is the nine-fold path which creates devotion to God. As soon as an unshakable faith is created, the I.A. Examination is cleared.

The preceptor then lays down the syllabus for the B.A. class: Worshiping His 'universal form' by means of practice, meditating on His embodied form externally, His glorious form within and meditate on the thought that He pervades the fourteen worlds. As the devotee progresses in his *sadhana*, he begins to see his God's image in the trees, the creepers, the worms, the insects, the birds and the beasts. The sight of flower, fruit and leaf reminds him of his God. The songs of the birds, the humming of the bees and the playfulness of the breeze remind him of his God. He is reminded of the feet of God by

47

the gurgling of the waters of the Bhagirathi and the full Moon reminds him of the face of God. As the new blades of grass remind him of the radiance of his Lord, tears well in his eyes. When he sees the ocean, he plunges in it, thinking of the Blue-hued Gem, that is his Lord. Seeing the cloud…Yes, listen to the song I sing. This was said by my loving Lord…

'I have seen him

A fair complexioned *sannyasi* has come here,

I have seen him,

Who sheds tears on saying Hari's name,

Who cries and makes other cry,

Who lights up the world with his beauty,

Whose head and body are covered with dust,

Who says, 'Where is Shyama Rai?'

Seeing the new cloud covering the sky

He calls the cloud and says, 'This is the Flutist'.

If you do not show yourself why did you play the flute?

Do you not know O Lord, I am the servant of your feet?'

Saying this he cries and faints in the dust;

He says, 'Where is Shyama Rai?

I have seen Him.'

(The madman sings this, two or three times)

Ah! Ah! So it happens. And if it does not happen thus, the illusion of the world is not removed.

Niranjan : The song is very sweet.

Madman : Yes, admiring this universal form of God, the devotee forgets his body, home, relations and dives into the ocean of God. His world vanishes. The B.A. course of study ends at this stage. Then one has to take the path of a *sannyasi* and prepare for the M.A. class. The M.A. course of study comprises receiving the doctrine of 'I am all' from the Guru and through listening, meditating and assimilating the knowledge, becoming fixed in the thought of 'I only am all'. A student of the M.A. class is the worshipper of the universal form or attributeless Brahma. After that, the syllabus for the Premchand Roychand Examination is; being established in the inexpressible, indestructible and attributeless Brahma. Do not dismiss this determination of order as the raving of a mad man; these are the words of a great man. Do you understand it, my son? To go up you must go step by step. You cannot do it in one leap. What will you cook if you have no rice, *dal*, oil or salt? Nothing will happen by saying, 'I am Brahma, I am the witness, I am the Soul,' without the required knowledge. Go on chanting the name of Rama. Once the world is wiped from your mind, then, if you like, enquire about Reality.

Niranjan : If we do not at all know about the soul, how will the longing for attaining it arise? Is there no need of knowing what I am, what I have become or what I am to be?

Madman : The preceptor has stated this right at the time of initiation. Right demeanour is developed through perusal of prescribed scriptures. The preceptor has briefly outlined that purifying the physical elements will give awareness of the soul, Kundalini-Shakti and the twenty-four Tattvas and, only after dissolving these as well, one will attain oneness with Shiva.

Niranjan : How can dispassion towards the world come without enquiring about the nature of Reality?

Madman : What have you heard till now? Has it been said that enquiry into Reality needs to be done lying down on a mattress and looking at the faces of the wife and children? Dispassion towards the world will only come through working without expectation of fruit and taking a vow to worship Hari.

Niranjan : Whatever you may say, thought has an independent power, which lifts the mind to a higher level. I have been enquiring about the soul for ten years and I can well understand that I am always free, pure, wise and the eternally joyful Reality.

Madman : Is it so? Let me see what sort of Brahma you are!

(The madman strikes a match and brings the burning stick near the Niranjan's clothes)

Niranjan . : (Rising quickly) What are you doing? What are you doing? The clothes will burn!

Madman : Sitaram Sitaram. Why do you flee? Is it possible that the Supreme Soul that cannot be burnt, wetted, dried, penetrated, that has no attribute and is changeless, will be burnt by a matchstick? Why are you giving up the tall talk of 'I am that', 'I am Brahma', 'I am Shiva' and running away? Can your ten years of enquiry into Reality be reduced to ashes by the flame of a match, my son? Mere words do not put out a fire; water is needed. Nothing will happen with a mind devoid of devotion; a greater state of mind is needed. You have no right to the Raja-yoga until you attain the elevated mood of the Mantrayogi, Mahalaya of the Layayogi and Mahabodha Siddhi of the Hathayogi. By enquiry, the mind will rise to a higher level but due to the want of infallible memory it will at once fall to the bottom.

Niranjan	:	What is meant by the right to Rajayog? Everyman has the right to whatever he likes.
Madman	:	A patient likes harmful diet and a lustful man likes wives of other men. Do you mean to say that they have a right to them?
Niranjan	:	No.
Madman	:	Thanks to the printing press, descriptions of Reality are easily available on the streets. A treatise on the Reality can be had even for two *annas* and by spending five rupees the reader can become an expert on Reality. Everyone reads these treatises. When this literature was not freely available, social order and practices were in place. Now almost all have become scholars and knowledgeable about the nature of Reality. There are many who have memorized the verses of the Gita but do not hesitate in doing unrighteous things. They take the help of the scriptures to justify their sins. Is this wisdom or a corruption of wisdom? The knowledge of Brahma should be kept hidden. Look at its miserable condition. Every house has an expert on Reality. No one is ready to perform a minor *sadhana*. All are worshippers of the formless Brahma. These inexperienced but well-read people are real scholars but the fire licking at their hearts is not quenched. A few days ago I met a famous Mahamahopadhyaya scholar. His disciples also were professors

of Vedantic subjects. He is a good orator, poet and publisher of books on scriptures. He said, 'I speak in meetings. People praise me and call me a Vedantin. But, alas! I am tormented by the fire burning in my heart. If someone shows me the way to peace, I am ready to be his disciple.' Tell me, son, what sort of wisdom this is. Do you consider him eligible for *moksha* because of his study of the scriptures? He likes the Vedanta, has mastered the scriptures, has repeated 'I am Brahma', 'It is I', but why there is still so much agony in his heart?

Niranjan : There are some 'realised' scholars among housholders.

Madman : A couple of great men do appear for deliverance of the world and to preach duty, knowledge and devotion. They too repeat, 'A man with poor eligibility should follow the path of devotion.' Jai Rama, Sitaram.

Niranjan : Suppose I want emancipation. I cannot embrace *sannyas* because I cannot find a good preceptor, what is the harm if I enquire about the Reality?

Madman : First judge whether you want emancipation or not. A dead body has no feeling of joy and sorrow. If you become like that even while alive, you may belong to Kaivalya Ashrama. Have you reached that state?

Niranjan   : No.

Madman   : Do you find yourself lost in the thoughts of your beloved Lord, wherever you look?

Niranjan   : No.

Madman   : Then you have not completed your first lesson. Your mind has not been purified. Follow the path your preceptor has advised you to follow?

Niranjan   : To follow the path shown by the Guru means that he will say what he likes and I shall have to follow that path.

Madman   : 'In Kaliyuga the path approved by the Agama is to be followed.' My Shankara has recommended the path of the Tantra for Kali. He appeared as the preceptor and gave Tantra instructions. Have you been initiated?

Niranjan   : Yes.

Madman   : The preceptor said, 'My son, chant the mantra 'Rama' and read daily the Ramagita, Ramasahasranama, Rama-kavacha, Rama-stotra and Rama-Hridaya. Devotion should be profound. Meditate on the Leela and perform Purascharana (ritual offerings) for Mantrasiddhi. There are three levels of Siddhis, the highest, medium and the lowest. If one attains the highest form of Mantrasiddhi one will see the deity of one's worship. Both Nirguna (having no attribute) and Saguna (having attributes) forms will become apparent. You yourself will become Shiva. By chanting the Name off and on for one or two months you taste a little joy of Japa, get some joy from meditation on Leela but before a deep devotion to God is established, you start believing that all deities are the same and that you are entitled to begin enquiry into the true nature of Reality. That is it! You leave your study of religious literature as well as your meditation on the Leela, and run after all kinds of Shastras like the Sankhya, Vedanta, Gita, Bhagavata and Upanishad. You study many scriptures and become a scholar but nothing real is accomplished. The agony is not removed and fearlessness is not acquired.

Niranjan : There is discussion on the Reality in the Ramagita.

Madman : That is to be done after purification of the mind and renunciation. After knowing about the Nirguna, Saguna, soul and incarnation forms, you will need to follow the one that increases your devotion. You will have to perform work without desire, service of God, Purascharan and such other things to gain Mantrasiddhi. If, instead of doing that, you only orally repeat statements like 'I am the attributeless Brahma', 'I am the soul' or 'I am not the body', you will lose both the worlds. Bhakti will not come without appropriate

55

practice and without Bhakti true knowledge (Jnana) will not come even in a million ages.

Niranjana : When all deities are Brahma what is the use of separating them and meditating on the Leela of Rama or reading the Ramagita?

Madman : The system of worshipping the five deities is included in the doctrine of Panchatatva. A man will worship the presiding deity of the Tattva that dominates his body.

'Vishnu is the presiding deity of Space, Maheshwari of Fire, Surya of Air, Shiva of the Earth and Ganapati of Water.'

So long as the mantra given by the preceptor has not been fulfilled you should understand that you have not yet risen above the Tattva. When the mantra will reach its end, the preceptor in the form of the mantra will give a new mantra for meditating on Brahma and depart. Only then will the understanding that all deities are one, be established.

Niranjan : What do you mean by saying that the mantra will depart?

Madman : The soul will remain permeated with the mantra. The power to pronounce the mantra will leave.

Niranjan : Is that possible?

Madman : All the Vedas, Upanishads, Sandhya, Gayatri

will depart when the Sadhana is complete.

Niranjan : You are saying something insane. I have my tongue, I can speak, I can do other things but my Sandhya and Gayatri will be lost! You are completely mad! You are completely mad.

Madman : Sitaram Sitaram. Not only am I mad, but my father and mother are also mad. The Father has gone mad and sings the name of Rama from his five mouths. He plays the *damaru* and dances. Father had been very calm but went mad only because of the Mother. She too has become mad and dances wildly on the Father's chest. She gets a chest like the Father's to dance on, which is why she can dance like this. She feels no shame and has no time to put on her cloth. When will the one who has to give birth to millions of worlds every moment, get time to wear clothes?

Mother Gourishankar, Mother Sitaram. Mother! Ever Joyful Mother! Jai Guru, Jai Rama, Jai Rama, Jai Ma.

Tears flow from the madman's eyes, he becomes overwhelmed. Niranjan keeps sitting, staring at the face of the mad man.

Jai Sitaram.

ॐ

4. A Terrible Dacoity

A grave trouble is about to visit Benida. The dacoits have sent a letter threatening to loot his wealth. I hear that Benida is very anxious. I am a little sorry to hear about it. I had a grievance in my mind about being poor, but now I have no complaint. I have no fear of dacoits. What will they come to take away? I have nothing. All that I have is want. The dacoits are not looking for want. Otherwise, why would they commit dacoity? How easy has God made it for me by making me poor! I have no anxiety about dacoits. My mind drifted, lost in these thoughts.

All of a sudden I saw inside my house; the dacoits had struck my place!! Six dacoits were fleeing with six pitchers of coins (*mohurs*). Alas! All is lost! I had only six pitchers of *mohurs* but the dacoits have taken away all of them. Is there anybody? 'They have taken away all that I had!' I began to cry aloud.

At that moment I became aware of a man, clad in white, wearing a garland of white flowers around his neck, with white sandal paste smeared on his body.

He gave a little laugh and asked me, 'Who are you? Why are you weeping?'

'I cannot say who I am. I have forgotten...forgotten my own self. Who are you, Sir?'

He said, 'My name is Guru. What is the cause of your weeping?'

I said, 'See, my Lord, six dacoits are carrying away on their heads, six pitchers of *mohurs* that belong to me. What am I to do? O Lord, what am I to do?'

The Guru said, 'Well, I will give you a solution. Will you be able to recognize your six pitchers?'

I said, 'Why not? All my pitchers have names written on them.'

He said, 'What are the names?'

I said, 'Forgiveness, Uprightness, Compassion, Contentment, Truth and Devotion. The dacoits also have some names written on their backs; Lust, Anger Greed, Delusion, Pride and Envy.

Guru Thakur said, 'Just see, which pitcher each of them is carrying.'

I said, 'There is Lust fleeing with Uprightness on his head, Anger with Forgiveness, Greed with Compassion, Delusion with Contentment, Pride with Truth and Envy with Devotion. Alas! Alas! All is lost, Guru Thakur, I pray to you, my Father, please find some way to save me.'

He said, 'Well, take this gun of the Name of God and pursue the six dacoits. Fire the gun of the Name continuously and hit the dacoits. Challenged by you, they will run, but will not be able to go much far along the way they have taken. Just a little further down, they will come upon a bottomless pit of Detachment (Vairagya) with an inaccessible mountain of Wisdom (Jnana) rearing above it. They will not be able to advance any more. Go, don't delay.'

I took aim with the gun of the Name and attacked the six dacoits. They ran and I went after them. I was not accustomed to holding a gun. Many shots missed their marks. Some shots did hit them. They were such hardened dacoits! They kept running even after being hit by gunshots! I now began to fire at every breath. After a while, on coming upon the bottomless pit of Detachment and the inaccessible mountain of Wisdom, they drew to a halt. There was no way forward for them. Seeing me coming up from behind, they sensed the danger and consulted amongst themselves. They quickly took the pitchers off their heads, collected their shields and joined them into one by a special mantra. The dacoits then took cover under the shield. I began firing again. I saw the words 'Attachment to the World' (Sansara Asakti) written in large letters on the shield. I fired relentlessly, targeting the dacoits under the shield. But gradually, I grew tired.

I invoked the Guru, 'O Gurudeva! Those six wicked dacoits are lying covered by the shield of 'Attachment to the World'. What should I do? Should I go near them or fire from a distance?'

Gurudeva gave me a sword and said, 'Go! Bring down those six dacoits with this sword of Meditation (Dhyana).'

Armed with the gun of the Name of God in my left hand and the sword of Meditation in my right, I fell upon the dacoits with the ferocity of a lion. I snatched away their shield. I saw that bullets (of God's Name) had pierced the shield and had riddled the dacoits' bodies. They were debilitated and deathly pale. I said, 'Wicked fellows! Will you decamp with my six pitchers of *mohurs*? I will slay you.' All of them fell at my feet, 'We seek your shelter. Do not kill us. We will do your bidding.'

I asked the first one, 'Well, what is your name?'

He said, 'My name is Lust (Kama).'

I told him, 'Well, crave emancipation and keep repeating, 'May I have emancipation.'

I asked another, 'What is your name?'

'My name is Anger.'

'Show your strength on these three objects of desire: Virtue (Dharma), Money (Artha) and Lust (Kama).'

'What is your name?'

'My name is Greed.'

'From today show your intensity towards the service of God.'

'What is your name?'

'My name is Delusion.'

'Well, use your power to exhibit the beauty of God.'

'What is your name?'

'My name is Pride.'

'Well, apply yourself to the thought 'I am the least of all'.

'What is your name?'

'My Name is Envy.'

'Well, show your prowess on the statement 'I am nothing, I am God's servant.'

Seeing the gun in my left hand and the sword in my right, they agreed to obey. I began the return journey with the six fellows carrying back my six pitchers on their shoulders.

I met Gurudeva on the way. I said, 'Here, take back your gun of the Name and sword of Meditation. I have conquered the enemies and recovered my stolen treasure!'

He said, 'No, son! The victory is not yet final. It is very difficult to conquer them. Do not think that you have conquered them. They are always on the lookout for a chance and at the first opportunity they will strangle and ruin you. Keep that gun of the 'Name' by your tongue, and keep the sword of meditation close to your mind. Then you will have no fear. When it is time for you to return the weapons, you will be unable to find me; howsoever hard you seek. Then, you will have no power to speak. Go, son. Do not forget to challenge these looters day and night. There is no harm if a few shots miss, but the reports of the gun must be heard. Only then will these dacoits remain under control.'

Suddenly my trance came to an end and I looked. Where were the dacoits and where were the *mohurs*? Hari...Hari! Was it a waking dream? Anyhow, since the Gurudeva has asked me to, I will continue to fire the gun as long as I live.

MADMAN'S JHOLI

Jai Jai Rama, Sitaram

Gauri Shankar Radheshyam

Radheshyam Sitaram,

Gauri Shankar, Jai Jai Rama.

ॐ ओं ॐ

5. Self-Rule

The madman was telling the beads of the Tulsi rosary, repeating the name of Rama. A patriotic gentleman came to him and said, 'Well Sir, all are working hard to attain Self-rule (Swaraj) and you are only sitting; silent and inactive.'

Madman : No, son, I am trying very much for Swaraj, but the result is in the hands of God.

Patriot : You do not carry out the instructions of the Mahatma. How do you claim that are you trying for Swaraj?

Madman : What has the Mahatma instructed?

Patriot : He has said 'If you want to be free of this slavery, join the non-cooperative movement. Shun violence, shun untouchability, spin the *charkha* and ply the loom. By doing so, you can get Swaraj.'

Madman : Even before the Mahatma preached this message, I had adopted these very means for the attainment of Swaraj. Sri Guru, the invisible ruler of the infinite universe, had given those very orders. I have been trying to attain Swaraj by following these orders since then.

Patriot   : I do not quite understand you.

Madman   : Well, I will explain. I do not remember how long I have been enslaved. I am serving as a slave, having accepted the bond of slavery. And is it the slavery of just one master? No! I am a servant to hundreds of feelings and objects. I have been serving my relatives and my friends as a slave. I have forgotten that I am a king. I have been waiting on them, as do bought slaves and dogs. Their smiling faces give me delight and a single sweet word from them makes me thank my stars for the success. I place at their feet without hesitation, whatever I get after the whole day's labour. In exchange for this, I get bondage upon bondage. That is about my slavery to human beings. In addition, I am slave to things such as houses, gardens and tanks, clothes, shoes and umbrellas, utensils, cows and calves, paddy, rice and straw. I keep watch over these all day and night, with a *lathi* (stick) on my shoulders, as if I am their unpaid guard. What a strange thing! One day I took off my shoes outside the temple and went in to see the Arati. O Hari! Glaring with blood-shot eyes, the shoes scolded me, 'I am left outside and you are watching the Arati? Come, out quickly.' Though my eyes were gazing at the image of the God, my mind was meditating on the shoes! What am I to do? I am a slave to my shoes. I hurriedly came running to my shoes.

From that day I developed contempt for this sort of slavery.

Whether willingly or unwillingly, I am serving these five things; sound, touch, form, taste and smell. I cannot live a moment without serving the eleven sense organs of ears, skin, eyes, tongue, smell, speech, hands, feet, rectum, genitals and mind. Say nothing of lust, anger, greed, delusion, pride and envy; which are standing on my head. They have thrown me down and are kicking me. Oh, what agony it is! A great deal of contempt rose in my mind at this sort of slavery. As I wondered if there was a way to gain deliverance from this, I saw Sri Guru before me. I held his feet with my hands and said, 'O, Lord! Put an end to my slavery, show me a way.' Then he advised, 'Be non-co-operative. Give up attachment; work and fight at being free from delusion. Then only will your slavery come to an end.' On hearing this I quietly began to withdraw cooperation from my relations, houses, money, from taste, smell, eyes, ears, nose, anger etc. This attitude yielded benefits. Tell me, am I not obeying the orders of the Mahatma? There is no way other than giving up co-operation if I am to conquer these enemies who are disguised as my friends. So I am abjuring cooperation through uttering the name of Rama.

Sri Guru then made the second commandment 'Be non-violent. Give up co-operation but do not be violent, remain aloof and never try to kill anyone. Rather take the blows while repeating the name of Rama. At this non-cooperation your former masters, will make terrible attacks on you. They will give you a sound beating. Do not retaliate in any way but take their blows lying down and continue to call upon Rama. They will grow tired and become powerless to beat you anymore. Give up violence and you will have no enemies.

'Prefer death to the abjuration of non-co-operation and to non-violence.' Son, do you follow what I say?

Patriot   : This is utterly confounding! A riddle at best!

Madman   : At first this seems puzzling but later on everything becomes simple and clear. Sri Guru then commanded, 'Give up untouchability. That means doing away with the sense of discrimination. When I am everything, how can you distinguish between touchable and untouchable? Look upon all as equal.'

Till you can look upon all as equal, your attachment and malice will not leave you.

What else has the Mahatma instructed?

Patriot : He has also instructed to give up foreign clothes and to wear *khaddar*.

Madman : Yes, My Sri Guru too has enjoined, 'You are wearing three foreign clothes. You will not be able to attain Swaraj unless you can give up the three coverings of the Gross, Subtle and Causal bodies.' So I am trying to burn these three attires. I have begun to use the *khaddar* of meditation. What else has he said?

Patriot : He has told us to spin the *charkha*.

Madman : My Sri Guru also has said the same thing, 'Spin the *charkha* of the mind always, spin yarn of the Name.' So I began to spin the yarn of the Name incessantly on the *charkha* of my mind using the cotton of karmic impressions (Sanskars). At first the yarn was not uniform; it was thin sometimes and thick at other times. It would break. But this problem did not continue for long. At first a long thread formed in the heart, which extended to between the brows and finally up to the Sahasrara. How bright it was! The *charkha* began to turn in the darkness. One day I found that a long thread of light had stretched from the base to the head. It was so subtle, that without great concentration, its thinness could not be perceived. See, I have lost the thought again! Yes! Yes, then I began to gather and wind that thread on the reel of devotion. Then I began to hear a big bell ringing at some distance. I would listen to the ringing of the bell and keep drawing the thread. What else has the Mahatma enjoined?

Patriot : He has told us to work at the loom.

Madman : I too, at the command of Sri Guru, began to weave the *khaddar* of meditation with that thread of divine Love. Oh, I have lost the thought again! Yes. When I put on that coarse *khaddar* of meditation, the sound of a cricket's chirp arose, the whole body became still; almost unmovable! Oh! I got lost again. Meditation became *khaddar*, Digambar became Self - the eternal being. Isn't this excellent?

He smiles to himself in his thoughts. He sings to himself, weeps and then sinks back in his own Self.

Do tell me whether I am trying for Swaraj or not? O son, why are you not getting Swaraj?

Patriot : The foreigners cite 'ineligibility' as the reason.

Madman : Crossing the point that marks the 'lack of eligibility' is Swaraj. This point is elusive and proving very difficult to transcend.

Patriot : Sir, now I realise that you speak of spiritual freedom!

ಲ ಓಂ ಜಿ

6. Encounter with a canine

Yesterday, as I was returning from Chandigaccha, three or four dogs began to follow me, barking and advancing upon me, in a rather menacing fashion. They would bite me any moment, it seemed! I told the beads of my rosary, chanting the Name of Rama, and purposely walked on slowly. One second I would fear that the dogs would bite me but the next I would think, 'You (God) are in the dogs as well.' But this thought would not stay for long. I made no attempt to look behind. The dogs went away, after following me for a while.

In the form of the dogs, You gave me such a teaching!

I did not understand then, but have understood since; happiness and sorrow cannot overwhelm, if one keeps remembering You (God); even if the faith is not as firm. If the belief that 'You (God) are everything' becomes firm, then there is no limit to the grace one receives.

In this world, grief, sorrow, disease, want, debt, happiness, wealth, praise, blame and such other things, keep barking at you like dogs. But if you ignore them and continue on your way chanting 'Rama...Rama', they will bark for a while and then stop following you. Ultimately they will be silenced. If the belief that 'Disease , grief, sorrow, heartburn, want, debt, riches, wealth, happiness and peace, are all your manifestations (of God)' becomes established, the mind can no more be troubled. It is a universal truth. If the thought 'You are all' is maintained in one's mind till the faith becomes firm, and 'Rama...Rama' is chanted whenever the mind vacillates, Your grace can surely be received and there is riddance from all types of 'dogs'. This world will continue to bark at you like a dog. It cannot resist barking, be it in happiness, sorrow, wealth, honour, insult, earning or spending. Let it bark. Don't pay any attention to it. Think of the Name and remember that 'You are all'. The world will become peaceful.

See, how many forms You assume to deliver Your teaching, encourage me and assure me, yet I am not able to become still. Whether in daily duties or in worship I become very ill at ease when I am not able to feel Your presence within myself. I feel that everything has become meaningless. However, next moment when I remember that You are everything and that You are the joy as well as the sadness; the despondent mood disappears. Remembering that You are listening to me makes me happy when I pray. There is no pleasure in praying without You in my thoughts. Again when I think that 'You are all'; 'there is nothing without You'; 'even my forgetting You is You', my mind gets a little quietened.

I well understand that nothing can come of my own efforts. It is foolishness to expect to find You by meditation. If my praying and worship is of no avail, as is my practice of Yoga and meditation, then what shall I do? With whom shall I seek refuge? Whom shall I let know of the agony of my mind? Who will listen to me? Who will understand my pain? No one! No one will give me assurance on any count. Rather, I get threatened! I am cast in the role of a doer and then, blame or praise is heaped on me! Now I see that I have no way of salvation but through You. Hence I want to know You! Therefore I want to catch hold of You! Therefore I want to speak to You! I cannot prevent my mind from speaking. Since the mind must speak, from this day I will speak only with You. Well, do You not feel inclined to talk? Please speak. Are You angry? Why are You angry? No longer shall I be disobedient to You. I will do what You ask me to do. Tell me what I am to do. I have said this many times before but am not able to keep my word. My work remains imperfect.

I am defeated, tired, oppressed by the constant battling with the worldly affairs, by the repeated 'coming and going' into and out of this world, birth after birth, and by the tyranny of endless desires. Today, I seek shelter from You! Give me shelter. Please speak, You must speak. Here while I am writing, You are all around me. Can You not hear me? If You can hear, why do You not respond? Where are You not? It is You, who are the earth, water, fire, air and space. You are the ears, the skin, the eyes, the tongue; the nose, speech, the hands, the feet and the other organs. You are the mind, the intelligence, the spirit and the ego. You are the directions, the Wind, the Sun, Varuna, the Ashwini twins, Indra, Upendra, Yama and Prajapati. You are the blood, flesh, marrow, bone, fat; You are all. You are the cricket that is chirping there. You are the palanquin, the bed, this paper and the pen. You are the expression. You only are the language. You were all that was; You are all that is and You will be all that will be. You will also be that which will not be; everything.

Do You hear me? I do not know what is good or bad for me. I cannot always understand the essence of Your goodness, and that makes me feel strange. Then I do not quite remain Yours and become my own 'I'. Make me Your own; You must, why not?

Please listen there is no one here now. Please appear, just once! Speak to me, just once! What is this? Who is calling whom? Are You calling me? If You know, why are You calling me by that name? Ah! The name of that I know as 'mine' is after all the name of this body! Is it then the name of this burden of the five elements? Therefore You are calling me by my real name? Yes, please call, loudly. When I hear You call, I remember many things, many deeds. Please do not become quiet, please call! Let me call You and You call me back.

'Rama, Rama, Rama, Rama, Rama, Rama, Hare, Hare

Rama, Krishna, Rama, Krishna, Rama, Krishna, Hare, Hare.'

Your call is very sweet. Speak to my mind, as my mind. Please call. My body reverberates when I hear Your call. It feels as if it has lost control. Please call again and again! Let me fall asleep listening to You. Yes! Yes!

'Rama, Krishna, Rama, Krishna, Rama, Krishna, Hare, Hare.'

ॐ

7. What God does is for our Good

The madman's joy knows no bounds. The madman's Guru has taught him one thing. As soon as he thinks of it, he forgets everything; sorrow and suffering, disease and grief, honour and dishonor. That thought remains in his mind as long as he utters the name of Rama. As soon as he forgets to utter the name of Rama, he no longer remembers his Guru's words.

Having fallen in great suffering he had said to his Gurudeva, 'Thakur, tell me such a word as will remove all the sorrow from my mind, when I remember it.'

Shree Gurudeva had said, 'Always repeat the name of Rama and maintain a firm belief that whatever God does, he does it for our good. Disease, grief, sorrow and such other things will not be able to overwhelm you.' The Madman has been thinking of this statement ever since and has been repeating the name of Rama. He is unable to hold his belief in the statement whenever his repetition of 'Rama Rama' becomes weak. He began applying this teaching to every situation.

He began to think, 'An incurable disease is not cured by medicine and even the physician admits defeat; what good does God do in this matter?' He remembered a man who started uttering the name of Rama only after he had been attacked with a serious disease. Then God surely does well by bringing diseases. A disease also is good because man learns to utter the name of Rama on becoming ill. He forgets to wail for the dreamlike world. The disease of uttering the name of Rama is also good. Man becomes devoted to God in disease and grief. Now I have got it 'Whatever God does is for the good'. Rama, Rama, Sitaram.

Well, there are men who are poor, have nothing to eat, who may get food but once in a day and have no provisions for the next; what good does God do for them? The madman began to think. When a man is poor he has no ego and can understand the misery of the poor. People hate the poor so he cannot approach other people. Whomsoever he approaches thinks that he has come to ask for something. Everybody avoids the presence of a poor man. A poor man has no place to live, other than in isolation. Living in isolation he senses the presence of his inner self. Then he talks with Him, becomes acquainted with Him and lives day and night joyfully with Him. The sadhus love the poor very much. The sadhus step into the house of a poor man to gratify him. They bring him nearer to God. He receives God's grace. God is the wealth of the destitute. God remains away from a man so long as he has something to call his own. As soon as the attachment to possessions is dropped, God comes and embraces him. This is the eternal way of God. The madman knows of a man, who, despite being poor, experienced great joy and by a miracle came to receive many things which he now uses for the service of his God. It is poverty that leads man towards God. Now I have realised it, 'Whatever God does is for the good of man.'

The madman began to examine all events howsoever little or great. He found every happening to be consistent with the statement 'Whatever God does is for the good'. In disease and grief, sorrow and pain, he saw that whatever God did was for the good. Even when he is not able to clearly identify the element of 'good' in a situation, he continues to believe that whatever God does is for the good.

He knew a woman. She had become a widow in her youth and had taken shelter in her father's house. For her, the world was a source of great suffering and continuous uproar. So he could not understand what good God did for the woman. After some time the madman heard that the woman was reciting the name of her Guru and later he saw that the she had attained *samadhi*. He understood. He danced and said, 'Whatever God does is for the good.'

Rama, Rama, Sitaram.

When he saw a licentious drunkard, he could not immediately relate it to the teaching. He could not understand what good had God done. After some time the drunkard lost his relish for wine and began to hate the company of woman. He became a great devotee of Hari and started spending his days in speaking of God. He was glad to become a servant of God. The crazy man's joy knew no bounds. He danced and said, 'Whatever God does is for the good.'

The madman sees a creditor saying very bitter things to a debtor. The debtor is shedding tears and silently calling out to God. There is no means of repaying his debt. What good did God do here? Being unable to decide anything the madman spoke out loudly, 'Whatever God does is for the good.' The debtor says, 'You are right. My master trusted me very much but I stole much money from him. This is the expiation of my sin. Whatever God does is for the good.' Glory to God!

One day the madman thought, 'A poor man reaches out to God if he is fortunate; otherwise he steals and commits fraud. What good does God do here?' Being unable to decide, the madman closed his eyes and meditated on the feet of God. He saw these words appear in his heart, 'They are destroying the fruit of their work by stealing and committing fraud.' The madman said aloud, 'Whatever God does is for the good.'

While reciting 'Rama Rama', the madman was thinking, 'Dacoits hit men on the head with a *lathi*, steal everything, bring about ruin, burn people to death, perpetrate inhuman torture, what good does God do here?' Being perplexed the madman focused inwards and saw that the dacoit is sitting in a solitary garden of Tulsi and is reciting the name of Hari. His whole body is marked with the name of Rama, he wears a garland of Tulsi round his neck and he is telling the beads of a Tulsi rosary.

'Hare Rama, Hare Rama, Rama, Rama, Hare, Hare

Hare Krishna, Hare Krishna, Krishna, Krishna, Hare Hare.'

His torso·is getting soaked with tears. The madman said, 'Well done sir, are you destroying the fruit of your deeds? Well done! Well done! Glory to Him! What God does is for the good.'

One day the madman saw that the son and daughter-in-law of an old man were beating him and driving him out of the house. The old man was crying aloud. The madman thought that perhaps this situation did not reconcile with the teaching. But he was not the man to retreat. He went to the old man saying, 'What God does is for the good.' The old man wiped his tears and said with joy, 'Truly what God does is for the good. I behaved in this way with my parents. I am expiating for my sin. O God, what you do is for the good.'

On a certain day the madman thought, 'Well, so many people are suffering from new ailments and ugly diseases like Kala-azar, beriberi, phthisis, indigestion, acidity, cholera, pox and plague. What good does God do in this?' After all, he is a madman. As he closed his eyes and sat down to utter the name of Rama, he saw the Howrah Station, crowded with people as if it was a great holy place. The tea-shop was heavily crowded. A youth drank tea from a contaminated cup and got infected. He went to the village and spread the disease in his country. The disease killed not only this youth but also the villagers. The madman thought, 'This disease is the result of not observing purity in life. Organisms carrying dreaded diseases are all around and are being ingested. Atonement matches the sin.' The madman decided, 'Good is being done by God, through the destruction of evil created by undisciplined and impure living.' Jai Sitaram.

This scene too disappeared from madman's sight. He now saw before him, a shop in which different curries of fish, eggs and meat were on display. He did not even know the names of all the items. Dogs, crows, beggars and greedy people had cast such glances at them that all the curries had got burnt. People who ate such spoilt food were falling prey to diseases such as indigestion, acidity and colic pain. The madman thought that diseases were indeed good for these gluttons. They were expiating for their sin.

The madman again saw a new scene. A Brahmin, toothless and reduced to mere skin and bone, was crying in hunger. He had no way of eating anything. He could not digest what he ate and suffered from acute pain. Although the madman was unable to decide what good God did in this case, he said, 'What God does is for the good.' The Brahmin said, 'True, He does no injustice. I am a Brahmin. I used to get up only after having my bed-tea, that too without washing my mouth. I never prayed. I had ever only eaten. So today, I have no digestive power and I am about to die of indigestion and acidity. Day and night I chewed betel leaves with tobacco like a goat. I exhibited my liberal attitude by accepting betel leaves prepared by anybody. As a result I have lost all my teeth. My head reels and I cannot remember anything, I speak rudely even when someone speaks sweet words.' The youth cried and said, 'You had rather commit suicide by taking poison than chew betel and tobacco and drink tea like me.' The madman no longer had any doubts. He said rejoicing, 'What God does is for the good.'

The madman thought, 'Well, even those who strictly follow the rules of conduct are also attacked with disease.' At once that question was settled. Evil deeds are the cause of disease. They might not have been committed in this life but how can their consequences be annulled? Deeds done in previous lives come in the form of diseases and affect even devoted persons. It agrees with the teaching, 'What God does is for the good.'

Madman's mind is gradually becoming confused. He is unable to identify any more evil. On reciting the name of

79

Rama, any evil he discovers and gets agitated about, turns out to be good-intentioned. The madman was floating in the sea of joy.

One day, the madman was going down a road, when he saw an old woman coming up, crying, 'O my darling son, where have you gone? I have no one else to call own who will look after me? Who will give me food? I have lost everything for you. I have been reduced to begging for you.' The madman realized that the only son of the old woman had died. Alas! What would happen to the old woman? Well, what good did God do in this case? But the madman did not give up saying. He went to the old woman and said 'What God does is for the good.' Hearing this strange thing at the time of her great sorrow the old woman stared at the face of the madman. The madman sat there and began to meditate on the feet of God. Slowly a man and a woman appeared in the space of his heart. The man said, 'Repay the debt in full with interest otherwise, the consequences will not be good. A great harm will befall you.' The woman said, 'How can I repay? I have nothing. I live by begging. In this situation how can I pay you back?' The man said, 'I do not know how you will pay me. If you do not repay my money you will not be saved. I will exact the money with interest, anyhow. I will make you suffer as you are making me suffer.' The woman said, 'How will you exact if I have nothing?' The man said, 'in my next birth I will be your son. You will bring me up by spending everything you have and with your own blood. Then after exacting my money, I shall die. As I am now crying in grief for my money, you too will have to cry in grief for me in your old age.' The madman's trance came to an end. 'Rama, Rama, he has exacted his money,' he said, 'What God does is for the good.' He stood up. The old woman was still staring at the face of the madman. Seeing the madman's face she had understood although his body was there, he was somewhere else. The old woman caught hold of his feet and said, 'Father! Why do you speak of repayment of loan in full?' The madman said, 'Leave my feet. Leave my feet. I am a madman. I dreamt that you were the debtor and your son was the creditor. He had come to exact his money.' Saying this, the madman recounted his dream. The old woman said, 'It is exactly that. He is not my son, he is indeed my creditor. What shall I do now? Where shall I stand? I have none to call my own.' The madman looked up at the sky and said, 'You are there with your love for all those who have been cast aside and have no one to call their own. O Lord, those who are homeless and without shelter also live in your house. O mother, say 'Rama Rama'. He is yours. The whole world is his abode. Call out to him. See the two eyes, how beautiful are they!' The old woman began to say 'Rama Rama'. The madman ran saying, 'Rama Rama'. Only joy! Only good! What God does is for the good.'

One day the madman went to the burning ghat and saw that a funeral pyre was burning furiously. Now and then there were cracking sounds. Those who were burning the dead body were hitting the pyre from time to time with a bamboo. A beautiful young woman was lying there, distraught with grief and crying. The madman understood that this woman's husband was dead. The madman's tongue uttered, as it had been accustomed to do, 'What God does is for the good'. To know what good God had intended, the madman closed his eyes, started saying, 'Rama Rama' and entered his inner space. He saw that a young man was standing with a pale face and a young woman was scolding him loudly, 'My misery knows no bounds as I have fallen in the hands of a poor man like you. I have nothing! Not even a piece of good clothing, a bottle of essence, a cake of soap or an ornament. Not the smallest desire of mine has been fulfilled. Who doesn't get food! Even jackals and dogs get to eat.' The young man said in a distressed voice, 'Look, whatever I earn I offer at your lotus-like feet. Because of you, my mother, father, brothers and sisters could not be happy. Because of you my world is on fire. Everything is gone. There is no one else now. Please be calm and let us live a pure life in God's grace.' The young woman became more furious and said, 'Shame! Shame on such a husband! Why did you marry? You could have lived with your parents. You speak of God, as if you are his great favourite. Let your God give me what I want, and then I will decide what sort of God he is. Die! Die! It would be better to remain a widow for seven lives than have such a husband.' The young man said, 'Let it be so. It will be so. You will remain a widow for seven lives. As soon as you will become an adult, you will be a widow.'

The madman's trance came to an end. Where was the young man and where was the young woman? The pyre began to burn more furiously. The madman said, 'What God does is for the good' and began to dance. The madman had forgotten all evil and he saw goodness in everything. All is good. Honour is good, dishonour is good, happiness is good, sorrow is good, a widow is good, a married woman is good, a son is good, a daughter is good, there is only good and nothing else. God who is 'all good' has created this universe only to do good. Glory to God who is auspicious! Hail! What God does is for the good.

ॐ

8. The Door and the Path

Disciple : Thakur, can you say where I will go after death, this time?

Madman : I certainly can, if you answer my question truly.

Disciple : Please ask what you want to know.

Madman : Look, Krishna has said that there are three big gates to Hell. They are called lust, anger and greed. Have you, given them up, my son?

Disciple : I have not been able to do so.

Madman : This time when you die you are sure to go to Hell.

Disciple : Well, Thakur, how can one keep clear of the gates to Hell?

Madman : If you give up desire, lust will perish. As soon as lust perishes, anger will not exist. If you think of perishable nature of all things, greed will cease to exist. If you follow the path laid down by the scriptures, greed can very easily be destroyed. Suppose you are very fond of fish and meat. But the scriptures have prohibited the eating of fish and meat for about sixteen or seventeen days, taking into account the eighth and fourteenth lunar days, the full Moon, the new Moon, the last day of every month, Sunday, tenth and eleventh lunar days of both fortnights; not to speak of meat not offered to gods and goddesses. If you follow the scriptures in this way the greed of fish and meat will automatically be destroyed. Why only greed? The three gates of Hell can be closed very quickly by following the scriptures in this way. Yes, Lord Shankaracharya has spoken of another gate -'What a gate of Hell is the carnal desire!'

Do you understand it, my son? So long as you are addicted to carnal desires, be ready to go to Hell; bag and baggage. You will go to Hell as soon as you die. Do you understand? Until you look upon all women as mother figures and bow to them knowing that Goddess dwells in all beings in the form of mother; until you are firmly convinced of that, there is no salvation for you. It is no use discussing this further. You will go to Hell as soon you die.

Disciple   : Well, Thakur, how can it be known where someone has come from?

Madman   : The very appearance of a man shows where

he has come from. If you see a man with illness, enmity towards honest men, envy, deprecation of Brahmin and Vedas, excessive anger and bitter speech, know him as a creature from Hell. Do you want to know the attributes of those who have come from Heaven?

Those have come from Heaven will have these four signs: giving, sweet speech, service of Gods and respect for pious people. In the Karma section of Garuda Purana the attributes of creatures from Hell and Heaven are described. The sign of those who have come from Hell are: dispraise of others; ingratitude; being offensive; cruelty; adultery; stealing what belongs to others; uncleanliness; dispraise of gods; deception; miserliness etc. The attributes of those who have come from heaven are: kindness; performance of rites for the next world; truthfulness and speech beneficial to creatures; belief in the authenticity of the Vedas; worship of the Guru, Gods and sages; keeping company only with honest men; doing good deeds and friendship. My son, know these signs well. If you see them, you will be able to understand who has come from where.

Disciple   : Sure. Now I can recognise them as soon as I see them. Well, Thakur, are there also gates to Heaven just as there are gates to Hell?

Madman   : Surely there are. There are seven gates
             called Penance, Charity, Peace, Self-control,
             Modesty, Simplicity and Kindness. If you see
             these in a person, know that he is on the path
             to Heaven. Krishna has explained these well
             in his Gita.

Disciple   : Well, Thakur, are there any paths of virtue?

Madman   : Yes, these are sacrifice, study, charity, penance,
             truth, patience, forgiveness and freedom
             from greed. These are the eight virtues. If
             you want to be virtuous, try your best to
             take shelter under these. If you are virtuous,
             Dharma will always protect you. Krishna
             loves the virtuous. So, for the establishment
             of order he has to incarnate again and again
             as the tortoise, the boar, Nrisimha, the dwarf,
             Parashurama, Rama, Balarama, Buddha,
             Kalki and Krishna. The other day, there was
             the birth day of Krishna. He was born on
             the eighth *tithi* of the dark fortnight of this
             month of Bhadra. He performed many feats.
             The acts and achievements of Krishna have
             been described in the Mahabharata, Srimad
             Bhagavad, Harivansha, Vishnupurana and
             Gargasamhita. If man reads or listens to
             these, and meditates on Krishna's Leela, he
             can quickly cross this ocean of the world.
             See, because Krishna incarnates in every
             Yuga, this land is today the crown jewel in
             spirituality and the haven of spiritual pursuit
             for adepts and yogis.

Disciple : Now I have heard of virtue. Thakur, what is the way for emancipation.

Madman : As there are three gates to Hell so there are three ways to emancipation. The Lord has said, 'Karmayoga, Jnanayoga and Bhaktiyoga are the three ways to emancipation.'

Disciple : Thakur, what are Karma, Jnana and Bhakti?

Madman : What is done is called Karma. What is done for the pleasure of the Lord, without any attachment to the fruit is called Karmayoga. Perception of Brahma everywhere, is Jnana. The way of Jnana is reason. To reason what Brahma is, what I am, what the world is, wherefrom the world has come, whether or not there is anything called the world except Brahma, is called Jnana. By means of this reasoning man can attain instant deliverance.

Disciple : What about those who cannot do this?

Madman : They will follow the path of devotion. Shandilya says that the highest love of God is devotion. Narada says, 'It is the supreme love of God.' Vyasa says, 'It is love of worship and such other things.' Garga says, 'It is love of *katha* (divine lore) etc.' Do you want to hear more about Bhakti? 'It is extraordinary love for God arising out of overflow of reverence.' Shankara says, 'Enquiry about the soul is called devotion.' Did you get it?

Disciple : No. Please explain in simple language.

Madman : Listening to His praise, singing His praise, remembering Him, serving His feet, worshipping, praying, serving, befriending and dedicating one's self; are the nine forms of Bhakti. Man fulfils the mission of his life by practicing Bhakti. There are other ways of developing devotion: keeping company of devotees, ceaseless service of God, fasting on the eleventh lunar day and observing religious festivals. People will adopt ways according to the inclinations determined by their previous births.

Disciple : Thakur, is there a gateway to emancipation?

Madman : Surely there is. There is one gate to emancipation: Non-attachment. Four monitors keep watch on this gate: Tranquility, Reason, Contentment, and Company of holy men. If you can make friends with any one of them there is no cause of anxiety as you are sure to attain emancipation. They are so powerful that each of them can throw the gate open.

Disciple : Thakur, do you know any way of gaining emancipation for a person who has no capacity for tranquility, control, reason and good company. You asked me many questions but I still find myself facing only a sea of doubts. I am incapable of practicing devotion or knowledge. I have no means of closing the gates of Hell. I am moving everyday towards Hell. How shall I be saved? Please tell me, Thakur. Is there any way out for me? Save me. I seek your shelter.

Madman : Yes, there is. There is a way. It is also not very difficult. If you always utter the two letters, there will be no cause of anxiety. Everything will be accomplished. A notorious robber became a Brahmarshi by uttering these two (that too reversed in order). The book composed by him is the only simple way for those who are incapable of religious practice in this Kaliyuga. Man attains the highest salvation by reading and meditating on that book. Lord Shankara while sitting in the cremation grounds keeps repeating the two letters. Not content with uttering them through one mouth, he has created five heads to utter the Name. Uttering the Name without cessation, Bhola becomes intoxicated with love and loses awareness of the outer world. By the power of the Name, he has even conquered death. He himself is engaged in uttering the Name and is giving salvation to the people dying in Kashi, by saying the Name in their right ears. Her consort is also crazy about the Name. That's enough about the mad man and his mad woman. Another God has been chanting the Name with his four mouths and by virtue of that, he has become the Creator. Another one said, 'Lord, I do not feel content by repeating your Name so please give me grace so that I can repeat your Name till the end of time.' Today, he comes to every place where the Name is being chanted. Teary eyed and with folded hands, he joins the singing of the Name. Another one to whom his wife was everything, crossed the ocean of the world with those two letters as his only help, and at the time of departing, left behind a boat (in the form of a book). By boarding that vessel, millions of the inhabitants of this land have set out on the voyage of emancipation.

Another person flooded Bengal with a deluge of devotion by chanting the two letters of another name of the Lord. Why should I speak of Bengal alone? Many continents were flooded by that great deluge. Navadwip, Shantipur, Nilachal and Vrindavana were totally submerged.

How much more shall I speak of those two letters? If you search carefully the Upanishads, Puranas, poetry, history and other Shastras, you will see those two letters constituting the seeds of emancipation, in every page and every line. Everybody will get whatever he wants. Do you know what those two words are? 'Rama' and 'Krishna.'

'Those who always chant the name of Sri Rama will attain emancipation and salvation and there is no doubt about it.'

As it is certain that a man will die if he be born; as night is sure to come after day, so it is certain that one who utters the name of Rama always, is sure to attain salvation and emancipation. Enjoyment does not require any prayer. It comes uninvited and destroys all merit. Therefore, always chant the Name and the gates of Hell will be automatically closed. Nothing remains unknown to him who chants the Name.

Brahmandapurana says, 'The heavenly light of this Name of Rama goes beyond the Vedas and the Vedanta. They, who cherish this Name always in their hearts, deserve to be worshipped by the three worlds.'

Disciple   : Thakur, may I say one thing?

Madman   : Say whatever you want to say.

Disciple   : What is the use of the Vedas, Upanishads, Samhitas, Purana, Tantras and such other scriptures if everything could be achieved by the Name?

Madman   : They are needed to bring about the love of the Name. How the Name is to be said, what can be done with it, His real nature and Leela, all these are described in the scriptures. How will the devotion to the Name come, if one does not read the scriptures? Why will faith in the Name arise? How will you dive into the Name? Reading the scriptures is therefore needed. See, simply by willing it, man cannot continuously chant the Name. His mind will need to be purified. The Smriti Shastras are meant for purification of the mind. The Smriti Shastras tell us in detail, as to when to get up, how to bathe, worship, offer oblations, serve the guests, serve the cows and what kinds of foods and travel purify the mind and make it devoted to God. The Smritis have not omitted to mention even a single instruction on how to live one's life from birth up to death. What kinds of occupation, conduct and thought are acceptable, are written in detail in the Smritis. If you disregard the sayings of the Rishis as rotten laws of the ancient times, the purification of your mind will be impeded. You will not be able to utter the Name continuously and you will suffer day and night. Have you understood the necessity of the Smriti Shastras?

Then, if there had been no Puranas, who would have pointed out to the distressed mind that if Ratnakar could get deliverance by repeating 'Mara, Mara' and Ajamil attained the salvation by calling his son 'Narayana' at the time of his death, there should be no reason to be afraid, and calling out to Him in whichever manner possible, will open the doors? Had it not been for Puranas, who would tell us that God always protects the devotee with His Sudarshan disc? Who would have narrated the holy story of King Ambarisha if the Purana had not been there? Who would have related how Draupadi was saved from dishonour if the Mahabharata had not been there? Who would have related how the Pandavas were saved and protected at every step? Who would have related how Savitri brought back her husband from beyond death, through the power of her devotion to her husband? The whole world today resounds with the sweet music of the Gita. Who would have created that music of the Gita? It is beyond my powers to give a full account of the scriptures. I am saying just a few things about them. But for the Puranas, who would have related how Prahlada's life was saved from weapons, elephants, poison, fire, water and from being crushed under a mountain? Who would have related how Indra was delivered? Who would have spoken of the wonderful devotion of Dhruva, the five-year old boy? Who would have spoken of the Krishna's grace on his friend Sudama? Who would have spoken of the devotion of hermits like Markandeya, Narada, Vyasa, Vashistha and Vishwamitra? Who would have spoken of the incomparable devotion of Hanuman, Sugriva, Guhaka, Jatayu, Vibhishana and Shabari? Who would have taught the devotees to worship Rama by showing how to chant 'Rama Rama' in happiness and sorrow, in the palaces of Ayodhya, in the dense forest, in the company of her husband and alone in the forest of Panchavati in the Ashoka forest, in separation from her husband? That is why I say that scriptures are necessary for chanting the Name. How will a love for the Name be developed without the study of the Shastras? If the Vedas and Upanishads had not existed, who would give teachings about Karma and Jnana? Who would have spoken of the Ascending and the Supreme? As the people of this age do not have the ability to understand the Vedas, the rishis have provided the teachings through the Samhita and Puranas. We cannot do without the Itihas, Puranas and the Fifth Veda.

If there had not been the Upanishads who would have said, 'See God in everything'? Who would have informed you through the allegory, of the struggle between the gods and the demons, that whatever glory there is belongs to Him? Your notion of being the doer is false; you have not the power to pluck even a blade of grass. Who would have told the story of Satyakama who received from the Gods, without asking, the gift of sixteen-dimensional knowledge about the Brahma? Who would have known that by knowing one, you know all? My son, nothing is to be ignored. Abiding devotion in the Name will not happen till the Shastra is understood and a practice, appropriate to one's path, is pursued. Man submerges into the ocean of Brahma with the aid of just one word. The Shastras are here to help us identify the truth and focus on the One. We have to immerse ourselves in one word 'Om…A-U-M'. Leaving the Vedas and all the scriptures, you take up Gayatri. Leaving Gayatri, you take up the Pranava and then at last when you merge 'A' in 'U' and 'U' in 'M', you can reach the state of oneness with Brahma. Have you understood the necessity of the scriptures?

Disciple   : Yes, at last, all my questions are answered.

Madman   : Then what else is left? Read, hear, meditate and sing the Shastras in a way that you are able to continue chanting the name of Rama. Only then will the mission of your life be fulfilled. If you can always remain engaged in the worship of the Name, you will be emancipated while you live.

Do you understand, my son? Go on chanting the name of Rama.

ॐ

9. The Human Skull

One day the Madman saw a human skull lying on the banks of the Ganga. As soon as he approached it, the skull revealed its rows of white teeth and began to laugh. The madman asked, 'O, skull, why do you laugh?' Then the skull smiled a little and said, 'O living man, why do you laugh?'

Madman : We laugh when we are glad. Why do you laugh?

The Skull : I laugh at your love of this dwelling.

Madman : What love! So long as there is the body we need a place to live.

The Skull : How long will your body last?

Madman : I do not know.

The Skull : Then why do you need a cottage? Sit on the banks of the Ganga and utter the name of Rama. Do not create any other impression in your mind. As you have taken up the path of renunciation, do not put the stamp of attachment on anything. Know it for certain, my friend, that you will have to suffer great agony through everything you stamp as 'mine'. Nothing is real, my friend. Everything is unreal! Listen to this. What did I not have in life? I had incomparable wealth, a handsome and healthy body, a devoted wife and an obedient son. I had all the elements of happiness in the world. There was a day when hundreds of people did whatever I ordered them to do. How many thought themselves honoured, to carry out my orders! There was a time when the citizens trembled at my power. Gangs of robbers fled at the utterance of my name. My kingdom, resources and wealth, kept me completely distracted. I enjoyed the best things and slept on a milky-white bed. I did not know of anything in the world, other than gratification of the senses. It never occurred to me that my body would perish. I thought that I would enjoy this pleasure till eternity. Is that ever possible? The body was attacked by diseases, my wife and son left, and my body also was destroyed. My house and wealth remained where they were. I am lying on the banks of Ganga since a long time. Jackals and dogs ate my flesh, and passed it the next day as excreta. I have been lying here for a long time, separated from my body. How much sunshine and rain, how many floods, storms, tempests and thunders have washed over me! I remain here still and think about the past and laugh. And I tell those who come near me, 'O, you will also become like me, so start calling out to God.' None can hear what I say or see me. Some do see me and say, 'Ah, there is a human skull.' I say, 'O mad man, once this skull belonged to a living man like you. I had not always been dead.' Who pays heed to me? All are engrossed in their own world. Although they cannot hear me, on seeing me, they pause; think of the emptiness of the world for a moment, and move on. Like waves crashing over waves, their worldly thoughts come in and drown their solitary fleeting experience of disenchantment with the world. Nevertheless I keep shouting, 'Everything is false, everything is false!' But who listens to me?

Madman : Well, friend, you are lying here. Has it a purpose?

The Skull : Surely it has a purpose! Not even a blade of grass can exist without any purpose.

Madman : By lying here, what are you doing for the world?

The Skull : God has kept me engaged in a very big task. I am lying here to impart detachment to the people.

Madman : You just said that nobody can hear you.

The Skull : Though many cannot, a few friends like you do come and talk with me.

Madman : Well, friend, do you mean to say that

meditation on God is not possible without detachment from the world? Everything can be done only by practice.

The Skull : No, that is not possible. Practice and detachment are both necessary. God has said in the Gita, 'It can be accomplished by practice and detachment.' Again, it is said in the Sankhya school of philosophy, 'From practice and detachment.' Without detachment none can maintain practice, and Sadhana cannot be permanent. Just by thinking 'I have been reduced to this condition for the sake of the loin cloth' the practitioner becomes attached to enjoyment.

Madman : Then what is the way? How can one be a seeker of truth?

The Skull : The real seeker is the one who is engaged in his quest, by keeping death before him. Without thinking of death, man cannot progress in his quest. Think for a moment; what creates impediment in your quest? It is the gross body and everything that relates to it. If you do not relate to the body and remember that it is perishable, then who can stand in the way of your quest? The gross only creates confusion. Do you know, my friend, that this body cannot be forgotten? As one chants the Name, an exalted mood arises and he forgets the body. After a little while when the mood dissipates and the thought of the body returns, the desire for beauty and pleasure rises in his mind. At this time it is necessary to give him teaching of detachment. Only then will he get into the habit of chanting the name of Rama. Then he will lose himself in the sweet touch of God.

Madman : Well, friend, we feel the touch but why can we not remain immersed in the touch forever? Can you tell me the reason?

The Skull : He who makes the effort can remain immersed.

Madman : What kind of effort?

The Skull : If you search for the reasons one gets touched by God, you find that repetition of the Name is the main. The more one does the Japa, the longer he can remain immersed in the grace. Meditation is the reason for receiving the touch. Increase the Japa and you will remain in touch for longer periods. If you do not give up meditation on God, you will remain immersed in His grace.

Madman : It is seen sometimes that although we meditate, we do not receive the touch.

The Skull : For times like these, calling aloud has been recommended by the *sadhus*. When you feel a distance from God, only calling him aloud brings him near. He comes near in response to repeated calling. Japa is the only way of salvation in this age. Immerse yourself while repeating the Name. By repetition of 'Rama Rama' you will find Him, in the form you seek. The edifice of the knowledge of Brahma is raised on the platform of Japa. If you attempt to raise this edifice without making the foundation progressively stronger, you will find that the knowledge you get is shallow and unstable. Let day after day, night after night, be spent in chanting the Name. Let your mind be steady. If you can make your mind steady in meditation, you can win over life. Then you will see that God will come and reveal himself to you. The Name is greater than God Himself. Chant His Name, you will find Him in whatever form you want, with or without attributes.

Madman : Well, my friend, does He show mercy even if one calls Him inconsistently? Suppose, I want to call him wholeheartedly, but the mind drifts. Is it not falsehood?

The Skull : No, it is not falsehood. Disguising as a *sadhu* and pretending to be a seeker, with the intention to deceive people, is falsehood. The attempt to conquer the mind cannot be falsehood. Practice is there to overcome the lack of focus on the target. There is sure to be fickleness of the mind during practice. Remaining still is called the state of Siddhi or control. You ask about His mercy? Surely He shows mercy. Suppose my name is Govinda and you are calling out my name, even without any real interest, will I not answer or come to you? After coming to you if I find you are not interested, I shall say, 'O friend, I have come.' Likewise, if you call Him even with disinterest, He comes smiling and says, 'Hello, I have come.' You know this.

Madman   : I know it very well.

The Skull   : O brother, Ratnakar uttered 'Mara, Mara' and Ajamil called his son, Narayana, still they were delivered, then why won't you find Him by calling him, in whichever way? Brahmapurana says, 'The name of Hari surely has an effect if it passes through the lips just as fire burns even though touched by mistake.'

In the scriptures He has given hope even to the greatest sinner. You see, friend? Just as the magically charged seeds of mustard, draw out a snake from its hiding, chanting of Name draws the mind, wherever it may be. However attached or great a sinner a man may be, he has no reason for fear. If he seeks Lord's shelter, if he calls Him piteously, 'God, I am a great sinner, I am very helpless. Be merciful to me as you are merciful', He will embrace the man. O brother, He is called 'Deliverer of the fallen and the depraved', even a great sinner is not deprived of His mercy.

Madman : Friend, what you say is very pleasing. Your encouraging message gives hope even to a despondent heart. Your company gives me great joy. I want to speak to you day and night.

The Skull : A great man says that talking is also a practice. If you speak to God, your turbulent thoughts can be driven away. You get to speak and at the same time progress on the path and find a way of salvation.

Madman : My Friend, I will live with you and talk with you.

The Skull : Alright. My friend, man cannot be happy till he gets into the habit of calling Him everywhere.

Madman : My friend, do all believe in God? Do all people call out to God?

The Skull : Yes, but there is difference in the name. It is seen that the vedantin calls God, Brahma, the Yogis call Him Paramatma, the devotees Bhagwan. The Shaiva call Him Shiva; the Shakta, Shakti; the Ganapatya, Ganesha; the sun-worshippers, Surya; and the Vaishnava, Vishnu. Sankhya philosophy refers to Him as the 'Adhi Vidvan Siddha Kapila'. According to Patanjali He is the 'Purusha untouched by suffering'. For Shruti community 'One who gives counsel and shows favours'. According to Mahapashupata He is, 'the creator of the world'. According to the Puranas He is Pitamaha. The believer in yajnas calls Him 'the yajnapurusha'. According to Digambars, He is 'Niravarana - having no body, unknown and unseen'. According to the believer in Mimamsa, He is the Mantras regarded as the object of worship. According to the Naiyayika, the 'one having virtue'. According to Charvaka, He is the Raja as acknowledged by popular belief. This was about the Aryans. Now listen to the views of the Non-Aryans. He is the God of the English, Allah of the Muslims, Brahma of the Parsees, Jupiter of the Greeks, Askuluskulu of the African people, Nayami or Nayamti of Bekuana and the Basutoes, Suki of the inhabitants of New Hebrides Islands, Manitu of the inhabitants of Tori Island and of the Red Indians of North America. Atua of Polynesians, Kat of the Bask Island, Dengi of the Solomon Island, Tavujarik of the Gilbert Island, Aihemi of the Vatayees, Tane of the Huahins, Tao of the Bolbolas, Tu of the Maruyas, Oro of the Tahayas, Rangi of New Zealand and so on. Now you have heard how people call the same thing by so many names. 'There is only one without a second.'

The universe floats on only the One

And into the One will it sink.

Or never did the Universe float.

He is changeless consciousness.

Madman : My Friend! Do not be silent, please speak on.

The Skull : Dive in me O mad man, I alone exist,

The skull remains silent. It says nothing.

Madman : Is this Your doing? Speak. Since you have already made me crazy, please make me totally insane. Say, how I shall spend the days.

The Skull : *When you go,*

Think of yourself

As a wave in the ocean of Reality,

As you sit,

Remember 'I am a pearl in the garland of knowledge,'

Seeing objects

Think that you see the Soul

When sleeping, think,

'I am immersed in the sea of joy.'

Think and be always content.

In this way

May your days

Be spent.

My Name, keep on thy tongue

Be as you are.

Madman   : Sweet, very sweet! Rama, Rama, Sitaram.

ॐ

10. Shalagrama's trip to the Ganges

The madman was getting up after bathing in the Ganga, and was chanting the name of Rama, when he saw a gentleman coming with a Shalagramshila (a stone with a natural holy mark) in his hands. Seeing him the man said, 'See Sir, my father and grandfather had no work to do, so they kept a god as a pet. Who should serve him now? Who should cook for him? So today, I have come to immerse this stone in the Ganga.' Saying this, the Brahmin prepared to throw the Shalagrama into the Ganga, but the madman stopped him and asked, 'who are you; a Brahmin?'

Gentleman   : Yes I am.

Madman   : Can a Brahmin ever cast a Shalagram into the waters?

Gentleman   : Why not? He can. He can throw everything. What is the use of worshipping those stones and pebbles? Sheer waste of time! So I have come to drop it into water. Arrangements are being made to put the Brahmin race together with their tools and the Shastras in a bundle, carry it across the Bay of Bengal and drop it into the Atlantic Ocean. The expedition will start soon.

Madman   : How long you have been suffering from dementia?

Gentleman   : Do you take me for a mad man? No, father, I am not a mad man. I am sane, hold a high post and maintain my family.

Madman   : Since you did speak like a mad man, I had asked. O Brahmin, are the Shastras as light as cotton that you will blow them away with your breath? No sir, they are not so light; they have an eternal existence. God is the protector of these Shastras. Who has the strength to trample on them? Fire has been here since the earliest times. Whoever kicks at it will burn his feet.

Gentleman   : Let it go. It is no good arguing with you. Revered Shalagram, please go and rest in the Ganga.

Madman   : Let me look at your Shalagram. (On seeing the Shalagram) This is a Lakshminarayan Shila! It is very auspicious. Lakshmi will remain forever in the house of the man who keeps it in his home. Brahmin! Who has given you the evil counsel? Do not drop it into water. No one should eat without worshipping the Shalagrama. He who eats his meals without worshipping the Shalagrama lives eternally as a worm in the stool of a lowly creature. This is said in the Padmapurana.

Gentleman   : Smritis, Puranas and other Shastras were

written by envious men. What is that speech worth?

Madman : Who says that Shastras were written by men? Man only remembers them but God is the creator of the Shastras. God revealed the Shastras to the sages whose hearts were submerged in Samadhi.

Gentleman : The person who advised me is an accomplished *sadhu*!

Madman : I do not understand what kind of *sadhu* he is! 'Itihas and the Puranas are called the fifth Veda'. The Puranas are mentioned also in the Chhandogya Upanishad. If he does not believe in the Puranas, then he does not believe in God also. What does he believe in?

Gentleman : He believes only in the Vedas. But I have got into trouble now! I had come to throw away the deity but have run into this hurdle!

Madman : You will surely get rid of the Shalagrama. Just listen to a few things I have to say. Wait a bit, and I will take that Shalagrama myself.

Gentleman : Please say quickly whatever you have to.

Madman : See sir, he was great man who established this deity in your family. By the grace of this Shalagrama you have no dearth of wealth. Look, the worship of Shiva and Vishnu is a daily duty of a Brahmin. Great ancestors established images of Shiva and Vishnu lest the descendants should be deflected from that duty. They understood that in the times to follow, no one would do anything except care for the body. Hence they tried this method to direct their descendants to the path of good so that they may, whether with faith or without, worship the Shalagram and attain the four-fold benefit of virtue, money, desire and emancipation. Please do not bring about your own ruin by dishonouring the forefathers and giving up the Shalagrama. If you listen to all that the Shastras have said about the Shalagram you will understand what an unrighteous thing you have come to commit.

Gentleman : Things have been exaggerated in the Shastras. Whenever the rishis spoke of anything, they always put it up there in Heaven.

Madman : Look here, my son, there is no effect without a cause. What good does the Shalagram do to the Brahmins that they will sing its praises? What do they gain by it? Has the Shalagram won over the Brahmins by bribing them? Why have they proclaimed the glory of only this stone for nothing? It cannot be put to any practical use! It cannot even be used as a weight. Then why do they praise it?

Gentleman : That is the fun! Let everyone establish Shalagram stones and let the Brahmins earn their living by worshipping it. This is the motive! Do you not understand this simple thing?

Madman : Shastras have prescribed praying thrice a day, worshipping Shiva and Vishnu and performing Shraddh and offering oblations to the departed souls, as the duties of a Brahmin. This has to be done by the Brahmin himself. Shastras have also proclaimed Tulsi, Ganga, the Gayatri, the Gita and the name of the Lord. Do you mean to say that they bribed the sages to sing their glory? Put to the test what the sages have said. I do not ask you to have blind faith. Personally serve the Shalagram with devotion and see whether you find joy or not. See what it does for you.

Gentleman : Please say what you want to. But don't vex me by speaking in Sanskrit. Please also explain the meaning.

Madman : The touch of the Shalagrama destroys the sins of crores of lives. Rebirth is avoided and contact with God is established. Padmapurana Patalakhanda says, 'The touch of Shalagramashila destroys the sins of millions of lives. How can there be rebirth after close contact with Hari?'

'Hari who pervades the universe is revealed in the Shalagramashila just as fire that is in wood is revealed by friction.'

Gentleman : How is that?

Madman   : Do you know the Fire-lens?

Gentleman : Yes, fire is produced when it is placed in the
              path of sunrays.

Madman   : Shalagramashila is also the Fire-lens of the
              omnipresent Hari. His light is always present
              in it. It kindles a fire in the hearts of those
              who worship it. Their ignorance is burnt.
              They become blessed by becoming aware of
              their true nature. Do you understand it?

Gentleman : Yes, today I remembered some things from
              long past.

Madman   : Who worships your Shalagramashila?

Gentleman : An Oriya Brahmin.

Madman   : Did you ever worship it with your own
              hands?

Gentleman : Yes, I used to worship it with my own hands
              about 5 or 7 years ago. My mother used to
              make arrangements for the worship and
              Bhoga. Every day I used to eat what had
              been offered to God and then go to office.
              None of us used anything that came to us
              before it had been offered to Him. Then my
              mother and my first wife died. My second
              wife is educated. As soon as she entered the
              home, she fixed the rations for the God and
              engaged an Oriya Brahmin to perform the
              rituals.

Madman : Well, my son, you are a Brahmin, so speak the truth. Which of the two situations, the past or the present, had made you happy?

Gentleman : I experienced enough joy when I prayed thrice a day, served God, did Shraddh and offered oblations with my own hands. Tears came to my eyes when I thought that God was pleased with my worship. My body was thrilled. My joy knew no bounds. Then my wife told me, 'All these are nothing. The tears that come to your eyes and quivering of the body are symptoms of nervous debility. Get yourself medically treated. You have got this disease from worshipping a stone. Give up all those superstitions, prayers and worship.' Since that time, the provision of a pound of rice for God and an Oriya Brahmin, have been in place.

Madman : Hari, Hari! It is when the mind touches God that tears come to the eyes and the hair stand on end. There is enough evidence of this in the scriptures. It is seen even in the philosophy of Patanjali. Is bestiality the symptom of the strength of the nerves? Let it be! The ancestors of that man who sees God in the Shalagramashila live in Heaven eternally at peace. Three Yojanas of land around the place where there is a Shalagramashila or Dwaravatishila, becomes a holy land. He who dies there, goes to the abode of Vishnu. Fruits of Japa and worship if performed

113

before the Shila become million fold. Those who worship the 'chakra-marked shila' do not have to take another birth. Even if a man is a great sinner and the murderer of a Brahmin, he will receive the benefits of the highest devotion if he only sips the water in which the Shalagramashila has been bathed. All the land within a *yojana* around the place where the Shalagramashila is worshipped by a pure man becomes as holy as millions of places of pilgrimage. 'A Brahmin, a sacrificing devotee and the Shalagramashila, all three are my manifestations.' The Lord awards the fruit of millions of 'Yagnas' to him who establishes and worships the Shalagramashila with a cheerful mind. Shiva said, 'O Mahasena! He who drinks the water touched by the feet of the Vishnu, in the form of the Shila, is exempted from the pain of living in the womb.' The sins of even he who has no devotion and is lustful are destroyed if he looks at the Shalagramashila every day. If a man remembers, sings the glory of and meditates on the Shalagramashila, he is pardoned the sins of murdering a million Brahmins. Just as the deer flee in fear when they see a lion in the forest, so do all the sins of men flee at the sight of the Shalagramashila. The man who worships the Shalagrama, with or even without devotion, is emancipated. It appears that you are bored. Give me your Shalagrama.

Gentleman : No. Please go on.

Madman : He who worships the Shalagrama shila
daily is freed from the fear of Yama in life
and death. Hari gives liberation from all
attachment to him who worships Vishnu in
the Shalagrama just once. Now, listen to the
merit earned by the wise one and a Vishnu
devotee who adores and worships the Shila
Chakra every day. 'Spiritual fruits that are
gained by worshipping a million Shivalingas
on the banks of Ganga and by living in Kashi
for eight ages can be had by worshipping
the Shalagrama for just one day. Therefore
my son, to earn my pleasure, my devotees
should always worship the Shalagramashila,
with devotion. Gods, Divine Beings, and
the fourteen worlds reside where Keshava
dwells in the form of the Shalagramashila.'

'There is no doubt that the ancestors of
those who perform Shraddh near the
Shalagramashila, dwells in Vishnu's abode.'

Hari and Lakshmi accompanied by the
holy waters, reside where Shalagramashila
is established. All sins, even murder of a
Brahmin, are destroyed by worshipping
the Shalagramashila. I give the meaning
of the *shlokas* without quoting them in
Sanskrit lest you should be confused. There
are many verses in the Padmapurana,
Shabda-kalpdruma, Pranatoshini Tantra,

Brahmavaivarta Purana, Tantrasara, Devi Bhagawata and such other scriptures. I have told you only a few of them. Give me your Shalagramashila.

Gentleman : Please tell me more.

Madman : Well, listen. As the magnet attracts iron, so this Shalagramashila pulls the hardened heart and takes it to the Purusha who dwells in the realm of the Sun. On reaching there, the heart loses itself and gets immersed in the ocean of light.

Shiva said, 'O Kartikeya, worshipping me in the Shalagrama shila is equal to worshipping me for seventy ages.'

Padmapurana says, 'Worshipping Hari in the Shalagramashila is equated to a thousand Rajasuya sacrifices, performed every day.'

'When one finds a Krishna-shila as a result of the merit earned in many lives, he is liberated.'

Here's what Harit Samhita says, 'By worshipping the Shalagramashila, even a man possessed by lust, anger and temptation can go to Hari's abode. A wicked man devoid of truth and purity or an unclean man can be made ever pure by the touch of the Shalagramashila. Even without going on a pilgrimage, without charity or without performing any sacrifice, a man can be made ever pure by the touch of the Shalagramashila.'

'Places of pilgrimages yearn to receive the man who always drinks the water touched by the Shalagramashila and eats what has been offered to the Lord. That man becomes pure and liberated in this life, and after death, attains a place in the abode of God.'

Did you hear? Give me your deity. What is this? Why are there tears in your eyes? Why are you trembling?

Gentleman : O Great man! Who are you? You have saved me today from a great sin and have corrected a great mistake of mine? What a ruin would I have brought about!

Madman : I am a mad man. I wander about chanting the name of Rama. However, if you do not want to give me your deity, throw it into water.

Gentleman : O great being! Do not put me to shame any more. I came to commit such a bad deed at the instigation of a person who has no devotion to the Shastras, Gods or Brahmins. Pardon me. I will not give up the deity. I will serve Him with my own hands. Today the clouds have lifted from before my eyes. You are my preceptor. I bow to you.

Madman : This is nothing new. The rishis had said that

such things would happen. This proves the sayings of the rishis are right. They said a long time ago that in Kaliyuga men will be void of merit, will be engaged in wicked deeds, will not speak the truth, will run after others' possessions and wives, will speak ill of others and will be envious of others. They will pamper the body mistaking it for the soul. They will be deluded, bestial and atheistic. They will disregard the parents. The Brahmins will be greedy and afraid, and earn their living by selling the Vedas. All will give up their duties and will often cheat others. Men will speak ill of the Shastras and will do whatever they like to do. Men, hostile to Vishnu, omnivorous and bestial, will trample upon the Shastras and create new wicked religions out of their own fancies. Please judge, my son, if these prophecies of the sages have not proved true to the letter. However, though such things may happen while Kaliyug pervades, the Sanatana religion will protect the virtuous. Do not be frightened at the terrible uproar created by the ghosts and evil spirits in the vast cremation ground that is, Bharata. Chant the name of Rama and all disturbances will be removed. See, O Brahmin! From the realm of the Sun, the Purusha resplendent with light and bearing the conch, the *chakra*, the mace and the lotus, is speaking:

'I appear in every epoch for the protection

of the holy men and the destruction of the wicked and the reestablishment of virtue.'

Do not be afraid, do not be afraid!

The madman departed swiftly, chanting 'Jai Jai Rama, Sitaram' and the gentleman with the Shalagramashila in his hand, stood looking at the sphere of the Sun, in bewilderment, his body quivering.

ଓଁ ଓଁ ଓଁ

11. Practice and Perfection

No sooner had the madman stepped out of his cottage than he saw a Babu sitting by the door. Bowing to the madman, the Babu said, 'I have come to take advice from you. Please give me some instruction about the true nature of Brahma.'

Madman   : (Laughs) Have you got direct perception of God?

Babu   : Nearly. First I had initiation from our family Guru. He is a householder. He does not know much. Thereafter wandering about in different places and after many attempts, I began my practice. Gradually progressing, when I crossed the stage of worshipping God with form and reached the stage of meditating on the attribute-less God, I met a *sadhu*. He initiated me into meditation of Brahma. Now I worship the form-less Brahma.

Madman   : What is the worship of the formless one?

Babu   : Sir, it cannot be expressed in speech.

Madman   : If speech and mind do not reach there, how do you worship?

Babu : Well, that is a state full of wonderful joy. I remain immersed in that state. It is a generous, profound and great state like the limitless sky.

Madman : I cannot follow you exactly. You are talking tall. Have you acquired Siddhi (special control) over the Mantra?

Babu : I do not want Siddhi.

Madman : How can you even have Siddhi just like that? It is not the dust on the road. What do you do?

Babu : I run a cloth shop.

Madman : Do you want profit from the business? Be truthful; if anybody gives you ten rupees, don't you take it?

Babu : I am a householder. I surely want money. The family as well as the business belongs to Him. I am only the instrument.

Madman : Is Siddhi the only thing He does not have? To whom do the shirt, the shoes and the fashionable shawl belong?

Babu : I have come to take spiritual instructions on the true nature of Brahma. What are all these things that you are saying?

Madman : I ask you if the mantra you received from your family preceptor has begun to show effects.

Babu   : Yes, it has.

Madman   : The fruits of initiation are of three kinds; good, moderate and bad. What kind of fruit have you received?

Babu   : The whole body would be filled with sensation, tears would come to my eyes and I would see a vague image of my deity of worship. Now the body becomes light and the heart is filled with a blissful mood.

Madman   : O God! I see you do not know what fulfillment of the mantra means. Tears in eyes, blissful mood, the thrilled body; these things have happened many other times in life, is it the fulfillment of the mantra? Listen to what is said in Tarkaratna. (Madman recites a passage in Sanskrit)

Babu   : Could you please paraphrase in our colloquial language?

Madman   : The best sign of the blossoming of the mantra is the attainment of the desired things without any struggle. The main signs of the fulfillment of the mantra are the ability to prevent death, to see God and to be able to use the mantra without any difficulty. The best signs of the fulfillment of the mantra are the ability to enter the bodies of the others, to rise up to the empty space, to wander freely everywhere, to meet the denizens of the sky, to hear what they say and to see the interior of the Earth.

On the fulfillment of the mantra one can attain fame, acquire conveyances, ornaments and live for a very long time. He can control kings and royal clans. He can live happily by performing miracles before people anywhere, and can cure all kinds of diseases. He can cure the effects of poison by a single glance. He can easily become well-versed in the four kinds of learning and can experience manifestation of the qualities of indifference to the world; the desire for emancipation; a spirit of sacrifice; the power to mesmerise people; the practice of the eight-fold yoga; giving up the desire of enjoyment; kindness to all animals and omniscience. All these qualities are characteristics of the medium kind of qualities. Attainment of fame, conveyances, ornaments and such other things, long life, patronage of kings and royal families, power of captivating people, incomparable wealth resources, wife and sons, all these are the indicators of the lowest kind of fulfillment. All these qualities begin to develop at the first stage of the fulfillment of the mantra. There is no doubt about this that he who attains real fulfillment of mantra becomes Shiva himself.

Did you listen to the signs of Siddhis? Have you seen your revered deity? Do you have the power to utter the mantra given by your previous preceptor? Have you got direct vision of God, not in meditation, but just as you see me with your physical eyes?

Babu : Is such vision possible?

Madman : It is surely possible. The statements of Tantra cannot be false. The philosophy of Patanjali also states 'One can see God by chanting the sacred words.'

Babu : My view is that by doing practices with faith, the ignorance is removed and the form-less Brahma is realized. To see God in a physical form is not possible.

Madman : At first He appears in physical form, gives us a boon and then comes the realization of Brahma. It is written in the Shastra that Dhruva and Prahlada saw God. Even in this age Goswami Tulsidas, Ramprasad Sen, Ramakrishnadeva and other devotees had direct vision of God. Bhargava Shivaram Kinkar has said this with great emphasis. Dayal Thakur and Swamiji Maharaj also say this. It is not long ago that the Krishna appeared before Karunamayee at Magra. Many other devotees have seen God in the present age. Physical perception of God does take place; there is no doubt of it. Leave this aside. Have your wishes come true without a struggle?

Babu : No Sir.

Madman : Have you gained omniscience?

Babu : Well, no.

Madman : Then you have not attained fulfillment of the middle order. Have you attained achievement, ornaments, conveyance etc?

Babu   : Well, no.

Madman : If you have attained nothing why did you give up the family mantra and become a worshipper of the form-less God? Look here, my son, worship of unmanifested Brahma is not an easy thing. If you concentrate on one thing, you can gain everything but if you pay attention to a number of things, you will lose them all. One must begin by getting initiation and then make sincere effort to acquire the powers of the mantra. If you do it the right way, your mantra is sure to fructify. Instead of doing that, you do nothing according to the Shastras; do not give up pleasure and luxury, worship according to your whims and expect to attain direct realization. This is impossible. 'In the Kaliyuga many will repeat orally, 'I am Brahma,' but no one will practice it.'

Babu   : Well, do you say that detachment and desire for emancipation is required for the fulfillment of the middle order?

Madman : Yes. From your dress and the cigarette box I can well understand that you have not yet attained the desire for emancipation. Would he, whose heart is restless for emancipation, like to engage in worldly matters? Will a

125

seeker whose inner fire is burning, want to marry a young woman? This does not happen. 'He alone is fit to attain emancipation, who does not feel joy or sorrow in life, just as one cannot know joy or sorrow after death.' Have you reached that state?

Babu : Well, no.

Madman : Then give up such tall talk. Follow with your heart and soul, that which can give fulfillment of the mantra. When you reach your goal and perceive God, the attendant benefits will appear on their own; even without wishing for them. As it is meaningless for a beggar to say that he does not want a lakh rupees because such a sum does not lie on the road; so it is meaningless for a man who cannot give up pleasure and luxury, has no faith in the preceptor, who is unwilling to worship God, to say that he does want fulfillment of his mantra. The appearance of powers will tell you that you are pursuing your object in the right way. Ignoring those powers you have to go on with your pursuit till you reach the ultimate goal. You will surely perceive God. If you get entangled in the possession of powers such as ability to control people and money, all your effort will go in vain. The vicious cycle will start again. One will suffer intolerable pain from the burning effects of poison and snake-bite, if one poses as Shiva before becoming Shiva.

Babu   : Then what shall I do?

Madman   : Rending the knot in the heart during mantra
repetition, expansion of all the elements,
tears of joy, inner thrill, loss of bodily
sensation and emotional speech: these are
the symptoms of mantra consciousness.
Perform *purascharan* after learning from
your preceptor the meaning of the mantra,
mantra consciousness and yoni-mudra.
'Through *purascharan*, the man without
desire can see God, and the one who has
desires, can have worldly gains.' If at first
you do not get mantra fulfillment, try
again, and failing even then, try for the
third time. If you cannot attain fulfillment
even after the third attempt, take support
of the seven methods laid down by Shiva
such as Bhraman, Rodhana, Vashikarana,
Pidana, Shoshan Poshana and Dahana. If
these are followed one by one, success will
be achieved.

Another way to gain the power of mantra
is to repeat the mantra duly stringed with
special energy sounds, during Anuloma-
Viloma, followed by the repetition of the
core mantra. One needs to do one lakh
repetitions. On completion of Japa the
mantra will yield its powers. Request your
Guru and he will facilitate everything.

Babu : See, my preceptor is not a sadhaka. He knows nothing of these things. Please prescribe something for me.

Madman : Fie! Fie! What are you saying? The preceptor is Shankara himself. He is all-knowing, he knows everything. You are seeing an unclean image of your preceptor in the unclean mirror of your heart, but that is not true. Repose faith in him and he will do everything for you. Without firm faith in the preceptor, mantra-fulfillment cannot be achieved. Listen to this story.

There was a sadhaka named Virupaksha in the district of Birbhum. The mantra that he was uttering was incorrect. But because of his firm faith in mantra given by his Guru and his revered deity, and the strength of his Sadhana, Mother could not remain unmoved. She assumed another form and said to him, 'There is a mistake in your mantra. Get it corrected by the preceptor.' Virupaksha said, 'Who are you to blame my preceptor? No, that cannot be true. Go away.' He went back to his Japa. Mother came again to him and said, 'Tell me what I am to do for you.' Virupaksha thought, 'Who is she? Could she be my revered Goddess? Why is she coming again and again?' He said to her, 'Will you be able to do one thing? Do you see this rock on which I sit? Can you carry this rock wherever I go? I have no other work for you?' Mother said, 'So be it.' In a few days, Mother's back began to hurt from carrying the huge rock. Many days passed in this way. Mother went to Virupaksha's preceptor and said, 'My son! Correct Virupaksha's mantra. Because of the mistake in the mantra I am not able to reveal my true form to him and as a result, have to carry a rock on my back.' The preceptor came to Virupaksha and said, 'My son! Chant this new mantra.' Virupaksha chanted that new correct mantra given by the preceptor and the mission of his life was fulfilled. His agony and cycle of rebirth came to an end forever. My son, the preceptor is Vishnu, Brahma and Maheshwar incarnate; the preceptor is the Supreme Brahma. No matter whether the preceptor is ignorant or learned, whether he follows the right path or the wrong path; he is the divinity and the only path of salvation. In brief, you should know that good conduct and purity of food are essential for a practitioner. Japa should be performed only after performing puja.

Babu : Well, *sadhuji* has said that external worship is the least in effect. Do I need external worship?

Madman : Surely you do. Though outward worship has the least effect, its practitioners are also seldom to be seen. You have adorned your body with clothes and ornaments and you run a business to maintain your family. You

129

live in great joy with your wife and son. You are always engaged in activities of the physical world and do not feel any difficulty there. Why does the question of higher form of practice arise only at the time of worship? This will not do.

As long as there is association with outward things, there is also the need for outward worship, which in turn, needs cleansing of the physical elements. There are three levels of Bhutashuddhi also. Therefore outward worship is to be performed only after mental worship. By performing physical worship as prescribed, one does not have to do this for very long. Very soon, the benefits of the higher levels also start appearing. Worshipper will not have to give up the worship; it will leave the worshipper on its own. The worshipper loses himself completely while doing the physical worship. He is unable to continue with the worship and the flowers remain in his hands. Tailanga Swami says, 'From the grossness of the mind comes gross realization of God, from the subtlety of the mind comes the subtle form and from the merging of the mind in God comes the highest realization of God.'

Babu : I cannot understand which of the concepts; Embodied or Form-less, Dualism or Non-Dualism, is true.

Madman : All are true. What is the need of so much
confusion, my son? The simple thing is
that you have been asked to call Him, so go
on calling Him. If you go on calling, He is
bound to come. When He appears, clasp His
feet. He will take you wherever He likes.

Yes, now listen to this. There can be no
worship without the Panchangashuddhi
- purification of the five limbs. This is the
purification of self, place, vessel, material
and deity. Purification of the physical
elements comes from bathing in holy waters.
Purification of soul is done by *pranayama*
and *shadanga nyasa*. Purification of the place
comes from cleaning and decorating the
place of worship with a canopy, incense,
lamps and garlands of flowers. By reciting
the mantra with Matrika-varna (sacred
energised sounds) twice, with Anuloma-
Viloma breathing, purification of the mantra
can be achieved. If the things used for puja are
purified according to the Shastraic methods,
Dravyashuddhi is achieved. After the
worship of Pithashakti, Sakalikarana is done
with the Moola-mantra and Sakalikarana
mudra. Devashuddhi is achieved by
purification of garlands, incense and lamps
by the moola-mantra. After worship one
needs to partake of the Panchanga.

Mantrayoga Samhita says, 'the masters call
the Gita, the Sahasranama, the Stavan, the

Kavacha and Hridaya; the Panchanga. We should read these every day, according to one's spiritual pursuit and practices of the community. Before the Japa, one should visualize Kulluka on the head; Setu in the heart; Mahasetu in the throat; Nirvana in the navel; Mahakundalini in the Mooladhara; Rakini in the Swadhisthana and Kamabija on the forehead. Japa needs to be done with full awareness of the meaning of the mantra and its nature, and imagining the Moola-mantra as a live entity located at the base of the Sushumna. Before the Japa, the mantra, prefixed or suffixed with Pranava, is to be recited seven times to remove the impurities due to birth and death. Then the japa of the personalized mantra is to be done.

Babu   : There are a number of things to be done!

Madman   : Removal of this huge world from your sight, and diving into the limitless ocean of intense joy, cannot be done by doing just a few things. If you cannot do so much, sing the name of Rama. God will lead you on the right path. If the knowledge of Brahma could be attained so easily, knowers of Brahma would be found in every home. You must toil and work with all your might. Keep firm your devotion to the feet of the preceptor and practice the Purascharan of the mantra according to his instructions. Only then can you reach your goal. Chant the name of Rama all the time.

What is meant is that you must repeat the name of your revered deity. Call aloud when God appears to be far, call Him softly when He is near and when He is felt within, call him mentally with the seed mantra given by your preceptor. But call Him you must. Then calling will automatically stop. He will then call you. On His call, you will leave behind your family and pride and plunge into the boundless ocean. Ah! He is the vast ocean of joy. See, while talking with you I was forgetting to call him.

Jai Rama, Sitaram,

Rama, Rama, Hare, Krishna, Hare, Rama.

ॐ

12. The illusion

Madman : Oh, how terribly dark it is! Where have you brought me? I am suffocating! My beloved! In what kind of hell have you left me? Where have you gone? I am yours! Protect me.

What did you say? There's nothing to fear? Well, if that's the case, I shall open my eyes.

Ah, what a beautiful land this is! Trees and creepers; how captivating! The birds are chirping sweetly! It appears that music plays with every ripple in the river! I see that this land too has earth, water, fire, air and ether. Every morning the Sun rises, illuminating the Eastern sky. The Moon too saturates the people of this land, with streams of nectar.

A path runs along the bank of the river. Let me follow this path. Here comes a man muttering something.

Hello, brother! Where does this path lead?

Stranger : Money! Money is the sole object of pursuit in the world. Nothing can be done without money. Whatever be the credit of your good deeds or virtuous living, you cannot achieve anything without money. He, who has no money, lives a life worse than animals. His parents do not love him; his wife and sons do not come near him; his kith and kin, friends and relations, flee from afar.

Madman : My brother, where does this path lead?

Stranger : Neither happiness nor peace can be had without money. Death is a boon to one who has no money. I want money! I want money! Money must be gathered by hook or by crook; by theft, robbery, fraud or villainy. Money! Money! Money!

Madman : What is this? Is this man insane? He goes away muttering 'Money, Money' without answering me. Here comes another gentleman. Sir, where does this path lead?

Gentleman : He who gives you money is venerable; whatever is his station in the society. He, who has money, is a god. We have fallen on such times that we cannot move a step without money. Only he who gathers money has a meaningful life, whether he does so by slavery or any other means. If you wish to be known as a man, gather money. Money! Money! Money!

Madman : This man too did not listen to me. He went away speaking of money. Here comes a Brahmin. He bears on his upper body a cloth with Ram-naam written all over…a Namavali, and he has marked his forehead with a long *tilak*. He seems to be uttering the name of God. No! No! It is not the name of God; he is also meditating on money! Yes Sir!

Brahmin   : *In this world man becomes strong and learned by virtue of money.* As a little pond dries up in summer, the deeds of a penniless man are destroyed. The writers of the Shastras have said this and it is an irrefutable truth, 'He, who has money, has friends and relations. He scatters pearls when he laughs and sheds rubies when he weeps. A penniless man has no one in the world to call his own. The four-fold path of virtue (Dharma), money (Artha), desire (Kama) and salvation (Moksha) is in the possession of the man who has money.' If you have money you can have peace; just as your hunger is satisfied when you have food. If I do not get peace in this life, what shall I do with it in the life to come? That a Brahmin should not take up service, is a worthless belief. Earn money by all possible means; by selling the Vedas, taking up service, stealing, lying, forgery or fraud. I am a devoted follower of this belief. My ideal is, 'Think always that money is meaningful.'

Madman   : Alas! This one also goes away without answering me. Every one speaks of the same thing: money, money and money. What is the matter? Is everybody insane? Ah, here comes a *sadhu*; a personification of peace, clad in saffron robes, with a water-pot in his left hand. He is telling beads of a rosary with his right. He is coming straight this way. O, Lord! Is 'money' his mantra as well?

Sadhu : I don't chant 'money, money, money' for my own enjoyment. I do not want it for my own use. Seekers and saints grace my house with the dust of their feet and it is to serve them that I need the money. Here, look at my saffron clothes, my *kamandalu* and my rosary. I have given up all enjoyments. Whatever I have, is for others. I shall go on a pilgrimage. Give me money.

Madman : O Lord! The reverend sadhu did not cast a single glance at me. He proceeded on his way, saying, 'give me money, give me money.' Where have you brought me, O Lord? I hear a distant chanting and the sound of drums and cymbals. A group singing the name of the Lord is coming this way. Whatever be it, let me join that group and chant the name of God. O Master! What sort of chanting of the Lord's name is this!

'Carry on chanting, money, money, money, money, money, money.

Carry on repeating, money, money, money, money, money, money.

Chant it! Chant the great mantra of

money, money. Chant it. Chant it.'

Madman : What has happened? Everybody says the same thing. From the mouths of many, I hear the cry for money and more money. Oh, the thousands that are running after wealth are not concerned whether they stumble, fall or even die. All are running; I am the only one standing and watching in wonder. Just tell me if I have gone mad or not, my beloved; my everything; tell me, tell me, tell me.

Voice : This is only a dream, so be steady.

Madman : Dream! O Lord, have I been dreaming while standing here since morning? I shall not follow this path now. Let me go the opposite way. Here comes a handsome youth. O brother! How far along this path is a human habitation?

Youth : I am born as a human being to enjoy. If one does not get intoxicated and enjoy sensuous pleasures in the company of women, it would be better to be born a bird or a beast instead. Since God has created you as a man, enjoy yourself; sing and play music; live with women and gratify your senses.

Madman : O Mother! This is a new malady! This person too goes away without answering me. Here comes a middle aged man. Sir, which way lies the village?

Middle-Aged man	:	Woman is the queen of this universe. He, who can satisfy a woman has a meaningful life; he alone is famous and is worthy of being remembered in the morning. Father and mother will die one day, so what is to be gained by serving them? Serve your wife and she will fulfill your four values of life. Instead of worshipping God with flowers, *tulsi* leaves and sandal-paste, you must worship the woman. Is she to clean the utensils of the God who dwells in a dark and damp room or lives in a nest of bats? Is this soft-bodied woman, a cook, meant to make bread everyday for that God who is the lord of lowly creatures? Do not put her to the trouble of serving guests. Serve the woman with dedication and sincerity. The entire world will be contented if the woman is contented. Woman! Woman! Woman!
Madman	:	This gentleman also goes away crying 'Woman, Woman'. Now whither am I to go? Here comes a learned Brahmin. I wonder if I can rely on the Namavali and Tilak. It could be just a show! However, let me ask him. Sir, how far am I to go to find a village?
Brahmin	:	Inquiring about relationship will not do. Enjoy all that is meant for enjoyment. There is no certainty when you will die, so enjoy while you can. Enjoy, enjoy, enjoy. If you have to meditate, chant the mantra of 'Woman,

Woman'. If you have to worship, worship the feet of a woman. If you are to serve as a slave, better be a slave to a woman.

Madman : The Brahmin goes away saying, 'Woman, Woman.' What has happened? Where I have come? Thousands of old and young men are running around, shouting, 'Woman, Woman'.

Is this the abode of Brahmacharis; the holy land of the Aryans? Or is this a vast *burning-ghat*? Are these men or ghouls? What a dangerous trend! Save me, save me, I am in your refuge. Is this truth that I behold? Please tell me.

The Voice : Wake up. This is only a dream, so be steady.

Madman : Rama, Rama, I have been dreaming again! Let it go. I shall go nowhere now. Whatever may befall me, let me sit here. There comes a woman. I shall not speak any more. But then, what is she saying as she is approaching?

Woman : Men get blinded by the desire for women, so they put them on pedestals and act as their slaves.

Madman : Oh what is all this! What terrible uproar the world over!! Enjoy, enjoy. You have come to the world only for a few days, enjoy everything. It seems as if the birds and the beasts, worms and insects; and the trees and creepers too are saying, 'Enjoy'. The breeze too says, 'Enjoy, Enjoy.' It appears that the waters of the rivers lap against the banks, saying, 'Enjoy, Enjoy'. Is it so? Is this the purpose of the noble human life?

I feel very sleepy….I seem to have become very small…A little infant!!

Who are you? You want put me in your lap and breastfeed me?

Mother   : I am your mother, suckle at my breast.

Madman   : But how did you become my mother? I have just come to this country. Everything seems to be scattering. Everything is getting mixed-up. It seems that I had someone who loved me very much. I used to play in His lap like a drop of water on the ocean.

I feel very sleepy.

Now, who are you?

Father   : I am your father.

Madman   : Father, mother, I don't seem to remember anything. I forget when I try to remember. I had someone who used to keep me always in his embrace. Well, tell me. What do you want of me?

Father   : One should learn to read and write. One should serve one's parents. One should earn money and accumulate wealth.

Madman   : Is that so? Where has that dear one of mine gone? Oh, I feel very sleepy. Who are you?

Woman   : I am your wife.

Madman   : Same old story! I cannot remember except that I had someone. Where has He gone? Who are these people that have come? Tell me what I am to do?

Woman   : I am your wife; it is your duty to provide for me, to love and take care of me, to earn money and indulge me.

Madman   : Father, mother and wife; all are speaking of wealth. I remember a kingdom of dreams. What a beautiful country it was! He was there and I was there. Now it feels as if I was never there!

I feel very sleepy. Who are you?

Crowd   : We are your sons and daughters and friends and relations. You should provide for us. Do not remain so indifferent. Earn money.

Madman   : Wherefrom have so many people appeared in the middle of this path? All are talking about money. Money is very essential. Well, shall I do as they say?

Well, where is He hiding?

How dear was He to me! But who was He?

What relation did He bear to me? How much He loved me!

Oh, oh…How terrible! All my relations have turned into snakes of expectation and are biting me. Death! Oh, I am dying, I am dying! O my mother and father, my friends and relatives, where are you? Save me! I am dying!

I am burning with poison. I am dying from the fire of the poison! Is there anybody here? Save me! Save me!

'Save me, O Lotus-eyed Hari, from the ocean of the world.'

Hari Om, Hari Om, Hari Om.

Hari : What is the matter? Are you frightened by my appearances? Don't be afraid.

Madman : Here you are! Now you have come. Were all those people, your own forms? You have now appeared as a Guru to grant deliverance. Who are you? Hari Om, Hari Om, Hari Om.

Hari : Are you dancing, madman?

Madman : Should I not dance? When you have appeared to me in the form of Shabda Brahman, why should I not dance? It is not only I that is dancing. My hands are dancing, my legs are dancing, my tongue is dancing and all the blood cells are dancing in my veins. I am immersed in the Ocean of Dance. Hari Om, Hari Om.

What? You have again become the Mother, the Father, a Woman and a Man….Glory to you!

Hari : You there! Hari Om, Hari Om, Hari Om.

Madman : O Lord! You only have assumed these various forms. You only appeared as father and mother, wife and son; everyone. See, I did not recognize you at all. How painful and agonizing my journey was! If you had sensed this agony, you would not have played such a game. You have appeared in multiple forms. You alone can assume so many shapes. You assume the forms of men and women, beasts and birds, worms and insects, trees and creepers, and play with us. Oh, why did you not tell me all of this beforehand?

Hari : Look, I am all. Those who come to this land and go to sleep are tortured with nightmares. Remain aware. Only then will the knowledge 'I am all' take root.

Madman : But sleep is so overpowering!

Hari : Chant. Chant 'Hari Om, Hari Om, Hari Om', incessantly and loudly.

Hari Om, Hari Om, Hari Om

Then nothing can make you sleepy. Those who are asleep will also wake up at your cry. They will join in and chant your tune of 'Hari Om, Hari Om, Hari Om'. No matter how many obstacles appear before you, do not be afraid and don't give up chanting the Name.

Madman : Afraid of what? You are and I am.

Hari Om, Hari Om, Hari Om.

Glory to Guru!

ॐ ఓం ॐ

13. Possessed!

'Rama, Rama, Rama, Rama, Rama.' The madman would chant the name of Rama and start dancing every now and then. At that time Haladhar came and asked, 'O mad Thakur, why are you chanting and dancing early in the morning?'

Madman	:	Rama, Rama, Rama, I am possessed by a 'pancho'.
Haladhar	:	What is 'pancho'?
Madman	:	A demon, a demon. Rama, Rama. What a beating has he given me! I am nearly finished. Rama, Rama, Jai Rama, Sitaram, Rama, Rama.
Haladhar	:	Only little children get possessed by ghosts. You are an old man. Why would you get possessed?
Madman	:	It is not a recent thing. I have been possessed for a long time.
Haladhar	:	Do you feel any pain? Is he present all the time or comes and goes? How did you get possessed?
Madman	:	He is always present. At first I did not know

at all that I had got possessed.

Haladhar : How did you come to know of it?

Madman : I heard him repeatedly shout 'money', 'wife', 'son', 'I will eat', or 'I want to be worshipped'. Hearing these cries, I became suspicious. I went to an exorcist. His name is Panchanan. I laid the facts before him. The exorcist said, 'you have been possessed by a ghost.' I asked, 'How can I get rid of it?' He said, 'Chant the name of Rama.' The exorcist cast a spell and gave me the mantra. Well, I started chanting but the demon did not leave me.

Haladhar : Perhaps he has left you by now.

Madman : Humph! Sometimes, under the influence of the name of Rama, he does become silent and I begin to hope that he has left me. Dear me! But after a few days, the shouting of 'I will eat, I will eat' resumes. Sometimes he also shouts the name of Rama. Once I did not hear from him for many days and thought he had finally left me. Hari! Hari! Then I heard him say, 'I will read Sankhya, Vedanta and Patanjali.' I knew it was the demon. He could hardly manage two words but wanted to read the Shastras! I began to utter the name of Rama with great intensity and thought that it would finish him off. O God! One day I heard him shout, 'I want to be worshipped.' I said, 'O wicked one, have you not died as yet?' I began to chant the name of Rama with greater effort. Again, hearing no sound for many days, I thought that the evil spirit had finally been finished. But, can a demon like him die? One day I heard him say, 'I will do good deeds for the world; I have developed equanimity.' I laughed and said, 'Panchu Gopal! Do you think that I have not been able to recognize you? No, I know you well. So long as you need even a loincloth, there is no trusting you. You may start with one thing and end up doing quite another. Out of a small seed of desire, a huge tree of worldly illusion will grow. Today you will start to do good for the people but tomorrow you will become eager to hear your praise. That will not do, my son.'

His face became grave. I said, 'Do not be angry. You can do no good so long as you have sense of shame, honour and fear. Don't you know it? Well, you say that you have developed equanimity. Put yourself to the test. For some time now, you have been experiencing great pleasure from getting praise and a great deal of worship from the people. Do one thing. Throw away the clothes you wear, smear dust on your body, and go to the street naked, and dance. Let the people call you mad, throw dust on you, abuse you, and beat you. See if you get as much happiness from it as you did when you got praise and worship. If you are equally happy, I shall understand that you have gained equanimity.' He sat with a long face. I said, 'Do as the Guru has said and you will see how everything becomes the same. Mastery over seven of the eight parts of yoga gives you Nirvikalp Samadhi. After crossing the six wheels, the Sahasrara is reached. The Fourth State is found only on the dimension on Jnana.' The wicked spirit was speechless. I tried to explain, 'Equanimity is not a glow-worm that goes into hiding. It is the autumnal Moon which lights up the world when it rises.' Do you know what the fellow says? It says, 'One also has to give as one receives.'

I said, 'For so many years you have been following the practice of giving as you received. Go naked; pick up excreta in one hand and sandalwood in the other. Narayana's *prasad* in one and food tasted by another person in the other; taste and see if you feel the same about both.' The ghost went quiet. He does not know how to do the sum but he has memorized the answer.

Rama, Rama, Rama.

Ah! What a good charm the exorcist Thakur had taught! As the demon, so the remedy!

Rama, Rama, Rama, go on chanting the name of Rama.

Haladhar   : Have you seen the demon?

Madman   : Surely I have seen it.

Haladhar   : What does it look like?

Madman   : Just like a man. He is three and a half cubits
tall. He has eyes, ears and a nose. He also
has two friends. They hunt together. Yes,
one day the fellow said, 'I have made the
world vanish by reasoning.' Hearing this, I
gave him a knife and said, 'Make this knife
vanish with your reasoning. Then I shall see
whether or not it can chop off your nose.'

The demon fell silent. He poses as Shiva,
though he is not. Do you know what
happened another time? The demon said, 'I
have attained the Samprajnata Samadhi'. I
said, 'What are you saying? By discriminating
between the object, the process of receiving
and the receiver, Samprajanata Samadhi
occurs with the Gross and, with or without
the use of reasoning, the Samadhi happens
with the Subtle. Engrossment with the
process of receiving, with or without
reasoning, is called Sanand. After gaining
mastery over these, the ability to meditate on
any form, from the minutest to the largest,
is born. After that, comes Asamprajnata
Samadhi.'

I asked the ghost, 'Tell me what one feels
in Sananda Samadhi? How does one move
from Sananda Samadhi to Sasmita Samadhi?
Where does one have to meditate to realise

that the atom is the greatest principle?' The
fellow ignored it and kept quiet. I said, 'Does
Asamprajnata Samadhi happen at the snap
of one's fingers? Only after crossing the
Samprajnata is the Asamprajnata Samadhi
attained. O, Pencha! Your Samadhi is nothing
but ordinary sleep.' The knave is tormenting
me in this way.

Haladhar : Why is he doing so?

Madman : Don't you understand? He wants to be
worshipped. He wants to go to Africa on a
ship to preach the Hindu religion; leaning
against a bolster, smoking a hubbly-bubbly.
Not only this, he has numerous faults but
is blind to them. He will criticize others
on their face but will be all ears to his own
praise. This way, he continues to torment me.

Haladhar : Can you show me the demon?

Madman : I can show you the fellow but the other two
are invisible. Rama, Rama, Rama.

Haladhar : Come, show me.

Madman : Rama, Rama, Rama, (pointing at his own
body) look here.

Haladhar : O Madman, this is your body, this is you.
How can it be the demon?

Madman : This very fellow is the demon. His den is
made of the five great elements. This is not

I, my son. Is he alone? No, there are three of them; one is coarse and the other is subtle. Having fallen in their hands I have been driven mad. I do not even remember who I am.

Haladhar : Is this your demon?

Madman : Yes, my son, this is the demon and his den. I have heard that the business is well spread. The beautiful world that you see before you is also this wretched fellow's doing.

Haladhar : O Madman, why do you abuse him?

Madman : I did not abuse him. He is not an infant that his ignorance can be overlooked. That, which scholars call 'the abode of that which has not been created' is called by ordinary men as 'the abode of ignorance'. By calling it names, I have not abused him but have spoken of his true identity.

Haladhar : Somehow I do not understand the statement that the world does not exist. I am seeing the world and I am seeing the body, then how can the world not exist?

Madman : That is the fun. I have heard that a great Master is at its root. He hides in the unfathomable waters and his whereabouts cannot be known easily. And there is also his consort. She too has been up to much mischief. Unless she is pleased, no work can be accomplished. To approach the Master, you need to do the Mistress' bidding. She is a very stern woman. She cannot be easily brought under control. But I know that she is very fond of being called 'Ma'. If you can call her 'Ma' she will carry you in her arms to the Master. Once you get hold of the Master, you escape from this cage.

Haladhar : Why do you call him a Master?

Madman : I don't call him a Master for nothing. Just see how he has prepared the cage. Is that all? Together, the two start playing the *dhaks*, *dhols*, *kansar*, *kamanagara*, drums, *khols*, cymbals and many other musical instruments. Their sound stupefies you and you are not able to breathe. Sometimes, you hear the sound of drums, cricket-like chirping, humming in a sweet voice or the plucking of a stringed instrument. The helpless mind becomes overwhelmed and restless.

Haladhar : What madness is this!

Madman : *It is not easy to be mad. A madman, who is rational, cannot find the Mother.*

You will never find the Mother

If you do not go mad for good,

A 'sane' madman by cunning,

Will never find the real 'Ma'.

Do you not know, this world around

Is a pure imagined thing?

It is the core of Shri Nath's tale

Open your eyes and see.

With detachment at your side

Set out to seek the Truth

Chanting the name of 'Kali'

Go mad in love and dance

The mad man began to dance.

Haladhar   : Stop, stop.

Madman   : He also has a flute. On hearing the flute, no one can stay still. The flute has seven note-holes; Sa, Re, Ga, Ma, Pa, Dha and Ni. There is also a Veena which has seven strings. See, by uttering the word seven I have got into difficulty. I am now reminded of the families of sevens.

Haladhar   : How?

Madman   : The master has designed everything with fives and sevens. See how many things are sevens. His own room has seven coverings; the primeval pulsation, Pranava, A-U-M, Nada, Bindu, that which is within reason and that which is beyond reason. There

154

are seven Gayatris which are vehicles for the offerings; Gayatri, Ushnika, Anustup, Brihati, Pankti, Tristup and Jagati. Agni has seven tongues; Kali, Karali, Manojava, Sulohita, Sudhumravarana, Sphulingini and Viswaruchi. The names change a little according to the special rites being performed. In Satviya yoga, these are called Hiranya, Kanaka, Rakta, Krishna, Suprabha, Bahurupa and Atirakta. For performance of Rajasic deeds, they are called Vishwamurti, Sphurlingini, Dhumravarna, Manojava, Lohita, Karala and Kali. Their presiding deities are Amartya, Pitru, Gandharva, Yaksha, Naga, Pishacha and Rakshasa. These have seven Dhatus; juice, blood, fat, marrow, semen, flesh and bone. The horses of Surya are seven. There are seven colours. There are seven divine rishis; Sanatsujata, Sanaka, Sanandana, Sanatkumar, Kapila, Sanatana, Narada. The rishis of the physical world are; Marichi, Atri, Angira, Pulastya, Pulaha, Kratu and Vashishtha. Their seven wives are; Sambhuti, Anasuya, Kshama, Priti, Sannati, Arundhati and Lajja. The seven currents of the Ganga are; Hvadini, Pabani, Nalini, Shivajala, Suchaksu, Mahanadi and Sindhu. Inside the human body there are these seven lotuses; Muladhara, Swadhisthana, Manipura, Anahata, Vishuddha, Ajna and Sahasrara. Bhu, Bhubah, Swah, Maha, Jana, Tapah and Satya, are the seven higher worlds. Atala, Vitala, Sutala, Talatala, Rasatala, Mahatala and Patala, are the seven under worlds. The seven schools of philosophy are; Nyaya, Vaisheshika, Yoga, Sankhya, Karma-mimansa, Daivi-mimansa and Brahma-mimansa. There are seven seas; Lavana, Ikshu, Sura, Sarpih, Dadhi, Dugdha and Jala. There are seven continents; Jambu, Plaksha, Salmali, Kusha, Krouncha, Shaka and Pushkar. Each continent has seven coasts and seven mountains and seven main rivers. There are seven bases of knowledge; Shubhechchha, Vicharana, Tanumanasa, Sattwapatti, Asangsakti, Padarthabhavani and Turyaga. There are seven bases of knowledge in Daivi-mimansa; Jnanada, Sannyasada, Yogada, Lilonmukti, Satyada, Anandapada and Paratyara. There are seven secondary Rasas; Hasya, Veer, Karun, Adbhut, Bhayanak, Vibhatsa and Raudra. Attachment to service, attachment to friend, attachment to wife, attachment to filial affection, attachment to surrender and attachment to singing glory, are the seven Rasas in Daivi-mimansa. Samadhi has seven parts; Yama, Niyama, Asana, Pranayama, Pratyahara, Dharana and Dhyana. There are seven parts of a kingdom; lord, minister, friend, treasury, country, fort and strength. The Ramayana has seven Kands. The Gita consists of seven hundred shlokas. The incapable person reads the Gita of seven shlokas. The Chandi has seven hundred shlokas. The reading of Srimadbhagavata is to be completed in seven days. The planetary system is of seven planets. There is a constellation of seven stars. Parashurama made the earth empty of Kshatriyas, thrice seven times. Rama Chandra lived in the forest for twice seven years. Raghunatha pierced seven Talas in a test before Sugriva. To rescue Sita, he started the worship of Durga on the seventh day of the Moon. The Vasanti Puja is held on the seventh Tithi. After coronation Sitadevi lived in Ayodhya for twenty-seven years. Krishnachandra held the mountain Giri Govardhana for seven days. Seven chariot-warriors surrounded and killed Abhimanyu. Seven days around an eclipse are inauspicious for any journey. The first and other case-endings are seven in number. Wild beasts are of seven kinds; the buffalo, monkey, bear, reptile, antelope, speckled antelope and deer. Country animals are of seven kinds; cow, sheep, goat, horse, mule, ass and man. The days are seven. Rich people build houses having seven stories; or seven palaces. The bird-hunter kills birds with a seven-barreled weapon. If the Abhimanyu of pride is to be killed, a seven-barreled weapon and seven charioteers are needed. There are seven streams of wealth for prosperity. The Mangalya thread is spun seven-fold. At the time of marriage ceremony, seven married women are present. Only after taking seven steps there is the change of the Gotra for the bride. Then after death, after placing the body on the pyre one has to go seven times round it before fire is applied to its mouth. In the mantras of the Shradh ceremony too, there is treatment of the seven obstacles. Did you listen to the story of number seven?

Haladhar   : How wonderful! So many sevens!

Madman   : I tell the ghost, 'You will have to fight in the Kurukshetra and overcome the seven chariot-warriors.' Duryodhana said, 'Keshava, I will not give up without war, even half of so much earth as is pierced by a sharp needle.' Not even as much knowledge as can be held on a needle-tip can be obtained from ignorance. Fight and overpower the seven chariot-warriors. Only then will you be saved. The naughty fellow flattened two or three warriors and then came and said, 'I am He'. Go appear in the test. Throw away the clothes. He looks at Kashi on a map and gives you such graphic descriptions as if he has just returned from there. The imp is tormenting me in that way. Rama, Rama, Rama.

Every one has to appear in a test. Rama went to the forest and when Ravana kidnapped Sita, he sought help from Sugriva and assured him that he would kill Bali. Sugriva said, 'Appear in a test'. In the test Rama had to pierce seven palm trees with a single arrow. Sugriva means one who has a beautiful neck. He whose body is perfectly aligned with his mind is Sugriva. Appear in a test before him. Let seven palm trees be pierced with one arrow. Only then Sugriva would understand that you have the strength to kill Lust in the form of Bali, the friend of Ravana, the ignorance incarnate. Let alone seven palm trees; no sooner he pierces three palm trees, and sees a little light, than Pencho starts saying, 'I am He'. He does not recognize that there are still four trees remaining. Midway itself, he starts to say, 'I am He!' Well, how many times will you say, 'I am He' with one tongue? If you really want to hear 'I am He', go to that land:

Where the heady music flows

And melodies playfully swell and hum

Where strings of a thousand veenas sing

'So'ham' 'So'ham' – the best mantram.

Pencho would not listen to this. After all he is a slave to lust, who pretends to be enlightened. Pencho has given me so much trouble that my anger will subside only when I can make him wear a loin cloth, and go from door to door begging with a coconut shell in his hand. Rama, Rama, Rama.

159

So you heard about the greatness of seven. Thinking of fives and sevens, I got angry. Rama, Rama, Rama.

Haladhar : Well, you say 'Rama Rama'; where does the number seven occur in Rama?

Madman : Seven rishis came and taught Ratnakar this mantra. The Fish, the Tortoise, the Boar, the Nrisinmha, the Dwarf, Parashurama and Rama; the seventh incarnation is Rama. That is how the number seven applies. Well, I was also speaking of the flute. Whoever hears the Maestro's flute, even once, gets smitten. There was a princess. Someone came and told her the name of Shyama. That marvelous name entered her heart through her ears and rendered her absolutely helpless. Radha began to utter the name of Shyama, continuously.

I know not how much sweetness has the sweet name of Shyama. The tongue cannot leave it.

Uttering the name I've grown helpless. .

How can I meet him?

'Where will you go?' So sang the flute.

And Radha began to say,

'Hark! He plays his flute!

Is it playing in the forest or in my mind?'

The deliverance was done.

Radha was lost for eternity,

Uttering endlessly;

The name of Shyama.

Nimai Pandit was a healthy, strong and beautiful youth. He went to Gaya to offer *pinda* to the departed soul of his father. As soon as he looked at the lotus-like feet of Gadadhara, the Maestro played the flute. Immediately, tears started streaming from his eyes and his body began to shiver. Nimai returned to his country. There was no word other than Krishna on his tongue and no other image other than that of a dark-hued boy playing a flute. He left his old mother, his young wife, his home and family. Nimai wandered through the lanes crying, 'O Krishna, O Krishna, O loving Radhe.' Krishna cannot be had without reaching Radha. 'Without the form of the Devi, the Formless One cannot be perceived.' Without the mercy of the intoxicated one, He cannot be perceived.

Haladhar : Where does She, the intoxicated one, live?

Madman : She has multiple forms and is present everywhere. She is Prakriti on the left side of Purusha, Durga on the left of Shiva, Sita on the left of Rama, Radha on the left of Krishna and the Kundalini in the Muladhara. She assumes the form of Pranava. My Mother has infinite forms, she is always joyful.

I run to hold your feet, O Ma.

But always fail and miss.

One thought of you, my mind dissolves!

What a difficult test is this!

Jai Rama, Sitaram!

ॐ

14. Breaking of the Bow

Madman	:	Rama, Rama. Release the arrow, break the bow!
Harihar	:	O Mad Thakur! Who are you targeting with your arrows this morning?
Madman	:	Him, him!
Harihar	:	Where is your bow? And where is your arrow? Are you verbally breaking the bow?
Madman	:	Everything is within me; the bow and the arrow. If I could just somehow break the bow!
Harihar	:	Will you get Sita? Ramachandra won Sita by breaking the bow. Do you have such a motive? Since everything is within you, Rama and Sita are also surely there. What do you say?
Madman	:	It is Rama who is breaking the bow. Till bow is broken, I cannot rest in peace. Rama, Rama. Please release the arrow, break the bow!
Harihar	:	Well, who has given you the bow?

Madman : Shiva has given it. Who else but Shiva can give the bow? Rama, Sita, Shiva and the bow; all are there. Only the bow remains to be broken. As soon as the bow is broken Mother will bring the garland and put it around Rama's neck. Being one with the Mother, Rama, Shiva, the bow and the arrow, is such a joy! Jai Rama, Jai Sitaram. (Dances) Jai Sitaram.

Harihar : Stop! Stop! You have started dancing early in the morning! What games this madman plays! There is nothing but he is going on dancing.

Madman : (Clapping his hands and dancing). Come if you want to see the meeting between Sita and Rama.

Harihar : This madness will not do. Tell me where your Rama is.

Madman : Why, my Atmarama lives in my heart.

Harihar : Where is Shiva?

Madman : Why, Shiva resides as the Guru in my Sahasrara.

Harihar : Where is the bow?

Madman : Why, the Guru has given the bow of Pranava.

Harihar : Where is the arrow?

Madman : Why, that is my soul.

Harihar : You just called your soul Rama and now you are calling it the arrow?

Madman : Yes. As Rama, he draws the bow, and then
becomes the arrow to meet the target. Break
the bow, break the bow. I cannot rest in peace
so long as the bow remains intact.

Harihar : Yes, I forgot the real thing; where is Sita?

Madman : Why, Brahmavidya is Sita.

Harihar : What are you saying, madman?

Madman : I am saying, Pranava is the bow, the soul is
the arrow and Brahma is called its target.
Look here, all these things are very complex.
When one thinks of breaking the bow, the
mind boggles. The bow only is Rama. It is
Sita. It is the Vedas, Vedanta, Tantra, Mantra,
Puranas, the Ramayana, Smriti, Bharata,
Itihasa and the fourteen worlds. During the
Night of the four-faced Prajapati, only the
bow remains.

Harihar : What a madman!

Madman : Am I the only madman? Shiva went mad
meditating on the Tattvas. He renounced the
world, and with a *damaru* in his hand, started
dancing and chanting the name of Rama from
his five mouths. Is it an ordinary dance? He
taps out the rhythm with his feet and chants
'Rama, Rama, Jai Rama, Jai Rama.'

Harihar : You have started dancing again! I have not
completed what I have to say. Stop. If the
bow is broken, how will the union between

Rama and Sita come about? What is the wedding garland?

Madman : As soon as the bow is broken and the arrow pierces the target, Sita will come and put the garland of Jivanamukti round Rama's neck. Just watch the kind of union it will be. Just watch. Just watch the union between Sita and Rama.

Harihar : Where is the union?

Madman : What! Can you not see the union? Watch how in the morning, mother Sita arranges flowers in a basket and worships Rama. Watch how as a bird, she sings praises of Rama, how she performs Rama's *arati* with the Sun as the Lamp and how she washes Rama's feet with the river Ganga as water. She fans Rama with the breeze which is laden with the fragrance of flowers. Why, so many things are happening and you are not able to see?

Harihar : Where, brother? I cannot see anything.

Madman : Take, take my hand and dance with me. Chant 'Sitaram Sitaram'.

Hand in hand, the madman and Harihar, begin to dance, chanting 'Sitaram, Sitaram'. The place becomes the abode of the Lord and unseen, the sage Narada, joins the chanting of the Name.

Jai Sitaram.

ಲ ಓಂ ಜಲ

15. Game of the Swan

The Madman came out of the cottage and cried, 'Jai Sitaram. Oh! This is a huge swan', and began to dance. Haladhar came there and said, 'O, mad baba! Why are you shouting 'Swan, Swan'?

Madman   : I do not shout for nothing. The cry of the big swan has made me restless. So I am shouting. Jai Sitaram. Jai Sitaram.

Haladhar   : Where is the swan? There is no swan here!

Madman   : Is it a tiny little swan that it can be seen?

Haladhar   : What a madman! Big things are visible first.

Madman   : Is it an ordinary, big swan? It is bigger, bigger, and much bigger than that. Jai Sitaram.

Haladhar   : Just tell how big your swan is.

Madman   : Then let me tell you. Will you be able to imagine it when you hear about it?

Haladhar   : Just tell me.

Madman   : The Bhuloka is found in the feet of the swan, Bhuva in his thighs, Swarloka at its waist, Maharloka, in its navel, Janaloka in its heart, Tapaloka in its throat and Satyaloka in between its brows.

Haladhar : This turned out to be an immense swan!

Madman : Yes, my son. He, who is Pranava, is the Swan. The Shrutis have commanded worshipping the Pranava as the Swan. There are four deities for the matras of A, U, M and Ardhamatra. The right wing is the first syllable 'A' and its deity is Agni. The left wing is the second syllable, 'U' and its deity is Vayu. The tail is the third syllable 'M' and its deity is the Sun. The head is the Ardhamatra and its deity is Varuna. Jai Sitaram. Jai Sitaram. Do you wish to hear more?

Haladhar : Yes, I would like to.

Madman : Each of these has three qualities. The right wing is 'A', its first *kala* or quality is called Ghoshini; the second, Vidyumala and the third, Patangi. The first quality of the left wing is called Vayuvegini; the second is called Namadhyeya and the third, Aindri. The first quality of its tail is called Vaishnavi, the second, Shankari and the third, Mahati. The first quality of the Ardhamatra is called Dhruva; the second, Mouni and the third, Brahmi.

Haladhar : Why are the qualities so named?

168

Madman : Ghoshini gives commands. If a man dies meditating on Ghoshini, he becomes a sovereign king. If one dies meditating on Vidyunmala, one becomes a powerful Yaksha. Patangi gives one the power to move in the sky. The man who dies while meditating on her is born as a knower of science and spells. If a man dies meditating on the Vayuvegini, he is born as a Gandharva. If a man is dissolved into the five elements while meditating on Namadhyeya, he is transformed into a God and is worshipped in the Somalok. If a man dies meditating on Aindri, he is absorbed into Indra. Death during meditation of Vaishnavi and Shankari, leads to the attainment of Vaishnavapada and Rudratva, respectively. Death while mediating on Mahati, leads to Maharloka; Dhruva, to Dhruvaloka; Mouni, to Tapoloka, and Brahmi, to the eternal Brahmaloka. Do you understand? Jai Sitaram.

Haladhar : Yes, I understand. But how is the quality or *kala* to be identified?

Madman : Take every movement of the wings to be a *kala*. Then he, who leaves the mortal coil while meditating on the *bindu*, attains Brahma; that is ever sacred, comprehensive, undivided, benign and manifested. This Supreme Brahma is the revealer of the Soul etc. 'His light illuminates all this.'

Haladhar   : Well, since it is known that Pranava is the last and ultimate goal, what is the good of uttering the other useless mantras?

Madman   : The last thing can only be had in the end; it cannot be taken up first. Just as one does not start eating the sour dish first and leave rice and dal, because it is the final item. Suppose my destination is the holy Kashidhama, I cannot avoid the whole path and reach Kashi by one leap. As no one wants to die ahead of time because death is the end of life, so nobody can take up Pranava first. It is incapable of being taken up first although it is the ultimate goal. If anybody tries holding it by force, the almighty Hansa Maharaj pecks on his head in such a way that he has to give it up at once and the path is lost forever.

Haladhar   : How is Pranava grasped?

Madman   : Pranava is accessible through the highest state. The highest state presents itself when 'Rama Rama' is chanted ceaselessly. The name of Rama is the trap to catch the Swan. In course of time, Prarabdha wears away and just as the Sun appears when the clouds have dispersed, through the union of Brahma and Pranava, the radiant Shiva, Atman and Nada reveal themselves. Jai Sitaram.

Yes, this 'king of swans' is very fond of living alone. When he does appear, he stifles everything; the Gita, Chandi, Upanishads,

Sandhya and Gayatri, and delivers the seeker to the beyond.

Haladhar : How does this happen?

Madman : Suppose you open the Gita and begin to read 'Dharmakshetre Kurukshetre' and at once Hansa Maharaj comes cackling and pulls your Prana into your Sushumna. Now that your mouth is shut, how can you read the Gita? Similarly, as soon as you begin to utter 'Shanna Apo dhanvanya' or 'bhurbhavaswah', he will enter the Sushumna; dragging your Prana with him, and start producing the notes of various musical instruments. Your mouth will be shut and you will have no power to say anything. People say he eats like a swan, so when he appears, there is no escape and he swallows up everything.

Haladhar : Well, the Shastras say that mantras should be uttered with the Pranava at the beginning or mixed with it. But who is entitled to chanting just the Pranava?

Madman : Pranava Kalpa says, 'Advanced seekers, who abjure Trikal rituals i.e. Gayatri, Savitri etc., through action, mind and speech, are entitled to the uttering of the Pranava.' The highest and complete Pranava is to be chanted only after giving up the pigtail, the sacred thread, the Gayatri, the home, wife and children. But the common man may read the Angas of the

Pranava like the Pranavakavacha, Pranava Panjara, Pranava Hridaya, the hundred and eight names, Angastuti, the garland of the thousand names of the Pranava, mantras, Gita and Anusmriti.

Haladhar : Nowadays everyone recites the Pranava!

Madman : If an ineligible person tries to play any trick, the swan will block his path.

Haladhar : We often see that just by practicing *pranayama* for a few weeks, sitting in meditation for a few hours and learning a few statements from Vedanta, people shun Sandhya etc., and call them activities of people with lower eligibility.

Madman : This is Kali's sport. Leave it. Let it be. Sitaram Sitaram. If a man intentionally gives up Shastric daily functions like the Sandhya-Ahnik, he becomes guilty of transgression and goes to hell. But as soon as Hansa Maharaj arrives, Sandhya, Ahnik and worship, themselves, leave the seeker.

Haladhar : Well, what do you say he does after dragging the Prana into the Sushumna?

Madman : He makes you listen to the Nada. You then ride the swan and journey into the single point of consciousness or dive into the ocean of Reality. Enjoy the ride. What else?

Haladhar : And go where?

Madman : There, from where there is no return.

Haladhar : How is one to get there?

Madman : You have to go by following the Nada. Nada Bindu Upanishad says, 'The mind lasts as long as the Nada lasts. At the end of Nada, when the audible Akshar fades away, comes the supreme realization. The mind and Vayu merge into the pure Being. Then the yogi is freed from the three states of waking, dreaming and sound sleep and becomes devoid of all thoughts; much like a dead person. There is no doubt that he is emancipated.'

Do you see the game of the swan?

Haladhar : I am getting anxious to see this swan of yours.

Madman : Why the anxiousness? Go on chanting the name of Rama and the swan himself will come running. You will not have to make any other effort. Prana and Apana cease to function.

Haladhar : Well, can a man be liberated even without wishing to be?

Madman : Yes! He who performs the japa of the Hansa Malika is liberated even without wishing to be.

Harihar : Could you please tell me the 'Hansa

Malamantra'?

Madman   : (Recites the Hansa Malika)

Harihar   : Is it not impossible that I will be liberated even without wishing to be?

Madman   : No. Shastras are never wrong. It is possible for an ocean to be bounded, a mountain to move or Moon and the planets to leave their orbits, but the Shastras cannot be wrong. The path of Shastras is like the royal road; safe and guarded from all sides. Those who take this path with a single-pointed mind, reach the Formless, Nameless King; smiling and fearless. Shastras are the truth. Shastras are the great truth. Shastras are the ultimate truth. Jai Sitaram. Jai Sitaram.

ॐ

16. The Speaking Tree

'No, it is no longer bearable. I can no longer bear the ill-treatment by men. I have endured much. Some remedy must be found.'

A man was sitting under a Peepul tree, speaking to himself. He got up saying, 'Unbearable, unbearable', and was about to leave, when he thought he heard someone say, 'Tolerate it'.

The man looked around but seeing no one said, 'I have tolerated much, but no more.'

A reply came from the tree, 'How much have you tolerated, my son?'

Since the man could not see any person, he assumed that the tree was speaking. He said, 'Look, Mr. Tree, you do not know how painful it is to be insulted by one's immediate family!' The tree answered, 'Do you think that the tree endures any less? In summer he has to take the heat of the Sun on his head and endure it silently. In the rainy season, storm and rain, wind and thunder pass over him but he stands still. He steadily spends the long night covered with frost in winter. Tell me my son, can you endure so much torment silently, like a tree does?

Man : The tree is inert so it endures, otherwise, it could not.

Tree : Who says that the tree is inert? The tree is as living as you are. The tree is alive due to the presence of the same Consciousness as you have. The tree can endure and you cannot? Let me tell you a story.

A man went to a *sannyasi* and took shelter with him. He was hoping that the *sannyasi* would teach him to pray and worship, and that he would see God and be fulfilled. He engaged himself day and night in the service of the *sannyasi*, without in the least caring for winter, summer or rains. Many years went by in this fashion, but the *sannyasi* did not show any grace. Gradually, the man became impatient and made up his mind to leave the place. One day when the *sannyasi* was absorbed in meditation, the disciple decided to flee. But as he was moving out, he heard someone say, 'have patience.' In astonishment he looked at the empty room and found that the pitcher of water was speaking.

The pitcher said, 'Don't be so restless; be patient and endure.' The disciple said, 'There is a limit to one's patience. I have been waiting patiently for about 20-odd years but I cannot endure it anymore.' The pitcher said, 'How much have you endured? Listen to my tale of endurance. At first I was earth. I endured so much of sunshine and cold. Countless men eased themselves on me. I silently endured this torment for so many years. Then one day a potter broke me into pieces with a spade, carried me away in a basket, threw me down there on the ground. He poured water on me and trampled me with his feet. I remained silent. Are you listening to the account of my endurance? Then he made round lumps of me and started to spin me on a wheel. You cannot imagine how terrible it was. When I was taken down from the wheel I was no longer earth; I had become a different shape. Then placing me in the sun he added something to me and began to beat with a wooden club. Under the pain of belabouring I cried aloud for mercy. Then I found that I had turned into a pitcher. After drying me in the sun, he burnt me in a fire. My hard life still did not leave me. I continued to endure. I thought now perhaps my sorrow had come to an end. O God! It was not so. He put me in a shop. Whoever came to the shop would examine me by knocking me with the knuckles. In this way I endured so much beating by so many men. After many days, this sadhu Thakur bought me. Now I carry Ganga water. Now this water is used to worship Shiva and Vishnu, and serve *sadhus*. Did you hear, my son, the fruits of endurance? The disciple understood and realized that the *sannyasi* Thakur himself had appeared in the pitcher to impart the teaching. The disciple prostrated himself and began to cry, 'Gurudeva, have mercy on me.' The Gurudeva came smiling and removed all his pains by one graceful touch.

Do you understand, my son? So I tell you, 'Endure, there is no quality equal to endurance.'

Man : How long am I to endure?

Tree : Endure till perfect detachment arises. Know everything to be illusion, go on chanting the name of Rama and endure the onslaught of the world.

In Kaliyug, there is much strife in the relationships, due to attachment to worldly objects and the desire to gain control of other people's lives. Even in their homes, people are in constant struggle for power and position. I have heard of great accomplished men who have suffered due to this. Who are you to complain?

Man : Then, what shall I do?

Tree : Endure it by chanting the name of Rama. Pray for detachment. When God shows His grace, wipe away this kohl of happiness from your eyes, snap these bonds of attachment and renounce the world; dancing in joy. There is water in the Ganga, there are fruits on trees, there is the ground for your bed, the arm for a pillow and people still give some alms. Then what is the cause for anxiety, my son? Anxiety is always in respect of desires. Set fire to your desires. Let them burn down. If you cannot do this, then carry on crying. Caught in that trap, you won't be able to do anything. If you can hold on to God firmly, all your sorrows will flee. Men of Kaliyug are very lustful. Hence my Lord assumes the form of Mother and kicks them to make them lose their lust. Everything is the Lord's play.

Man : O, Mr. Tree!....

Getting no more response, he climbed the tree and saw the Madman sitting within a hollow of the tree, telling beads and chanting the name of Rama.

Man : O Thakur, is it you sitting in the tree?

Madman : Yes, I had thought I would spend some time in solitude. So I sat within the hollow of this tree in the forest. You came from nowhere and began to fret and fume with discontent. Seeing your sorrow I could not remain silent and had to say a few things. Go away straight along the road. Do not give up the name of Rama.

Rama, Rama, Sitaram.

ॐ

17. The auspicious Maheshwar

The Madman was sitting alone chanting the name of Rama, when some women came and made obeisance to him and said, 'Father, we offer you our *pranam*.'

Madman   : Jai Sitaram. Jai Sitaram. Are you all well, mothers? Jai Sitaram.

Woman 1   : Yes, father, we are all well. By your grace, my grand-daughter has been married.

Madman   : Sitaram, Sitaram. Why do you call it my grace? Sitaram.

Woman 1   : It is indeed your grace, father! When we searched around and could not find a suitable bridegroom, we came to you and you said, 'Ask the girl to worship Shiva every day in an idol made of earth.' We did so. She had barely worshipped Shiva for a few days than she got married to a good bridegroom. They are well-to-do and the boy has a good character.

Madman   : That was very good. (To the girl) My daughter, you have given up worshipping Shiva?

Woman 1   : Yes, father. She no longer worships.

Madman   : Sitaram, have you defied the crocodile after getting upon the bank? If you become averse to Shiva, you will only get sorrow. Shiva is auspicious! Can any good come to those men and women who shun that fountain of goodness? Sitaram, nowadays grown-up girls cannot get married; bridegrooms cannot be found. The cause of all this is that they and their parents have become averse to Shiva. Sitaram, a number of parents today are inclined to bring up their children in a completely modern way, abandoning the age-old practices, traditions and culture.

In earlier days, as soon as the daughters were five-year old, the mothers taught them to observe Vrat in the months of Baisakh and Kartik. In the month of Baisakh, the girls got up early in the morning and did worship of Shiva, the ten dolls, Hari's feet and Gokal. Jai Sitaram. Since they could not pronounce the mantras, special prayers for Shivapuja were given:

(Sings a song in Bangla)

After worshipping Shiva with these prayers, they would sing about Hari's feet and the ten dolls. Jai Sitaram. The mantra of ten dolls was:

(Sings a verse in Bangla)

Coming across the names of Rama, Lakshman, Sita, Kaushalya and Dasharatha in the song, the girls would be interested in knowing more about them. Their grandmother and mother would tell stories of Rama and Sita. A girl grew up keeping ideals of Sita in her heart. With growing maturity, she would learn to meditate on Shiva, sing hymns and develop devotion towards Guru and Brahmins. Duty and love towards her husband became ingrained in her. Sitaram, this is not the case anymore.

Jai Sitaram, Jai Sitaram.

Listen, my daughter, if you want to live in happiness, show devotion to Gurus and worship Shiva every day.

The girl showed consent with a nod.

Woman 1 : Look, father, we are doing what you ask us to do. But everything seems to have been turned topsy-turvy.

Madman : Sitaram, Sitaram. There will be a decline. If people of Hindu families abandon the customs and practices, they will have to suffer. We are beginning to see various diseases and sufferings due to inappropriate conduct and lifestyle. It is sure to happen. Will not anybody get punished if he goes against the constituent elements of his body? Let it go. Sitaram Sitaram.

Woman 2 : Well, father, should everybody worship Shiva?

Madman : Yes, mother, all human beings should worship Shiva. Without worshipping the Linga, no other worship should be performed.

Linga Purana says, 'Prayers of the person who performs other *pujas* without first worshipping Shiva, are wasted. He goes to hell in the end. So, O consort of Mahesha, Shiva should be worshipped first. A country devoid of the Shiva worship is considered a waste land full of filth. O Goddess! People of all parts of the society should worship Shiva. O Parvati, the house where Shiva is not worshipped is to be considered filthy. People should worship any other deity only after worshipping the Linga with the leaves of the Bilva tree and praying to Shiva. The person, who does not do this, turns into a creature, powerless to speak.

My dear! Make an earthen Linga to worship Rudra; the destroyer, Ashutosh; the one easy to please, Mahadeva, Shankara and Vrishabhadhwaja. Know as the city of Kashi, is the house of that man where Shiva is always worshipped. One can get the fruit of all *pujas* if one worships the Shivalinga.'

Sitaram Sitaram.

Woman 2 : O mother! I did not know that the worship

of Shiva has such benefits! I worship a Banalinga every day. O father! Is it better to worship Banalinga or an earthen image?

Madman : Matrikabhedatantra says, 'Worship of earthen Shiva gives all-round fulfillment, worship of stone-made Shiva yields two-fold fruit, worship of golden Linga destroys the enemies, a silver Linga gives four-fold fruits and makes one lord of all Siddhis. A copper Linga fulfills the *puja* and a bronze Linga leads to accumulation of wealth. Worship of Shivalinga made of the earth of the Ganga multiplies the benefits a lakh times. Linga made of lac gives freedom from diseases. Crystal and emerald Lingas give all-round accomplishment. An iron Linga destroys the enemies and one made of ash, gratifies one's desires. A Linga made of sand fulfills the worldly desires and worship of a Linga made of cow-dung destroys the enemies. Worship of all Lingas gives Dharma, Artha, Kama and Moksha. Lingas made of stone and such other things are to be purified before worshipping.' Did you hear that, mother? Sitaram.

Woman 1 : What should be the size of the earthen Shiva?

Madman : Matrikabheda Tantra tells us, 'An earthen image of Shiva, of the size of a thumb and weighing one or two *tolas*, should be made and worshipped.' After worshipping Shiva specific sounds should be made through the mouth. He who utters Matrika letters five hundred times, through Anuloma and Viloma and then makes the special sounds, attains fulfillment. He is Shiva.'

In Lingarchana Tantra, Lord Shiva says, 'I conquer death because of the Mukha Vadya, the sound made through the mouth. He, who does not do this, suffers and becomes a crocodile in the next birth.'

Woman 2 : We just make sounds of 'Bum, Bum, Bum, Bumbo'm Bum.' Is that alright?

Madman : Yes, that will do. Sitaram.

Woman 2 : Well father, if the clay from Ganga is not available, what can we use in its place?

Madman : Shivalinga should be made of clay collected from the places of pilgrimage. That not being available, ordinary clay also will do.

In Matsa Sukta, Shiva says, 'One that rises from the mountains is called a river. A river rising from a spring also gives all kinds of benefits. In the absence of these, the mud from under the foot of a cow or from a place that gives you a sense of peace can also be used.'

The earthen Linga should be made with a ring, should be without gravel and beautiful to behold. Shiva has said, 'Linga is Rudra, the Supreme God and the Kundali encircling him, is the supreme Goddess.'

The worship of Shiva is the worship of the God and the Goddess. The worship of the earthen Shivalinga should not be performed without ash, without making three horizontal marks, a Rudraksha rosary and Bilva leaves. This worship of Shiva yields eternal fruit. Those who spend their time without worshipping Shiva, undergo suffering.

Skandpurana says, 'On the one hand, there are charities of all kinds, various vows, places of pilgrimage, discipline and Yajnas, and on the other hand, there is the worship of Shivalinga. The two give equal fruit.' It goes on to say, 'At first there was no worship other than the worship of the Linga in the four Vedas. This was the principle of all Shastras.'

Worship of Linga produces enjoyment as well as emancipation, and counteracts numerous troubles and calamities. Through daily worship of Shiva, man achieves union with Him.

According to Skanda Purana, 'A learned man discards all other practices and devotes himself to worshipping the Linga only.' Sitaram Sitaram.

Woman 2 : Oh, worship of Shiva yields so much fruit! I will begin this puja tomorrow itself and continue doing it for the rest of my life.

Madman : That is not it! Matsa Sukta says, 'A thousand Ashwamedha Yajnas, a hundred Vajapeya Yajnas are not equal to the one-sixteenth of the fruits of the worship of Shiva.'

One who worships Shiva is himself called Narayana. As per Matrikabheda Tantra, 'All the deities that reside in heaven, on the earth and in the underworld, get worshipped if only Shambhunatha is worshipped.'

Woman 2 : Alas! People who are deprived of this beneficial worship are indeed unfortunate.

Madman : Mother! There are four substantial things in this insubstantial world; living in Kashi, society of holy men, Ganga-water and the service of Shambhu.

Woman 2 : Father, we fail to express in words how much we have benefited by coming to you today. Shiva-worship is so beneficial! We never heard that. We continued doing the *puja* because it had to be done.

Madman : Mother, I am incapable of describing the glory of Shiva. Sitaram, it cannot be completed even if I speak for ten or twelve years. Shiva is easy to please. There is no difficulty in worshipping him. He has said in the Linga Purana, 'If I am worshipped with fragrance, flowers, obeisance and Mukh Vadya, I am instantly pleased.'

In the Mahabharata it is said, 'By thinking of Shiva, even the one without virtue and tainted with sin, is set free.' Sitaram.

Woman 1 : O Father! Which Shastra says that women can worship Shiva?

Madman : Shiva says in the Skandapurana, 'I accept the worship of everyone; whether they are clean or unclean. I accept the worship of all who perform their own daily rites as laid down in the Shastras.'

Women are to worship Shiva by saying Namah Shivaya. By knowing Savitri, Pranava and Lakshmi-bija, women can gain eternal freedom at the time of death.

A, U, M, Nada and Bindu is the unexpressed five-letter subtle pranava, which is to be used by a Jivanmukta. But all can chant the great mantra Namah Shivaya which gives deliverance in this life. Jai Sitaram.

Woman 3 : Well, father! Please tell me which direction should one face to worship Shiva.

Madman : Shiva should be worshipped facing the north during day or night. Shiva has five heads. Shiva should not be worshipped facing the eastern side. Shiva is the destroyer of the world. His main face is turned towards the east. Shiva should not be worshipped sitting on the northern side because there is Shakti on that side. He should not be worshipped sitting on the western side because the back is turned to that side. So He should be worshipped sitting on the southern side. Then one faces the north. In day or night Shiva should be worshipped facing the north. The same rule is prescribed for the worship of Shiva with a single head.

Woman 2 : Well, father, if one is to worship the earthen image of Shiva, is the image to be made while saying 'Haraya namah Maheshwaraya Namah'?

Madman : Worship of the earthen image of Shiva comprises collection of clay, putting the image together, establishing it, invoking it, bathing it, worshipping it and immersing it.

Collection of earth should be made by saying 'Haraya namah'. Image should be made saying 'Maheshwaraya namah'. It should be established by saying 'Shulapani'. It should be invoked by saying 'Pinakadhrik'. It should be bathed by saying 'Pashupataye'. It should be worshipped with 'Shivaya namah', and immersed while saying 'Mahadeva Kshamaswa'.

Woman 2 : Yes, father, I do this. I meditate by saying 'Dhyayenityam Mahesham'. Well, father, is there a separate hymn for Shivalinga?

Madman   : Sitaram. Yes there is.

(Recites the Lingastava from Bhavishya Purana)

Woman 1   : Well, father, it is said that one gets very good result by making the Shivalinga with only one hand.

Madman   : Sitaram, if one makes the Shivalinga with any one hand only, the result one gets is increased one lakh times. In Lingarchana-tantra Shiva says, 'O, Maheshani of fair complexion! The devotees should, on the bright or dark fourteenth lunar day, and especially on the New Moon, make a Linga using one hand only and worship it. Those who make the earthen Shivalinga either with the right or left hand and then worship it, get the result equal to that of the worship of one lakh Shivalingas.'

Woman 2   : Well, father, it is said that the remains of an offering made to Shiva are unacceptable. What does it mean?

Madman   : There is a secret to it, mother. The Goddess asked Shiva, 'O Parameshwara! O ocean of mercy! The remnants of offerings are rare to obtain even for Brahma and the other gods, then how is it polluted?' Shiva said in Lingarchana Tantra 'O Supreme Goddess! My middle face is the dark-hued Ishana and is turned upwards. It embodies the Blaze of

Time so always know it to be all-powerful, effulgent and upward-turned.

O Goddess! A potent venom rose to the top when the ocean of milk was churned. I took that universe-destroying, subtle and dangerous venom in the palm of my hand and drank it. That venom remains always in my throat. The venom creates a fire in my throat. The remnants of leaves, flowers, water offered in my mouth become unfit for consumption, because the offering becomes Brahma himself. By consuming it, the person becomes corrupted and he has no escape. Remnants of the offering of leaves and flowers made to me should be placed on one's head. First they should be offered to Vishnu with the Vishnumantra and then consumed. O Goddess! The remnants of offerings made to me are acceptable only to Vishnu. The Gods, Asuras, men, Gandharvas and Kinnaras are poor in wisdom. How can they be entitled to the remnants of the offerings to me? Sitaram Sitaram.

Woman 2 : Then why is it said that the leftover offering is purified if it comes in touch with the Salagramashila?

Madman : Sitaram. Yes, mother that is prescribed for the Vaishnava in the Padmapurana. It says, 'Do not touch anything offered to Shiva be it material, grains, fruit or water. Throw them into a well after offering to Shiva. The one who out of temptation or illusion, takes even the tiniest bit of the remnant falls into hell for all births up to the end of the Kalpa.' Shiva says in the Purana-Samgraha, 'Leaves, flowers and fruits offered to me, are unacceptable but they become purified if they come in contact with the Shalagramashila. If the offerings are partaken of without bringing it into contact with Shalagramshila the expiation of Chandrayana is to be performed.'

Woman 1 : Father, you say that the *nirmalya* of Shiva is acceptable but again some Shastras say it is not acceptable. Please explain it clearly.

Madman : Sitaram, mother, there is no confusion in it. Devotees of Shiva will freely accept the *nirmalya* of Shiva, but the devotees of Vishnu will take it after bringing it in touch with the Shila. It is said in the Shaktananda Tarangini, 'The *nirmalya* of Shiva takes away diseases, the water of His feet takes away grief and offerings made to Shambhu take away endless sin.'

Once, the Goddess said to Shambhu, 'O Maheshwar, we have heard from your utterance in the Vedas and the Puranas that only by your *nirmalya* can the final emancipation be obtained. King of Yogis, O Mahadeva! Why do you falsely state that your *nirmalya* is unacceptable?'

According to Matrikabheda Tantra, Shiva said 'After going through eighty four lac births, a creature attains final emancipation. O, the one revered by the gods! If in the middle of his journey, the creature acquires great wisdom, he attains emancipation. Then who completes the journey? How can he whose cycle of births has not been completed become fit for *moksha*? How can he who has much sin, reach the Heaven? So, Mahadevi! I have created the concept of unacceptability of *nirmalya*. One can reach the Heaven through *nirmalya*, and Nirvana through the nectar. Even a sinful person becomes like Shiva and attains Moksha when he partakes of *nirmalya*. This is true and it never happens otherwise.'

Sitaram, did you see, mother, the cunning of the Innocent One?

Woman 1 : O Hari! I thought that the Innocent One was simple-minded and innocent of everything! This is his doing! He resorts to so much verbal juggling lest man should attain Moksha by partaking of *nirmalya*!

Madman : There is no restriction in respect of Banalinga. One gets the result of performing Chandrayana by partaking of the offering made to Banalinga. It is best not to partake of things placed on the Shivalinga. Chandesh is entitled to the worship of the Shivalinga.

193

Nothing should be taken back after offering it to Chandesh.

Woman 1 : O father, is there a specific mantra for meditation on Banalinga?

Madman : Sitaram, Sitaram. Yes mother, listen to the mantra for meditation on Banalinga.

(Recites the Dhyana Mantra for Banalinga)

Woman 1 : Father, I wish to hear you sing the hymn to Banalinga.

Madman : Sitaram. Listen. (He sings the Banalinga Stotra from Yogasara)

Woman 2 : Father, could you please write out for me the meditation mantra and the hymn?

Madman : Very well. Sitaram Sitaram. Yogasara says, 'He, who rises before dawn and thinks of the Banalinga, is always victorious.'

Kedar Khand says, 'Nothing as holy as the Banalinga is seen in this world. His worshipper gets all things in this world and the next.'

Woman 1 : Please tell me which kind of Banalinga should be worshipped by a householder and what things are auspicious and inauspicious in respect of the Banalinga.

Madman : Sitaram. The worship of rough or rugged Banalinga leads to the loss of sons and wives.

That of a flat one leads to disruption of the family. The worship of a one-sided Banalinga leads to the loss of sons. Banalinga with a broken head is the cause of disease and death. A perforated linga brings about wanderings in foreign lands. The sight of a linga with earrings causes diseases. Lingas with sharp ends, bent-head and three eyes should be shunned. Excessively fat, excessively thin and very small lingas should be shunned by householders but these are beneficial to those who wish to have Moksha. Two lingas should not be worshipped together. Sitaram, a brownish linga gives money. A deep-coloured linga is the object of worship for one who wants final emancipation. No householder will ever worship a light or deep brown linga. A householder should worship a linga having a colour like a big black bee. A Banalinga needs no purification by mantras. It gives fulfillment and deliverance.

Woman 2 : Father, which flower does Shiva love most?

Madman : Sitaram. Leaves of the Bilva tree are Shiva's favourite. Offering of a thousand flowers is equal to that of just one Bilva leaf.

Woman 3 : Well father, what is the reason of the glory of Bilva leaves?

Madman : There is a wonderful anecdote about the Bilva leaves in the Brihad-dharmapurana. Listen to this.

One day Lakshmidevi asked Sri Bhagawan, 'Who is your most favourite? I had thought that I was your favourite but the other day I realized that Nilakantha was dearer to you than I. Is there anyone you like more than Nilakantha?' The Thakur said, 'I don't have many favourites. There is only Shiva. He alone is as dear to me as the body is to the owner of the body. A man loves his wife because of sons, youth and home. The son is dear to him for *pinda* and fame. Wealth is dear for deliverance from danger and for happiness. The virtuous people love the body for virtuous deeds. Everyone's love has a reason. Love for love's sake is not to be seen. Genuine love happens between one man and another because friendship is based on equality. So due to difference in nature, similar feelings arise in respect of woman. In the past I travelled in all the directions with the desire to find genuine love. I would look at everyone and think that I could have genuine love for him. This time I met Shankara. He too was traveling like me to find his beloved. As soon as we glanced at each other, due to deeds of previous births, a great love sprouted between us. There was no difference between Shankara and me; like water kept in two pitchers. The person, who worships Shankara with devotion, is dear to me. He, who is averse to the worship of Shiva, is never dear to me.'

Hearing this from the mouth of Keshava, Kamala said, 'I am averse to the worship of Shiva. Then I am not dear to Keshava. Fie on me! Fie!' Sri Bhagwan said, 'Goddess. Do not be sorry. I am saying so to induce you to worship Shiva. Begin to worship Shiva from this day and be the object of my love.' Kamala said, 'O Thakur! Which flower satisfies Shiva specially?' The Thakur said, 'worshipping him with Oleander flowers is as fruitful as donating one hundred and eight milch cows to Brahmins. The offering of red Oleander flower is doubly effective. Offering Parijat flowers is as effective as the offering one crore silver flowers. Jasmine is a hundred times more effective than that and Mallika is a hundred times still more effective. The offering of the Drona flower is as effective as worshipping the bare linga with pearls. The Champaka flower is as effective as the worship with flowers of gold. To worship Shiva with Shirish flowers is as fruitful as fanning Shiva with chowrie in the waking fortnight of Vaishakh. The offering of Nagkesara flowers is a fruitful as the Ashwamedha Yajna and that of Muchkunda flowers is as effective as the performance of the Shradh ceremony at Gaya. The offering of Tulsi leaves is a hundred times more effective than that. The Tagar flower is as fruitful as the Chandrayana Vrat. Dhatura flower offering is as fruitful as a hundred Ekadashi fasts. Ketaki and many other flowers are dear to Shiva. However, no other flower is dearer than the lotus. You must worship Shiva with the lotus only.' Following Lord's advice, Lakshmidevi began to worship Maheshwar daily with one thousand lotuses culled from the lake. She would count them three times before offering them. Nearly a year passed, when one day Kamala found that two flowers were missing. She could not at all understand the reason for the shortage. She thought, 'Everyday I count the lotuses three times. Did I not count them today? What am I to do now? How shall I maintain the resolve to worship Shiva daily with one thousand flowers? The seat cannot be left at the time of worship. To gather flowers with the help of others would be breaking the vow. What am I to do?' Then it occurred to her, 'God calls my breasts a couple of lotuses. What He says cannot be false. I will worship Shiva with these two breasts. Let that make up the number of one thousand. Deciding thus Lakshmidevi took hold of the left breast with the left hand and taking a knife in the right, cut off the breast. With a cheerful mind she offered that bleeding breast on the Shiva-linga saying, 'I bow down to Shiva.' Again, as the Goddess was about to cut off the right breast, Maheshwar appeared from the Golden Linga and said, 'O Mother, daughter of the ocean! Do not cut off the breast. May your left breast be restored. I am extremely pleased with your supreme devotion. May your desire be fulfilled! The breast that you cut off and offered on my head will become the tree called Sriphal or Bilva on the earth. This embodiment of your devotion will live in the world, as long as the Sun and the Moon exist and will proclaim your glory. O Goddess! That tree will become most dear to me and I will be worshipped with its leaves. Gold, pearls, coral, flowers and such other things will not be worth even a billionth part of a leaf of the Bilva tree. The Sriphal is as dear to me as my three eyes and Ganga-water are dear to me.' With eyes filled with tears of love and voice choked with devotion, Kamala circumambulated Shiva and bowed to Him. Then with folded hands she prayed to Him. Maheshwar said, 'O consort of Vishnu! I am highly pleased. Ask for a boon.' The Goddess said, 'O Shankar! By your grace today I have really become the wife of Vishnu. I am contented by your rare vision. What boon is greater than this? Lord! O God! I pray at your feet only for reverence and devotion.' Maheshwar said, 'So shall it be,' and disappeared. Jai Sitaram. Did you hear that, mother?

Woman 1 : I feel fulfilled on hearing the story of origin of the Bilva tree. I did not know that there was so much history behind the Bilva tree. I only knew that the Bilva is really called

Sriphal.

Woman 2   : What happened then, father?

Madman   : Jai Sitaram. Then Kamala got that tree planted
in the field named Kapala-mochana. This
tree was created on the Dvitiya Tithi of the
fortnight of the waking Moon in the month of
Vaishakh. When the tree sprouted, Brahma,
Vishnu and other gods, accompanied by
their wives, came to that place. They bowed
and watered this fruit-bearing and effulgent
tree which was resplendent like Shiva
himself. Then Lord Vishnu said, 'This sacred
Bilva tree will have these nineteen names;
Malur, Sriphal, Shandilya, Sailush, Shiva,
Punya, Shivapriya, Devavasa, Tirthapada,
Papaghna, Komalachhada, Jaya, Vijaya,
Vishnu, Trinayana, Hara, Dhumraksha,
Shuklavarna and Shradhadevaka. Space
up to a distance of hundred cubits above,
below and around the tree, will be like a
place of pilgrimage. Know that its top leaf
is Shankara, its left leaf is Brahma and its
right leaf is I. Jumping over its shadow will
decrease longevity. He who will touch it with
his feet will lose prosperity. The offering of
Bilva leaf with mantras will be as fruitful as
offering one thousand lotuses. Seeing the
Bilva tree in the morning is as beneficial as
the sight of Shiva. It is forbidden to climb this
tree or break its boughs. The leaves should
not be picked on the day of the new Moon,

the day of the full Moon, on the twelfth lunar day, in the evening and at noon. It is good to pick its leaves by climbing it but taking care that its boughs do not break. Shiva may be worshipped with all Bilva leaves, whether whole or torn. Where there is a grove of Bilva trees, there is Varanasi. Hara Himself resides where there are five Bilva trees. Gouri and Shankara reside where there are seven Bilva trees. Shankara resides in company where there are ten Bilva trees. Maheshwar lives with me where there is only one Bilva tree. If a householder has a Bilva tree on the north-east of his house, the place is never visited by troubles. A Bilva tree on the east gives happiness. That on the south dispels fear of Yama. That on the west is said to increase the lineage. The place beneath a Bilva tree in a cremation ground, on the bank of a river, in a meadow, or in another forest is a place where austerities have been performed. No Bilva tree should be planted in the middle of the courtyard. If it grows there by divine will, it should be worshipped as if it were Shiva himself.

Offering a single Bilva leaf to the Supreme God Maheshwar during the four months beginning with Chaitra is equal to the donating one lakh cows. The men who go round a Bilva tree at noon may be said to have gone round Mount Sumeru. The Bilva tree should not be hewn and its wood should not be burnt. The person, who sells a Bilva tree, except for the purpose of a Yajna by a Brahmin, becomes fallen. Yama has no power over that person who places Bilva sticks, Ghee and Sandalwood on his head. Shankara keeps Bilva leaves, fruit, seeds on his head lest they should fall on the ground and get destroyed. The ancestors of that worthy person who waters the roots of a Bilva tree during the four months of Phalgun, Chaitra, Vaishakh and Jaishtha are pleased just as the tree is cooled. During the four months beginning with Chaitra, Shankara; the Guru of devotion and emancipation, always wanders in search of new Bilva leaves.' The Thakur was speaking thus when Maheshwar arrived there. Brahma and Vishnu worshipped Shiva with Bilva leaves. Then the gods went to their respective places.' Jai Sitaram, Jai Sitaram, Jai Sitaram, Sitaram, Sitaram.

All   : Hearing of the Bilva tree we are satisfied, our lives are fulfilled.

Woman 3   : I did not know that the Bilva tree has so many qualities. Bilva trees grow here and there. Nobody takes care of them. Nobody knows their glory. Man could be fulfilled merely by serving the Bilva tree. Alas! I never took any care of this tree that gives devotion and emancipation. What a mistake have I made!

<table>
<tr>
<td>Madman</td>
<td>: Sitaram, Sitaram, Sitaram. Mother, I cannot speak anything of the glory of the Bilva tree. Purascharanullas says, 'O Mahadevi! The Bilva tree is Shankara himself. The wise man who breathes his last underneath a Bilva tree is instantly emancipated. What need is there for him to go on a crore pilgrimages?'</td>
</tr>
</table>

Vaha Dasham Patal says, 'My dear! Any place which has a Bilva tree in its vicinity is comparable to Kashipur. If one dies there what need is there for one to go on a crore pilgrimage or to live in Kashi?' Sitaram, Sitaram. There is no end to the glory of the Bilva tree. It is seen in the tantras that the Bilva tree is Lakshmi Herself. Yogini Tantra states, 'O Devi! The roots of a Bilva tree up to sixteen cubits are like my dreadlocks. The three leaves of are like the Rig, Yajur and Sama Vedas and all the branches are all the Shastras. This tree which stands for Brahma, Vishnu and Shiva, is like the wish-fulfilling Kalpa-vriksha. Mahalakshmi appeared as the Bilva tree on Sri Shaila Mountain.'

The Goddess asked, 'Why did the consort of Vishnu become the Bilva tree?

Maheshwar replied, 'Brahma and the gods always pray for a small ray of my divine light. Vani, as speech, becomes dear to all, only due to my grace. The same Saraswati becomes dear to Vishnu. Keshava had no such fondness for Lakshmi. She, being aggrieved at such slighting by her husband went to Sri Shaila Mountain, where she established a Linga and engaged in severe penance. O Supreme Goddess! Still when she did not receive my grace, Lakshmidevi assumed the form of a tree and worshipped me for a million years with leaves, flowers and fruits. She then received my grace. By that grace she found a place in the heart of Vishnu forever. She is my greatest devotee. For that reason I have made that tree my shelter, and I stay there day and night. O Supreme Goddess! Therefore the Sri-Vriksha is always the essence, of all the places of pilgrimage and all divine grace. There is no doubt about that.'

Jai Sitaram.

Woman 3 : Baba, this is confusing. First you say that the Bilva tree is the breast of Lakshmi and then you say that Lakshmi is the Bilva tree. For this reason, the educated youngsters of these days do not want to believe in these things. They say, 'Many men; many minds. Nothing is definite.'

Madman : Sitaram, Sitaram. Let go what the educated young people of these days say. They have thrown away the jewels of their own home and are dancing for bits of glass from the others' houses. I have neither the power nor the patience to make them understand this. Jai Sitaram.

Woman 3   : Whatever you say, father, it seems to be ...

1st Woman : (To the third woman). Please stop!

.   (To the Madman) Father, please explain to us.

Madman   : Jai Sitaram. Mother, the Shastras say that the creation happens in every Manwantara and in every Kalpa. Satya, Treta, Dwapar, and Kali yugas have come and gone unknown number of times. The seeds of the preceding Kalpa remain and similar things happen in the succeeding Kalpa. Minor changes take place due to difference in Karma and time. The difference in Leela occurs with the changes in Kalpa. They cannot understand this and so they make a row. In one Kalpa the Bilva tree arose from the breast of Lakshmidevi. In another Kalpa, Lakshmidevi herself became the Bilva tree. Thus the anomaly is removed. Sitaram, Sitaram.

Woman 1   : What are Manwantara and Kalpa?

Madman   : What is one year for a man is one day-and-night to the gods. The Uttarayan is the day and the Dakshinayan is the night. Twelve thousand years of the gods is equal to four ages. The four ages repeated seventy-one times are equal to a Manwantara and fourteen

Manwantara make one day of Brahma.

Woman 2   : Then how many human years make up one day for Brahma?

Madman   : Sitaram. One day of Brahma is equal to four hundred thirty-two crore years of ours. The night also is of equal duration. A total of eight hundred sixty four crore years is equal to one day-and-night of Brahma. According to such calculation Brahma's longevity is one hundred years.

Woman 1   : It is inconceivable! One day is equal to eight hundred sixty four crore years and then a new creation follows!

Madman   : Sitaram, one day is called Kalpa. There are thirty Kalpas.

Woman 2   : What are they called?

Madman   : Jai Sitaram. Shvetavarah, Neel Lohita, Vamadeva, Gathantara, Rourava, · Prana, Brihad Kalpa, Kandarpa, Satya, Ishana, Dhyana, Saraswat, Udasa, Garuda and Kurma are the full moons of Brahma. Nrisinmha, Samadhi, Agneya, Vishnuja, Soura, Soma, Bhavana, Suptamali, Archisha, Valmi, Vairaja, Souri, Mahadeva and Pitri are the new moons of Brahma. Now Brahma is 51 years old and the Sweta Varaha Kalpa is going on.

Woman 2   : You spoke of Manwantara. What are the names of the Manus?

Madman : Jai Sitaram. Swayambhuva, Swarochisha, Uttama, Tamasa, Raivata, Chakshusha, Vaivaswata, Savarni, Daksha Savarni, Brahma Savarni, Dharma Savarni, Rudra Savarni, Deva Savarni and Indra Savarni. The seventh Vaivaswata Manwantara is in progress. Sitaram, Sitaram. O Mother, saying, 'we shall not understand and shall not try to understand' and brushing it off as nothing, is the reason for today's upheavals. The virtue, wealth, desire and final emancipation of the Aryans are all connected to the Shastras. The abjurer of the Shastras becomes blind. Can he be stopped from falling down a well? Shastras are true to the letter. Doubts can be removed by putting them to test. Shastras have enjoined on us to worship Shiva to attain complete fulfillment. Do so and see. Then there will be no doubt.

Woman 2 : Today our life has become meaningful. We heard today for the first time that man can so easily be blessed by worshipping Shiva.

Madman : Sitaram, Sitaram. Mother, my Thakur is the Ocean of Grace. He is assuming so many forms; trees, rivers, stones and other things, and calling out to us to receive his grace. It is we, who turn a deaf ear to his call. See, Thakur in the form of the river Bhagirathi is calling out to us, as she flows across the lands. Just through devotion to Ganga, a man can have self-realisation. Our Thakur only

207

has manifested as the Peepul, Tulsi, Banyan, Bilva and Dhatri trees and is beckoning to us by shaking their leaves. The Shalagramashila and Shiva in the form of the Linga are always calling us. Alas! Man is unable to hear this call. Sitaram, Sitaram.

1st Woman : The more we listen to you, the more we want to know. We are not satisfied to our heart's content. Father, please tell us which tree is loved both by Hari and Hara. Is there any such tree?

Madman : Jai Sitaram. Surely there is, mother. One day the gods went to the place of pilgrimage, Prabhasa, with their wives. Parvatidevi wished to worship Narayana with things created by own self. Kamala also wanted to worship Shiva with things created by own self. Both of them expressed their wishes to each other. At this time, pure tears of joy fell on the earth from their eyes. Thus was born the Amalaki tree. It is called Amalaki, because it came from Amala tears. All the properties of Tulsi and Bilva trees exist in the Amlaki tree. Hari and Hara are both worshipped with its leaves. Jai Sitaram.

Woman 3 : Amalaki is dear both to Shiva and Vishnu! I had not known this. Father, you have given us so much knowledge today. We don't know what to give you in return. We offer innumerable salutations to your feet.

Madman : Sitaram, my Thakur is the sole authority to give advice. He only gives advice and He only listens and draws everyone up into his lap. He has said. 'O look at me just once.'

Woman 2 : Yes, father. Please tell us one thing more. How did the Shivalinga originate?

Madman : Sitaram. At the end of a game, the force of Shiva and Shivani fell on the earth. The Shivalinga originated from that. He is the cause of creation and destruction of all things, hence he is called the Linga. Good resides in him, so he is called Shiva. He is called Shiva also because he destroys what is inauspicious and bestows the eight kinds of Siddhis. Man becomes one with Shiva by repeating the name of Shiva. A person suffering from even a great disease is cured by worshipping the Linga and by chanting the name of Shiva. Infinite are the good effects of establishing a Shivalinga. If a man establishes a Shivalinga in the Holy Kashidhama, he is freed from re-birth. Sitaram, Sitaram. Where there is the Linga, there is the Yoni; where there is mother, there is the father. In absence of mother, the father cannot be found. Again, there is a mother only because there is a father.

Woman 3 : Yes, father, who is Mahadeva?

Madman : Mahadeva is our Gourishankar, Mahadeva is our Sitaram, Mahadeva is our Radhagovinda and Mahadeva is the Pranava. Did you hear, my daughter, who Mahadeva is? Mahadeva is Brahma, Mahadeva is the beginning of the world; the whole world is the image of Mahadeva; that is why he is not clothed. He has the trident of the three qualities hence He is called Trishuli. This world is a cremation ground. He lives in the cremation ground out of mercy for those who pray to Him. Dharma has the shape of a bull, so He rides a bull. Anger and the other faults are snakes, so Mahadeva, who is the world, brings those snakes under control and wears them as His ornament. The three kind of discernment are His three eyes. The body having the three qualities means Tripura and He burns it to ashes so He is the destroyer of Tripura. Why will not those who come to know Mahadeva so minutely, worship Him? Did you hear, my daughter, who Mahadeva is? Sitaram, Sitaram. This visible world is Mahadeva; we are immersed in Mahadeva. Mahadeva is above, below, before and behind us. Mahadeva is within and outside us. He is the still ocean and we are the waves of that ocean. We appear on His bosom and again merge with Him. Nothing other than Mahadeva is present in the innumerable universes. There is nothing else! Jai Mahadeva! Jai Mahadeva! Jai Mahadeva.

The Madman and the others, bow to Him.

As he chants, 'Gourishankara, Sitaram, Gourishankara, Sitaram', the Madman becomes still. Jai Sitaram.

ఇ ॐ ಖ

18. The Bathing Water

The Madman was sitting in the cottage, clapping his hands and saying, 'Sitaram, the bathing water is beautiful, it is very good', when Haladhar came and asked, 'O Mad Thakur, now-a-days, don't you draw water to bathe? Where is your bathing water?'

Madman : This water cannot be seen. It gushes down from Hari's feet and falls on my head. It enters into the body through the Brahmarandhra and washes away all the dirt and grime, and makes us clean. Sitaram Sitaram.

Haladhar : Is the outer and inner dirt washed away if we bathe in that water?

Madman : Certainly.

(Quotes a verse in Sanskrit)

Haladhar : What does it mean?

Madman : I meditate on the One, who is as dark-hued as a large black-bee, wide-eyed, ever-conscious and joyful. I bathe in His grace and I am cleansed.

Haladhar : Please explain it properly.

212

Madman : Ever-present, Shining and Dear; these are
three of His qualities. The blue sky itself is
the eye of the Nameless, Formless Being. He
is looking unblinking at us. We are bathing
and getting cleansed in His light. Aha! Aha!
Aha!

The Madman's body shivers with ecstasy and tears flow
from his eyes. After a while Haladhar speaks.

Haladhar : O Mad Baba, you said that your bathing
water was not visible, but your bathing water
is flowing from your eyes and drenching
your body.

Madman : Sitaram, Sitaram.

Haladhar : Well, what is the inner and outer dirt?

Madman : The gross body made of five elements is
the outer dirt. The subtle body made of
the five pranas, mind, intellect, and the ten
senses and *karana deha*, the embodiment of
ignorance, is the inner dirt. Both have to be
cleansed.

Haladhar : What is to be done after washing them?

(Madman speaks in Sanskrit)

Haladhar : Please translate this and explain to me.

Madman : I am Achyuta. That is, I am always the same.
I am boundless; I am joy; I am eternal; I have
no decay or rise; I am the sole being; I have
no alternative; I am formless; I am the eternal
knowledge and bliss; I am unborn; I am the

manifest; I am the Reality and I am free from the cycle of birth and death. I am eternal and free. Think of it in this way.

Haladhar : Is it easy to conceive this? I have a tongue, so I can somehow utter the name of Rama. But I am unable to think in these terms.

Madman : O, My Thakur has said, 'If you cannot conceive of it, keep repeating these qualities of God. If you practice this for a year, you will surely become free.'

Haladhar : I do not understand it. How can I be freed by simply uttering these words?

Madman : Inside you, an upward current flows. These words are infinitely powerful and, carrying them around, the Prana becomes helpless. When the billions of universes are illuminated by the mere light reflecting off His little nail, how can His feet be located and reached? These are His names. The prana becomes powerless to proceed further, falls in the source and is immersed in nectar. Jai Sitaram, Jai Sitaram.

Haladhar : Where is it immersed?

Madman : Yoga Taravali says, 'In the human heart there is an empty space called Trikuta. If the life-breath is fixed on that place, only Kumbhaka remains and the Prana, leaving Ida and Pingala disappears in it.' Do you understand

Sitaram, how freedom is achieved?

Haladhar : This is like shifting one man's burden to another. Yoga Taravali says that by performing the Uddiyana, Jalandhara and Mulabandhana, the serpent-like Kundalini is roused from sleep and Prana Vayu enters the path of Sushumna. Are you telling me something else?

Madman : This kundalini is very difficult to find. She cannot be found simply by practicing these locks. In Mantrayoga, it lives in the image of the deity. In the Layayoga it exists in the point of meditation. Its abode is also in light in Hathayoga. It is roused by the chanting of the name of Rama as well as by the Japa of Gayatri. It also wakes up if one can cry 'Mother, Wake up Ma' like a child. As soon as it rises, the task is done, the citadel is conquered. Sitaram Sitaram. One bathes in the confluence of the three streams.

Haladhar : What needs to be considered is the distance between me, the tiniest worm, and God, full of infinite godliness.

Where is my godliness? Where is my power? Where is my omniscience? If I still say that I am Brahma, is it not a mad man's raving? He is the Sun, I am a ray. He is the Ocean, I am a wave. So great is the difference between Him and me.

Madman   : Is not the sunray, the Sun? Is not the wave, the ocean? Where have the ray and the wave come from? Where will they go?

Haladhar   : The ray has come from the Sun and will merge in the Sun. The wave has risen from the breast of the ocean and will settle back in the ocean.

Madman   : Then if the wave thinks that it is the ocean, is there any harm in it? Which other path is there? When the mind returns to its source it will be absorbed in it. Sridharaswami refers to 'Both, the soul and the supreme'.

When Krishna disappeared from the dancing arena, the gopikas, while searching for Him, attained a state of engrossment in Him. The feeling of being Krishna arose in all of them. Prahlada forgot himself, and could not know anything other than, 'I am the changeless, eternal supreme soul.' These are not tales about enlightened beings, but devotees. The person will become what the mind accepts. When hit by the arrow of Ramachandra, Marich fell into the sea and saw Rama everywhere. He said, 'I see Rama everywhere.' Kansa reached a similar state. While sitting, standing or moving about, Kansa thought of Hrishikesha and saw Krishna everywhere in the world. Shishupal also reached absorption by the route of malice. Marich, Kansa, Shishupal and such other asuras were not devotees and in spite of being in His physical presence, could not have the realization that 'I too am He.' Salwa became four-armed while meditating on Vasudeva. Go on worshipping; 'Be God, Worship God.'

In Tantric Sadhana, the phrase 'I am He', is used for Bhutashuddhi etc. Whatever Sadhana you engage in, you must remember that you are not the material body but the consciousness. Sadhana is there to realise that despite not being separate, you have started treating your self as separate. You are a creature because you are caught in a snare. Your supreme aim is identification with Shiva.

Haladhar : I do not want to be Shiva. I want Shiva, I am His servant.

Madman : As you go on repeating 'Daso'ham, Daso'ham' (I am His servant, I am a servant), God shows grace and takes away the syllable 'Da' so only 'So'ham' (I am He) remains. But utterance of 'So'ham' and 'Brahmasmi' (I am Brahma) by those who remain tempted by the world and who do not perform any *tapasya* or have devotion, is mere lip service. If after attaining indirect knowledge, no attempt is made to turn it into direct knowledge, no good comes of it.

Haladhar : I cannot understand Jnana. I do not derive any joy from it.

Madman : What need have you of Jnana? Surrender at His feet. Seek shelter with Him. Let Him do what He pleases. Sitaram.

Haladhar : What shall I do? Should I take a vow of following a practice of chanting for a year? I doubt if I shall be able to do it even for a month. There is no end of the obstacles one has to face. There are diseases, grief and poverty. Show me a simple, easy way and let me follow it with all possible effort.

Madman : Have you been initiated?

Haladhar : Yes.

Madman : Make the mantra your stay. Chant the name loudly when your mind becomes restless. When it settles down, chant the mantra silently. My Thakur has proclaimed that contemplation of the play of the divine is the only way out for this Age.

Haladhar : Will the chanting of the Name of Rama alone take me to the ultimate goal?

Madman : Lord Shiva says, 'O Parvati! The benefit from chanting of the name of Rama is a million times more than that from chanting all the mantras of the Vedas. He who utters the name of Rama even once at the time of breathing one's last, crosses the realm of the Sun and goes to the Supreme Abode. Do you understand it? Jai Sitaram, Jai Sitaram.

Haladhar : Sri Rama, Rama, Rama, Sitaram, Sitaram.

Madman : Absorption comes while one performs Japa.
During chanting; when God, unseen, comes
and embraces, tears, thrill and trembling
are experienced. The devotee then reaches
an unprecedented state. He softens and
sinks in it. What separation then remains?
When the spell is broken, the devotee
becomes a true devotee. The embodiment
of Love, Sri Chaitanya Mahaprabhu, while
chanting 'Krishna, Krishna', used to burst
out saying, 'I am He, I am He.' About Sri
Radha Ji, Vidyapati says, 'She forgets herself
while meditating on Madhava. She no more
remembers her own feelings and nature, and
indentifies herself with Madhava. The pangs
of separation rose in her mind. With eyes
filled with tears, with the voice half choked
she calls out the name of Radha again and
again. Her own body is afflicted with the
pangs of separation from herself. It is not love
if it does not produce this state. O Madman,
you just love. You need not perform any
Sadhana or Bhajana. Just keep on loving.'

The madman began to cry loudly saying, 'Lord, fill us with
love' 'Fill us with love.' Haladhar too could not remain
unmoved. He also began to cry, saying, 'Give me your love',
'Give me your love'. Jai Sitaram.

ॐ

19. Maid in the Quest of the Beloved

The Madman was chanting 'Jai Sitaram' when Ramdas appeared and said to him, 'O Madman. I have gotten into deep trouble.'

Madman   : What trouble?

Ramdas   : My Guru has given me a mantra. As soon as I start repeating it, my body starts trembling; I get a strange feeling in my heart; tears stream from my eyes and I feel feverish. What is happening to me?

Madman   : Jai Sitaram. This is very good! Your mantra has awakened. Jai Sitaram.

Ramdas   : It is easy for you to say 'this is very good' but I am dying due to this trembling. I am quivering from head to toe; how terrible is this! I am unable to control it. When I bend down in salutation, my head hits the floor. I perspire sometimes and other times I get goose bumps. Sometimes during meditation my hands involuntarily start touching my body or my mouth opens and shuts, as if, eating something. Sometimes I see lights or hear a knocking or some other strange sound. What does all this mean, Baba? I have been noticing for the past few days that something within, tugs at the space between my eyebrows, like a fish dragging a fishing-line. Many other things happen as well. I do not remember much, but it feels pleasant. If I go to attend a Kirtan, my hands start waving about and I involuntarily begin to go through strange motions. Strange noises escape from my mouth. My body gets up and starts dancing. It moves about, rocks and even falls at times. Sometimes I become rigid and lifeless as a log. What should I do, Baba?

Madman : O Sitaram, you are very fortunate. You have attained Siddha-Yoga and your mantra has awakened. The 'lady' has started her journey. A union will follow soon and then the merging will take place.

Ramdas : Baba, what is Siddha-Yoga?

Madman : Your Guru has infused energy into you. This is called Diksha-Sara, also known as Shakti Diksha. The mantra is activated and Kundalini is awakened. Your body has been permeated by the Divine Being. You have nothing to fear now and you do not have to do anything more. Everything will happen on its own. Go son, you have a bright future. Keep repeating 'Sitaram.' The union is near.

Ramdas : But why is there such trembling before the union?

Madman : Man despite being part of the Absolute, considers himself separate due to the notion of 'I'. This is made up of three bodies; Gross, Subtle and Causal. When the Guru gives the benediction of Siddha-Yoga, the dormant energy wakes up and starts refining these bodies. Listen, O Sitaram, on immersing a pot in Ganga, despite the fact that the water in the pot and outside is the same, the barrier created by the pot prevents the water inside to mingle with the river. The union is possible only on breaking the pot. Similarly, despite the fact that man remains immersed in the Divine Ocean, he remains separate due to the barrier created by the body. Instigated by the Guru, the Kundalini awakens, but the union becomes possible only after breaking through the Gross, the Subtle and the Causal bodies. The centre of the Gross body is the Brahma Granthi by the navel. After synthesizing the Gross body, the Kundalini reaches the empty space in the heart. Here one begins to feel the vibrations of the primordial sound. From here, the Kundalini moves on to the extra deep space in the throat called Vishnu Granthi, which is the centre of the Causal body. When this centre is pierced, the sound of pipes or drums is perceived. After this, the Kundalini pierces the Rudra Granthi, at the centre of the eyebrows and merges with the

Supreme Soul. When the Kundalini pierces
the Gross body, the physical body feels the
effect. On its piercing the subtle body, the
heart fills with joy. These are the deeds of the
Kundalini. Narada Bhakti Sutra says, 'After
the piercing of the three bodies, one has to be
nothing except being in service as a constant
servant and loving as a beloved.' You can
call the triad Gross-Subtle-Causal, Brahma-
Vishnu-Maheshwar, Sattva-Rajas-Tama,
Shravana-Manana-Niddhidhyasana, Shabd-
Anuman-Pratyaksha or Guru-God-Devotee.
What else? Pierce the three, make them one
and enjoy the bliss. Jai Sitaram. Yes, I was
saying that when the Kundalini wakes up
and starts demolishing the barriers, it starts
manifesting as physical signals. Did you get
it? Jai Sitaram.

Visible physical trembling, appearance of
goose pimples, palpitation, trembling of lips
and throbbing in the forehead, tingling in
the spine, pulsation in various parts of the
body, feeling of being pierced by a needle,
hearing patting noises, beginning to dance
and moving on hearing a hymn, moving
one's hands in extraordinary ways and
uttering 'Hum...Hum', are some of the signs
of Kundalini refining the Gross and moving
on to the Subtle body. Gross body is made up
of Earth, Water, Fire, Air and Ether. When the
Kundalini passes into the Earth element, one
is rendered immovable. On her going into

the Water element, tears flow uncontrollably. One feels feverish on Kundalini's .passing into the Fire element. Trembling and goose-bumps are experienced on her entering the Air element and loss of senses occurs, when she passes into the Ether element. The Gross body is refined in various ways. If any part of the Gross body is found to be lacking in strength, the Kundalini stops at that place and remains there till the weakness gets removed. Certain processes can refine the entire Gross body in one go. A refined Gross body experiences the divine words, sensations, sights, tastes and smells. The body having become stilled, one perceives luminescence as if emanating from a full Moon, a crescent, red and blue dots, stars, a flame, lightning, fireflies, fireworks, a cremation pyre, a lamp or a glowing thread. Apart from this, visions of Kali, Krishna, Rama, Shiva, Durga and various other gods and realized souls, are perceived. A sweet taste in the mouth and a pleasant sensation within, are felt. Effulgence resonating with the sound of 'Shiva' is experienced.

Ramdas   : Thakur, are you quoting the Shastras?

Madman   : Certainly. These are described in the Shastras. However this is not a mere repetition of the Shastras. These are experienced by those who have been blessed by their Gurus.

Ramdas : What is Nada?

Madman : I would not be able to describe it in words. Nada is of a thousand types. Mantra resides in the Hansa which in turn resides in the Pranava. The sound of 'M' in the Pranava resonates with Nada. In this context, Nada-Bindu Upanishad mentions the roar of the ocean, a clap of thunder, a drum beat, gushing of a waterfall, beat of a hand-drum, tinkling of an anklet, notes of a flute and buzzing of a bumble bee etc. as being resonant with Nada. Hamsopanishad says that Nada appears on a thousand repetitions of the Hamsa mantra as the sound of a Chinchini, a bell, a conch-shell, Tantri, Tala, a flute, drums or thunder-clouds. Shiva Samhita and Tripurasara Samuchaya have recommended blocking one's ears while undertaking the Nada practice. Here Nada is described as buzzing of the bumble-bee, notes of the flute and the veena, sound of a bell or a thunderclap. Gurutatvadhrut Shivapurana, Uma Samhita and Dharma Samhita contain tales where Nada appears as a roar, clinking of bronze vessels, ringing of a bell, notes of a veena or a flute, blare of trumpets, blowing of a conch-shell or a thunder. All these descriptions prove inadequate to describe the millions of forms in which Nada appears. No language in the world is capable of describing the ways in which Nada is experienced. The Almighty is Nada. It is the radiant Shiva. Nada, the primordial sound, appears in the heart of the seeker in different forms and cuts the noose of the world. One seeker hears the tinkling of anklets and the notes of the flute while another hears only the flute. Someone hears a metronomical repetition of 'Hare Krishna Hare Krishna Krishna Krishna Hare Hare', while someone else hears the same mantra being sung in different voices or played on various instruments. One could also hear the chanting of 'Radhe-Govinda, Jai Radhe Govinda', notes of various instruments, drone of string instruments, boom of a drum beat, vibration of 'So'ham', sound of 'Guru… Guru' or 'Jai Guru', songs, buzzing of bees, percussion instruments etc.

Coming from distant skies, is heard, the enchanting song of 'Guru…Guru', sound of 'Si…Si' or tinkling as if coming from the anklets worn by a small child. How many melodies and tunes! The sweetness of the Nada cannot be described. Who can express in words, the incomparable, limitless and incomprehensible joy felt while experiencing the Nada? In this manner, Shiva takes the form of the Nada and picks up the seeker in his arms.

The mind endures as long as Nada remains, after which comes Manonmani stage, when the body grows stiff as a log and the yogi loses all sense of heat or cold, weal or woe, esteem or scorn. He goes beyond the pale of the three states called waking, dream and deep, dreamless sleep. By Jyoti and Nada is achieved the purification of the Sukshma Deha. As the Karana Deha is purified, one cultivates the realisation of the idea that 'All is You'. The realisation, 'As the observer, you permeate all things and I have come to you for refuge', does away with the illusion of duality. Jada Samadhi and Chaitanya Samadhi go on, happening automatically. The long and the short of it is that so long as you have language to use and a mind to brood with, you have to hold fast to that supreme Mantra, 'I have come to you for refuge'. This by itself shall set everything right. This is how one comes to feel absolutely secure. A deep peace wells up from within. It is bliss and joy all over. Jai Sitaram, Jai Sitaram, Jai Sitaram.

Sri Shankaracharya says in Prabodha Sudhakara, 'Though the sky is void yet as cloud it fulfills the Chataka's hope and as the Moon, it gratifies the Chakora; such is the potency of firm faith!' Although inaccessible to sight, speech and thought, God does gratify the devotees out of His unaccountable grace, appearing in visible form; embodying profound truth and ineffable joy. Rama, Rama, Jai Guru!

Ramdas   : Well, Crazy Father! If the body does in fact split, how does it continue to function?

227

Madman : Though the Crazy dear breaks it up and turns it upside down, the karma of the previous birth holds up the body. When the path of Sushumna is purified, no trace of physical existence remains during Samadhi. The Kundalini becomes one.

Ramdas : Thank you, Father! I am much heartened by what you say. I was afraid that I had contracted a disease.

Madman : Jai Sitaram. Not you alone, but many other men, blessed with Siddha Yoga, often mistake spiritual symptoms for disease and undergo medical treatment. A young seeker wondering why his limbs should apparently be numb, and feeling something creeping near the spinal cord, consulted a physician who suspected that it would develop into Pthisis. One day as the vital breath got into Sushumna, an utter exhaustion seized him and he thought that his end was near. His anxious father ran about frantically for medicine, to prevent a heart-failure. The gentleman began to experience transcendent light and tastes. Yet he thought that his health was being impaired by Japa and abandoned it. If his head shook and body shivered, that was not due to disease but the result of Yoga. Vision of light is no hallucination, but genuine perception. Only after consulting the Shastras, could the youth bring himself to believe it.

Look again at this case of a female aspirant. Admitted to Siddha Yoga, she came to have many experiences such as a creeping sensation along the spine, the mouth gaping wide or becoming distorted, the eyes assuming weird expressions and unusual and disquieting feeling within the chest. She of course took all these as symptoms of neurosis and got very nervous. She had difficulty in being convinced that it was not a case of disease at all but the symptoms of her progress in Yoga. Yet another woman seeker practicing spiritual exercise for a pretty long time came to be similarly afflicted. She felt out-of-sorts, complained of something abnormal going on within the chest and had fits of fainting. Medicine could be of no avail. Subsequently it came to be known that the so-called disease was really a case of Yoga.

A seeker had an attack apparently of dyspepsia. Many doctors were consulted. But the disease would not respond to medicine. He was very much run down. He would often wonder whether or not he was actually alive and remained steeped in a sort of intoxication. The poor man was beside himself with anxiety. After being administered Havishya by his Guru, he was cured. Jai Sitaram.

It is the duty therefore of a seeker to inform the Guru of anything unusual that may happen after initiation and then to follow the Guru's instruction.

Spiritual symptoms, big or small, do happen in most cases, but they go unheeded, with the result that the spiritual progress gets arrested. The seeker himself should take note of every reaction. After the Diksha, until there is some manifestation of a thrill of joy, shivering of the body, the hairs standing on end, occasional changes in tone of voice or expression of the eye, it should be understood that the mind is not stilled and the Kundalini has not been awakened. When these signs appear, resort should be to the Guru and proper steps taken, so that the mantra may be activated. It is the chosen deity who comes as Guru and resides within the seeker as the mantra. When the mantra attains fulfillment, it merges with the deity.

Using Mantra-Siddhi, the yogi achieves Samadhi by merging his mind with the deity and destroying the distinction of the subject, object and relation between them. At first there is distinct awareness of the mind, mantra and the deity, but in the end, the mantra merges with the deity. The moment this is achieved, the three factors of the subject, the object and the act of meditating get dissolved. Once this stage is reached, Sattvika signs like hairs standing on end, shedding of tears in joy etc., appear. The seeker arrives very soon at final gratification through Samadhi. The supreme aim of mantra yoga is the attainment of Mahabhava, the grand psychic state. With the awakening of Kundalini, every form of Yoga comes to be intimately realised; no branch of it remains unknown. Jai Sitaram.

Ramdas   : Well, Crazy Father! How can the three; the Guru, the mantra and the deity become one? The Guru is human in form, the deity is the mental image of the form and the mantra consists of a few letters of the alphabet. How can they become one? Is not that a puzzle?

Madman   : As stated in Mundamalatantra, the very same question had also occurred to Parvati. Shiva says, 'By one form and type, is meant, the formless. It is Mahakala, the formless being, who in essence is every body's Guru. As for mantra, it is sound and the deity's form is self-assumed. All three are therefore formless. That explains why the three are one and the same. Out of the Guru comes the mantra; out of the mantra, the deity. So the mantra is the deity's father while Guru is his grandfather. Meditation on the father pleases the grandfather as well. Son and Grandfather are the same essence as the Father, hence they are the essentially the same form or the way of approaching each of them is the same. The Guru, the mantra and the deity can therefore be described as one.

In the Matrikabheda Tantra Shiva says, 'The best of the Sadhakas obtain the supreme mantra from the lips of the Guru, and out of the Bija grows the form of the deity. Other forms however may also evolve at the Guru's bidding.'

'One can realise the idea that Guru is the origin, if one seeks to do so'.

That is why I affirm the identity of the three; the Guru, the mantra and the deity. Without knowledge of this identity, there cannot be fulfillment of mantra. The Guru, undoubtedly, is mantra; the Guru, of course, is the deity.

By virtue of being with or without attributes, the Supreme Being gets two aspects. His formless aspect is described in the Shrutis, which state that three of His parts remain unmanifested, while the fourth becomes the spaces within which, the infinite number of universes are formed. That indeterminate Absolute creates each universe with all its creatures through his own power, as a sport for himself. And to deliver these creatures, he assumes determinate and 'with attribute' forms like Brahma, Vishnu, Maheshwar, Rama, Krishna, Sita, Radha, Durga etc.

He incarnates as Guru to demonstrate how

the formless may be found. As it is not always possible to remain with the Guru, He installs himself in the seeker as the mantra, in the form of mystic syllables like 'Kleeng', 'Hreeng' etc. The sound of mantra awakens the great-great-Guru namely, the Kundalini. Her awakening is another name for the mantra getting charged with life. Many psychic experiences start occurring, both without and within. The deity grants vision of himself. The mantra merges in the deity's form and the awareness is admitted to the Sushumna. He becomes a liberated spirit. Entering the Sushumna, Hamsa resolves into Soham, where the 'Sah' dissolves and leaves the 'Om'. Then the 'A' and 'U' also go away, leaving the 'M' imbued with Naad, which continues to rise. Then follow the stages called Bindu, Kala and Kalateeta. Bindu is Ahamkara, Kala is Mahat Tattva and Kalateeta is Prakriti. At the final stage, the Supreme Brahman appears. Every faculty of perception gets dissolved and merged. What that stage is like, can hardly be conceived. The yogi turns stiff as a log. He wakes up only to feel baffled and bewildered. Words fail him to express his joy.

Ramdas : Tell, in what manner should one meditate on the Supreme Brahman?

Madman : Well-asked indeed! Pray, how can there be meditation on the Supreme Brahman?

However, listen:

The sphere called Swar is His head, the sky is His navel, the Sun and the Moon are His eyes, the different directions are his ears and the earth is His foot. Jai Sitaram!

Ramdas   : Is the earth His foot? So we reside right within Him, eh?

Madman   : Sitaram, if a man is thrown into the sea, he is immersed in it and has nothing but the sea on all sides; it is the sea that lies above, beneath, beside and before him. Similarly all creatures are immersed in the sea of the Supreme. The only difference between this sea and that is that the Supreme is not just outside us but also inside us, even as the sky is. Immersed in Him as man is, he believes himself to be separate and the precise point of Sadhana is to eliminate this sense of being separate. During Samadhi, the mind merges in Him; the poor doll of salt loses itself while trying to plumb the depths of the sea and the seeker loses his identity. Madman starts to sing.

Dive, O, Mind, with 'Kali' on your lips,

Into the unfathom'd depths of your heart.

That mine of gems, the sea, is no blank, you know;

But can riches be fished with two dives or

three?

With one long dive, O Mind, proceed,

To the shore of your Kula-Kundalini.

Jai Sitaram, Jai Sitaram.

Dive, dive, do dive, I say.

[Madman begins to dance]

Ramdas : Enough of your dance, Crazy Father! I still have questions to ask.

Madman : Wait, Sitaram, let me dance for a while.

'Sitaram...Jai Sitaram...Jai Gopi Vallabh Sitaram.'

[He shouts, claps his hands and dances in ecstasy. Having danced, he resumes his seat.]

[A long pause; then Ramdas speaks]

Ramdas : Oh Crazy Father, have you returned to a normal state?

Madman : Yes, Sitaram. What have you got to ask?

Ramdas : Well, it is held in certain quarters that until joy and enlightenment is found, one can go on accepting new Gurus. Is this supported by the Shastras?

Madman : Yes, the Shiva Purana says, 'If initiation by a Guru does not fetch even a slight joy or enlightenment, the disciple may, on the expiry of a year, approach another Guru.'

Ramdas : What if the second too should fail? Should the seeker get a third and if that does not work, should he continue accepting Gurus? If his life is spent in changing Gurus, when will he do his practice? How can one serve so many Gurus? And how can one manage so many mantras? I have heard that a man dies if he abandons his mantra and becomes poor if he abandons his Guru. If he abandons both, I have heard, he is confined to Raurava hell. Wherever the seeker goes, he has to listen to something different. How can even a Siddha Guru block the doors of hell for the seeker?

Madman : Jai Sitaram. It is of course for the meanest of seekers that the Shastras prescribe these retributions. The respectful disciple never abandons his Guru, no matter how the Guru may be. He knows:

'Be he learned or ignorant, the Guru is a God to the disciple. No matter whether he follows the right or wrong course, he remains the only resort for the disciple.' *Nigam Kalpadrumah*

He knows that 'to look upon the Guru as an ordinary human being, to look upon the mantra as a mere string of letters and to look upon the image of the deity as a block of stone is the way to hell.' *Jnanarnava*

'He, who is lured by a false sense of Dharma to abandon the line of his father's Guru, has to live in hell as long as the Sun, Moon and stars exist. But then if there is no one competent to initiate, in the ancestral line of Guru, that line may be abandoned with immunity.' *Pischila Tantra.*

The respectful disciple knows, 'The letters comprising the mantra are indeed the deity and the deity is none other than the Guru. He who cares for his own welfare will make no distinction between the mantra, the Guru and the deity.' *Tara Pradeep*

So you see; the respectful disciple holds on to the mantra even if it does not grow sentient all at once. He looks to his own shortcomings and tries to correct his own failings by right observances, pure food, study of sacred texts, holy association and so on; and thinking that his Guru is incompetent, he will not lay his ears open to be whispered into by anyone and everyone. He lays bare his soul's distress at the feet of his own Guru and asks him how his mantra may grow sentient. The Guru too leads the respectful disciple along the way laid down in Shastras, for having the mantra activated. That is how his mantra becomes instinct with life and the seeker is gratified. Shraddha or reverence is the soul of all Sadhana. Where this is wanting, achievement is impossible.

Ramdas : Pray, what is meant by Shraddha?

Madman : Shraddha means faith in what the Guru or the Vedanta says.

The word is derived from the root 'Dha', preceded by the word Shrt, meaning truth. Shraddha, then, is the deity that presides over the intelligence out of which comes conviction as to the immutable and unalterable character of Dharma, Artha, Kama and Moksha; the four principal pursuits of man. The presiding deity of this intelligence is Shraddha. The Creator has ordained Truth to be her eternal shrine and has installed her in the Truth.

Shraddha is the source of all fulfillment; Shraddha is the cause of genuine knowledge. For, truth, knowledge and Shraddha mean the same thing.

So you see, the disciple who has faith in Guru and mantra does have his mantra vitalised, irrespective of the quality of his Guru. While millions of Gurus may be found, scarcely can a true disciple be met with.

Shiva says in Yamala, 'The only Guru is Shiva, I am that Shiva. Oh Goddess! You too are Guru, the mantra also is Guru.'

In another Mantra you have:

'He who gives mantra is Guru. Mantra is

Parama Guru (Grand Guru) Prakriti or Kundalini is Parapara Guru (Great-grand-Guru) while the Indeterminate Absolute in Paramesthi Guru (Great-Great-Grand-Guru).'

The respectful disciple resorts first to Guru and Parama Guru and throws himself heart and soul into spiritual exercise. When his reliance comes to be absolute and the Mother cannot hold-off any longer, she wakes up. It is she who unites the seeker with the Paramesthi Guru and relieves him of the bondage of life.

Ramdas : Many receive Diksha, but few ever achieve anything. Pray, why?

Madman : If you enquire, you will see that the vast majority of men take Diksha just on the impulse of the moment; a month or two and they give up their practice. They somehow complete barely ten or at best one hundred and eight counts of the mantra. Not even a Siddha Guru can be of much use to such disciples. Work you must, or how can you expect to reap the harvest? Very often again an ignorant Guru gives an incorrect mantra, which necessarily leads to no tangible result.

Ramdas : Is it possible for a mantra to be incorrect?

Madman : All mantras come from Shiva, who uttered them first. Any arbitrary combination of words cannot attain to the status of a mantra.

For example, an oddly constructed mantra like 'Om Namah Sarasva Kleem Gopinath Vallabhaya Namah' cannot give any joy to the seeker. If ever proper Japa should fail to fetch bliss, joy or some other tangible result, it is to be presumed that something is wrong with the mantra itself. An incorrect mantra may be abandoned in favour of a new one. If the Guru lives, the correct mantra ought to be received from him. In case, however, it is obtained from another Guru, it does not amount to change of Guru or mantra. For, he is the Guru who gives mantra and an incorrect mantra is a faulty combination of letters without sense; it does not enjoy the sanctity of a mantra. None-the-less, the mantra ought to be taken from the previous Guru. A little alertness on the part of the Guru and that of the disciple can prevent much trouble.

One who draws water from a well, makes it available to all and pours it out freely, can of course, gratify any thirsty man that cares to approach him. So the Siddha Guru, having attained fulfillment after spiritual exercise, infuses power into his disciples, out of his own infinite mercy, and rescues men scorched with the heat of life. Thanks to that power, a disciple can easily attain Jivanamukti. But a Siddha Guru of this category can rarely be found. It is only the accumulated austerities of many previous births that can bring you to the feet of such a Guru.

It is incorrect therefore to resolve not to drink water unless it is already drawn and kept in readiness. One should rather tie the bucket of mantra received from the Guru with the rope of Japa and with the words 'Jai Guru' on the lips draw the refreshing water from the well. There is always a reward to honest effort. If thirst be there, my son, water will not be wanting. Found wanting is a genuine thirst. My Lord says, 'whoever but once prays saying, 'I am yours', is promised every security by me; whoever he may be, I assure him of complete safety.' Only say, 'I have come to you for refuge' and go on with Japa, night and day. All shall be well. The crazy wench will wake up, you know. If you take refuge, the lord will not be able to hold himself but come in some form and vitalise your mantra.

'Out of Japa comes Mukti, out of Japa comes Mukti, out of Japa comes Mukti, there can be no doubt about it.'

Naam Kirtan accomplishes everything.

Bhakti of every category; secondary as well as primary, comes from the recollection or chanting of the Name. My son, as long as you have power of speech, you go on chanting 'Rama Rama'.

Ramdas   : Do all seekers exhibit the same symptoms?

Madman   : There are differences at the outset. Once you get to the root or centre, however, all come to be alike. External manifestations such as shivering, hairs standing on end, shedding of tears, etc. are common to seekers of every school; Vaishnavas, Shaktas, Worshippers of Surya (Sun), Worshippers of Ganapati, Yogi and Jnani. All roads lead finally to Sushumna. Spiritual experiences should not be generally disclosed. Publicity arrests perception and causes disease.

Ramdas   : What should be done in case of doubt?

Madman   : Doubts should be referred to, and resolved by, one's Guru, in case he is alive, or else an advanced practitioner should be consulted. A mere scholar will find it hard even so much as to trust you, if ever you take him into confidence about your experiences. He will measure your realisation with the yard-stick of his own second-hand knowledge and probably opine that you have gone off the track, or else oblige you with the news that you have developed a disease. Beware! Do not speak about your realisation.

Rarely do we meet an honest man candidly confessing, 'I am only a beast of burden, bearing the precious lore of the Shastras, I have no experience in that line.'

'Yogena Yogam Janeeyat'. Yoga is to be known by Yoga, that is, by practice. A seeker should go on with his spiritual exercise strictly according to the rule. As soon as one stage is won, the next will come of itself.

Amazement and suspicion are particularly detrimental to spiritual progress. The thought, 'Is it possible for me to have such an experience' is an amazement disorder. 'Why should it not be possible in my case? Since other seekers do acquire such transcendental experiences, why should they not happen to me?' Queries like these would need to be resolved with the help of the Shastras. Should pride assail you, remember it is your Ishta, who is present in all these various forms and experiences. To whom should you brag then? 'All's you, all's you'. Knowing this itself can solve all the problems. To sum up, Sitaram, pure food, pious conduct, morning and evening worship at the proper hour, study of sacred texts, association of Saints, are sure to bring about fulfillment. For this Kali Yuga, the best method is chanting the Name always and meditating on God's Leela. At the end, reflections on Leela do not evoke images of any kind; language passes through Bhava into Pranava and sets the seeker at rest.

Ramdas   : Well, Crazy Father, can you suggest how one can attain to Jivanamukti with effortless ease?

Madman : Yes, I can. Men, who by luck, get to serve a
Guru, meditate on him, sing hymns in praise
of him, do Japa of 'Guru', worship him, earn
his pleasure and get to revere him; can attain
to fulfillment of mantra: They indeed become
Jivanmukta. Got it, Ramdas?

Ramdas : Is there any other way?

Madman : He who constantly does Japa of the Supreme
Mantra 'Durga Durga Durga' is Jivanmukta.

Ramdas : It is not possible for a Vaishnava to be
Jivanmukta?

Madman : Oh yes, it is!

They undoubtedly are Jeevanmuktas who,
oblivious to all sense of shame, joyfully
sing the perpetually fresh nectar-nourished
Names of Murari, such Names, i.e. as Hari,
Keshava, Govinda, Mukunda, etc.

Ramdas : How do they fare who say 'Rama Rama'?

Madman : That wise man who is deeply devoted to
Rama and always utters 'Sri Rama' becomes
a Jivanmukta. Jai Rama, Sitaram.

By saying 'Shiva Shiva' too one can become
Jivanmukta. What is needed, my son is one
who can do it. The way, for this, degenerate
age, is to sing the Name, which is a very

quick way, indeed. Jai Rama, Sitaram, Jai Jai Rama, Sitaram.

Ramdas : Well, Crazy Father, does every seeker's body behave in this manner?

Madman : Jai Sitaram. Listen to what happened to our Srimati Radharani who, as you know, was all love.

Our Radha, continuously weeping for her darling Shyam, has been in a state of living death, when suddenly the flute is heard, there is freshness in the morning. Appears that Kala (Krishna) had come and expressed his love to Radha. She would hurry to meet him but the mere thought renders her immobile.

When slowly the warmth and consciousness returned, Radha said to herself;

An emerald mirror is my heart;

There I ever see your dark lovely image.

Like a sable cloud is your green boyish form!

How sweet you play on the flute!

The lovely face; how it beams!

More than the autumn Moon!

He smiles bewitchingly, the sportive youth.

Lovely rich is his cluster of hair with hanging locks

A peacock plume on the crest.

Winningly he looks; Oh what gestures!

Soft but arch; no silly lass can guess.

With malati garland dressed, his yellow cloth waves,

His loveliness is more playful

Than the light of the Moon.

Hearing the anklet's tinkle,

Radha, dressed as a bride

Followed the sound.

Radharani felt thrilled,

Words flowed uncontrolled;

Play no more on your flute, O Shyam.

Its tune drives me mad

And I know not how to keep my family's honour.

Radharani's limbs began to shiver, she could not move, her body turned pale. Out of her lily-eyes rained incessant tears and soaked her lotus-heart. She could not hold herself any more. She lost her consciousness and dropped down. She did drop, but not on the ground for, there came Shyam and spread his arms and clasped her to his bosom.

At last, after a hundred years,

The bride has met her groom.

Great is the exultation in Radhika's heart.

'My lost treasure I've found,' she says

And clasps him to her bosom,

Their meeting is unique

The Chakor has caught the Moon, and

The lotus meets her honey-bee.

In ecstasy their two bodies shiver,

Each in the other being rapt.

The morning breaks.

On the bejewelled couch the two sit,

Each seeing the other's face with joy.

Tears of joy drop a curtain over their sight

Try as they might, they cannot see clearly

Yet they gaze unwinking at each other,

The warm spring wind rises gently

The spotless Moon is up.

Choked with joy, Chandidas stands by

Waving the holy tail-fan for them.

As he sings, the Madman feels overwhelmed; tears stream from his eyes and his half-closed eyes become still.

After a pause, Ramdas cries, 'Oh Crazy Father!'

Madman springs to his feet and claps his hands, as he sings:

Radhe Govind, Jai Radhe Govind

Radhe Govind Bolo Radhe Govind

Ramdas joins him:

Radhe Govind, Jai Radhe Govind.

Radhe Govind Bolo Radhe Govind.

Jai Sitaram.

ॐ

20. God in Trees

The Madman had come out of the cottage and was dancing to, 'Jai Sitaram Jai Sitaram' when Haridas Babu came and said, 'O mad Thakur, can you tell me why our ancestors planted Peepul trees when they could choose good trees like mango or jackfruit? O Rama! It is just a big tree; without any fruit, flower or scent. It also occupies one or two *bighas* of land. There is no way of cutting it down and planting a few grafts. It is said that this is a ceremoniously established tree. It must not be cut down or burnt. What a problem! Tell me father, do the Shastras say anything about this?'

Madman   : Jai Sitaram. Surely they do. Do you believe in Shastras?

Haridasa   : I believe a little.

Madman   : How much do you believe? Jai Sitaram.

Haridasa   : I believe in things that can be understood easily.

Madman   : Do you believe in the Gita?

Haridasa   : I believe in that.

Madman   : God says in the Gita, 'In trees, I am the Peepul.'

Haridasa : God says, 'I am whatever is great.' The Peepul tree is very great so God says, 'I am the Peepul tree'.

Madman : Jai Sitaram. Not so. Sitaram, God is established as the Peepul tree.

Haridasa : Say, in which Shastra is it said that God incarnated as the Peepul tree?

Madman : Jai Sitaram. Listen. In the Uttar Khanda of Padmapurana, the Rishis asked Suta, 'Why have you called the Banyan and Peepul trees the most worthy of being worshipped?' In reply to that Suta said, 'Vishnu has assumed the shape of the Peepul tree, the Banyan tree is similarly the embodiment of Rudra, and the Palash tree is that of Brahma. If you see, touch and worship them; they take away your sin. They surely destroy sorrow, danger and pernicious diseases.

Haridasa : Why did God become a tree?

Madman : Jai Sitaram. The rishis put that question to Suta, who explained that at the time of the union of Hara and Parvati, the Gods entered the fire and created a disturbance. Parvati became angry and placed a curse on them, 'Even worms and insects enjoy the pleasure of union. You have spoilt that pleasure of mine. So you be transformed into trees.' Thence Brahma, Vishnu and Maheshwar have become trees.

For that reason Vishnu and Maheshwar have been transformed into the Peepul and Banyan trees respectively. It should not be touched on any day other than Saturday.

Haridasa : Is there anything else in the Shastras?

Madman : Sure there is.

'Parvati resides in the Bilva tree and Lakshmi in the Tulsi plant. At first the universe was created full of trees. These great trees were born of Gods. Their very touch makes one free from sin.' *Skanda Purana Nagar Khand, chapter 247*

Especially, during the Chaturmasya, they are particularly effective in destroying the sins. God has taken abode in trees out of compassion for all creatures. Chaturmasya brings about mercy for all creatures. The Peepul tree should be always served, especially on Saturday. 'By the daily touch of the Peepul tree a thousand kinds of sin are destroyed.' The ancestors of those who serve or worship the Peepul tree with milk mixed with sesamum are satiated. 'Sin is destroyed at the mere sight of the Peepul tree.' Specially, if the Peepul tree is worshipped, meditated on, seen, and served during Chaturmasya, it destroys sin and disease. Worshipping and watering the Peepul tree brings happiness, removes diseases and destroys all sins.

Haridasa   : Does the Peepul tree have so many qualities?

Madman   : 'Only by doing service to the tree, the man who sings the name of the Peepul tree, has no fear on the way to my world.' The man who chants the glory of the Peepul tree is not afraid on the way to the world of Yama. People, who apply *kumkum* and sandalwood paste to the Peepul tree, are freed from three kinds of sufferings and they become equal to Vishnu in Vaikuntha. Their nightmares, troublesome worries, fevers, humiliation and sins are all destroyed.

Dharmaraj shows his grace to people who worship the Peepul tree with a mantra. Utterance of the word Aswattha itself, brings knowledge to man. If one hears the word Aswattha, one's sins from birth to death are destroyed. The service of the Peepul tree is the creator of merit, especially· during Chaturmasya. When Gods fall asleep, Vishnu takes shelter within the tree and consumes all the water on the earth. Water is Vishnu. Being water, Vishnu is the great Rasa (juice). So, Vishnu, who resides in the trees, is the destroyer of sins during Chaturmasya. Vishnu, who is present in creatures, grows the world. Therefore, he who bows to Vishnu residing in the Peepul tree does not go to Hell.

'A disciplined man, who plants a Peepul

tree, is rid of a thousand sins, in an instance. When compared to the other trees, the Peepul is more pure, beneficent and emancipating. If planted and meditated on during Chaturmasa, it destroys the sins.'

Haridasa : Oh, for this reason the ancestors recommended this tree! Now I understand why they planted the Peepul trees instead of mango or jackfruit.

Madman : 'Touching the Peepul tree with one's feet is tantamount to the killing of a Brahmin. One surely goes to hell if one hews down a Peepul tree without any reason. There is no doubt that Vishnu resides in its roots, Keshava in its shoulders, Narayana in its branches, Hari in its leaves and Achyuta along with all gods reside in its fruit. Especially if a man worships the tree during Chaturmasya he gains emancipation.'

Therefore, if a man serves the Peepul tree always with devotion and care, his sins committed during the day are destroyed. This tree is a physical manifestation of Vishnu. Worshipped by saints, it is the root of merit, fulfills desires and is full of qualities. Under its shelter a thousand sins of men are destroyed.

Haridasa : Why should not the Peepul tree be touched, and why is there no sin in touching it on a Saturday?

Madman : Listen to what Suta told the rishis. (Quotes in Sanskrit) 'Kaustubha is the best of all pearls that Gods obtained from churning of the ocean and which, they gave to Vishnu.' *Padma Purana, Uttara Khanda*

Haridasa : I don't understand Sanskrit. Could you please speak in Bangla?

Madman : Jai Sitaram. I am speaking in Sanskrit lest you should think that I am concocting these things. If you go through the Padmapurana you will understand that all these are contained in the Shastras.

Haridasa : No...no, it is right that you are speaking according to the Shastras.

Madman : The Gods churned the ocean and of all the pearls they got, the Kaustubha pearl was the best. The Gods gave that to Vishnu. When Vishnu prayed for Lakshmi as his consort Lakshmi said, 'How can you marry the younger sister so long as the elder sister remains unmarried? First give my elder sister Alakshmi in marriage and then marry me. This is the sanatana dharma.' Hearing Lakshmi say this, Madhusudhan gave that Alakshmi in marriage to the Uddalaka, the rishi known for his long and intense austerities.

Haridasa : How does Alakshmi look?

Madman : Thick-lipped, dry mouthed, ugly, lachrymose red-eyes and rude. As per Vishnu's wishes, the rishi accepted Alakshmi and took her to his hermitage. On arriving at the hermitage, Alakshmi saw the place full of smoke and fragrance from the sacrificial fire and resonant with the chanting of Vedic mantras. Alakshmi was very much pained and said, 'Brahmin! Since the Vedas are being read here, I cannot stay in this place.' The Muni asked her where she could live. In reply Alakshmi said, 'I do not live where there is the sound of the Vedas, entertainment of guests, Yajnas, charity etc. I do not live there where the husband and the wife love each other or the ancestors and the deities are worshipped. I love that place where charity and purity do not exist, thieves and adulterers live. I live perfectly there where the elderly, good people and Brahmins are insulted. I live in the place where cruel speech is uttered.' On hearing this, Uddalaka Muni said with a sad face, 'Alakshmi, stay for a while underneath this Peepul tree till I return after finding a suitable place for you.' Uddalaka went away and never returned. Alakshmi waited for a long time. When Uddalaka did not return, she became sad on being abandoned by her husband and began to cry piteously. Hearing her lament, Lakshmi, residing in Vaikuntha, said to Vishnu, 'Lord, My elder sister is unhappy at being abandoned by her husband. Please go there and console her.' Arriving there with Lakshmi, Vishnu assured Alakshmi and said, 'O Alakshmi! Please reside permanently in this Peepul tree. It was created out of a part of me and I have now made this your abode. Only on Saturdays, Lakshmi will come here.' So the Peepul tree should not be touched, except on Saturday.

Haridasa : Then, it should not be touched on other days as it is the abode of Alakshmi. How will you serve what should not be touched six days in a week? One can be free of anxiety by cutting it down; at least Alakshmi will no longer be there.

Madman : Can it not be served without touching it? It can be saluted, gazed at, and watered without touching it. All these services also bear fruit.

Haridasa : Tell me what fruit is borne by watering?

Madman : Padma Purana says, 'In the month of Vaishakh, devotees of Vishnu should offer water to him via the Peepul tree, to gain the fruits of the four human pursuits. Offering even a palmful of water frees the person from billions of sins and takes him to the supreme abode.'

Haridasa : Oh, that is why crowds gather around the Peepul tree during the month of Vaishakh.

Madman : Listen. People, who safeguard the root of the Peepul tree by building a stone platform around it, receive untold benefits. Longevity of the man, who bows to a Peepul tree, is increased. His wealth grows. Religious rites that are performed below a Peepul tree do not suffer from shortfalls or excesses. Triveni and all other places of pilgrimage are present at the place where even a single Peepul tree, grows. He who worships a Peepul tree is a worshipper of Hari because God himself has assumed the image of the Peepul tree.

Haridasa : This means that even without touching it, worshipping it by salute, sight and watering; longevity and wealth are increased, and religious ceremonies held under it do not become defective. Worship of a Peepul tree is the worship of God. Please tell me more.

Madman : There is not a large enough meritorious deed in the world which could eliminate the sin of the person who destroys the Peepul, thinking it to be an ordinary tree. Peepul, the king of trees, is glorified as the personification of Hari. So there is no saviour for the destroyer of a Peepul tree. Hari destroys the bodily sins of the person who sees, touches, remembers and salutes a Peepul tree.

Haridasa : Dear me! Is the hewing a Peepul tree so great an offence?

Madman : Jai Sitaram. Further; Yamaraja himself

destroys the eyes of the person, who, does not prevent another person from destroying a Peepul tree, even though he could have stopped it from happening. Bhaskara himself chops off the tongue of the person who does not say, 'Do not cut a Peepul tree.' The man, who destroys even a small Peepul branch, suffers the consequences of murdering a billion Brahmins. A hewer of a Peepul tree is guilty of the sins of murder of a Brahmin, adultery with the wife of the preceptor, drinking, stealing, embezzlement, slaughter of a cow, murder of a wife, adultery, murder of a refugee, murder of friends, betraying confidence, killing others, slandering and eating on the eleventh day of bright and dark fortnights. The person who destroys Peepul, the personification of Vishnu, has no equal in sin.

Haridasa : O Hari! That is why a Peepul tree is not hewn. I see that Shastras are at the root of all the popular beliefs. Luckily I have not cut a Peepul tree.

Madman : Jai Sitaram. Kriyayogasagara says, 'The glory of the Peepul tree that I relate, destroys all sins. Peepul tree is the lord of the whole universe; Vishnu Himself and his devotees do not come to any harm. God is pleased with the pious man who serves the Peepul tree regarding it as Vishnu, and bestows on him the supreme state.'

Haridasa : What do you say? By serving the Peepul tree a man gains the supreme state? Is there anything more to say about this? What more do your Shastras say?

Crazyman : Jai Sitaram. The Peepul tree should be worshipped during the forenoon. After this the Peepul tree should not be worshipped. The prayer to Peepul is, 'O Peepul tree! Please take away the weakness of my limbs and eyes, my nightmares and the growth of my enemies. May Janardana in the form of the Peepul tree, be pleased with me. Looking at you, my sins are destroyed and I am blessed by Lakshmi. Circumambulating you bestows longivity. I bow to you.'

Haridasa : The Peepul tree is Vishnu, the Banyan tree is Shiva and the Palasha tree is Brahma. What is the Bilva tree?

Madman : It is said in the Brihaddharmapurana that the Bilva tree originated from the breast of Lakshmi. It is seen in the Yoginitantra that Mahalakshmi assumed the form of a tree and worshipped Shiva with leaves, flowers and fruits for one crore years, and was established in the heart of Vishnu by the grace of Mahadeva.

Yoginitantra says, 'O Goddess Maheshami! Forever present in the Sri Vriksha (the Bilva tree) are all the holy waters and all the gods. There is no doubt about it.'

Tantra Purashcharmollasa says, 'O Mahadevi, the Bilva tree is God Shankara himself. Dying at the foot of the Bilva tree gives final emancipation. Then what is the need of a crore pilgrimages? Brahma and other gods reside here for increasing their powers. Even if the place around the Bilva tree is physically unclean, it remains the domain of Shiva; the Pure.'

Nagarkhanda of the Skandapurana states, 'Under the effort of travelling, drops of perspiration formed on Girija's forehead. Bhavani dropped them on a mountain called Mandar. These grew into the Bilva tree.'

Haridasa : Different saints hold different views. Which one of them is true, O Mad baba?

Madman : Jai Sitaram. All are true. There are differences as the shape of creation in each Kalpa is a little different.

Haridasa : Please let that go. Could you tell me about Dhatri or Amla (Indian Gooseberry)?

Madman : One day the gods went to Prabhasa. While there, Parvati had the desire to worship Vishnu, with things created by her. Lakshmi also had a similar desire. Both expressed their wishes to each other. At this, tears of pure joy fell on the ground from their eyes. From these tears the Amla or Dhatri tree was born. Properties of both the Tulsi and Bilva leaves are present in the Amla leaf. Both Shiva and Vishnu are pleased if they are worshipped with Amla leaves. This is said in the Brihaddharma Purana, 'By planting a Dhatri tree a man becomes comparable to Vishnu. The space of three hundred and fifty cubits around the Dhatri tree becomes like the Kurukshetra.'

Haridasa : Dear me! The area of three hundred and fifty cubits of ground is like Kurukshetra? O father, are not all these things exaggerations?

Madman : Jai Sitaram. Not at all! All these things are true.

'Sixteen cubits of ground from the root of the Tulsi plant is a great place of pilgrimage, worshipped even by gods. Tulsi is indeed Vishnu himself.'

Haridasa : Well, O mad baba, why do the people of the country where gods reside, suffer? Peepul, Bilva, Banyan and Dhatri trees are God, the Ganga is God, the parents are God, the Shalagrama and the Banalinga are God, for a disciple his Guru is God, the husband is God to the wife, the guest is God and fire is God. Why don't the troubles of the people of the land which has the image of one God or the other at every step, go away? Why do they wail?

Madman : It is also said, 'The sky, air, fire, earth, the

Moon, the Sun and other heavenly bodies, creatures and the directions, are the body of Hari.'

Haridasa : Well, I admit everything. Why do those who have God all around their houses, suffer so much pain?

Madman : They don't know, recognize, take shelter with or serve God. So sorrow is not removed.

Haridasa : Is sorrow removed if one knows and recognizes God?

Madman : Surely it is. One should regularly do Sandhya and Puja. Speak the truth. Practice religion. Be devoted to your mother, father and the guests. Can sorrow exist if these commandments are followed? One's parents are the Father and Mother of the universe themselves. By treating them thus, can there be pain? There can be no anguish and pain, if one sees the Shastras, Guru and revered Deity as one, and seeks their grace. Living and serving all with this knowledge 'My revered deity dwells in all creatures', can keep away the three kinds of sins. But the man remains entangled in worldly things. He hopes to receive from his wife and sons, takes shelter under non-belief and serves the objects of enjoyment.

Haridasa : Well, the Peepul tree, Bilva, the Tulsi plant, the Ganga the Shalagrama, Shivalinga etc.

are inert. How can self-realization or the knowledge 'I am Brahma', be had from worshipping trees, rivers and stones?

Madman : Jai Sitaram. You make me laugh, my son. Is the knowledge of Brahma a piece of vegetable that you can quickly buy it from the market?

Haridasa : The knowledge of Brahma will arise out of listening to and contemplating on the scriptures.

Madman : Jai Sitaram. Now see who is entitled to the knowledge of scriptures. According to the Varnashrama, the mind is purified by doing actions without attachment to the outcome. When the mind becomes pure, the attachment to the world goes. Then one becomes entitled to receive knowledge. Otherwise, discussion of knowledge remains confined to the mouth. It cannot remove the anguish of the heart. I want everything; my wife, my son, my house, honour and dignity and money, but still 'I am He'. If I am not addressed with respect, tears come to my eyes, but still 'I am He'. If someone shares a little lime from my *paan*, I become furious, but still 'I am He'. My son, do you call this knowledge of the Absolute?

Haridasa : Let it go. How can even the purification of the mind happen through the service of inert trees, rivers, stones and such other things?

Madman : The Bilva, Peepul and Tulsi overflow with Sattva qualities. The person who serves them with concentration loses his Rajas and Tamas elements. He gains the Sattva and becomes contented.

Haridasa : O, then is Sattva quality increased by serving these forms?

Madman : Jai Sitaram. Increase in Sattva-guna increases the joy one experiences. When the Sattva-guna permeates the entire being, he merges with the Absolute.

Haridasa : Well, could you please tell me what does this statement from Gita mean? 'There is an undecaying Peepul tree where roots are turned upward and whose branches spread downwards.'

Madman : Lord Krishna has said that the world is like an eternal Peepul tree, whose roots rise upwards and branches spread downwards. The Vedas are its leaves. He, who knows this Peepul tree well, knows the Vedas.

The branches of that tree spread in both vertical directions. The tree grows due to Sattva-guna. The objects of enjoyment like beauty and juice are its leaves. Its roots are the good and bad deeds. It expands the material world in the downward direction. The shape of this tree is not visible. It has no beginning and no end. It cannot be known as to how it remains in its position. Dissect the tree with the tool of non-attachment and look at its core. If one finds that core, one is freed from the cycle of birth and rebirth. One has to hold the thought, 'I seek the shelter of the First Purusha' in one's mind while one seeks.

Haridasa : Look, mad father, do not take me to be an absolute atheist. I believe in God. I want to find Him. Can you show me some easy way?

Madman : Jai Sitaram. Make Him your refuge.

Haridasa : How is one to seek shelter?

Madman : Say, 'I come to you for shelter' and chant the Name. You will receive His grace.

Haridasa : Is it true? Can God be found by chanting his Name, even in today's age?

Madman : Man can find God even now by chanting His Name. I say not once, but a million times that man can see God even in this age.

Haridasa : Is the Name effective even without mental concentration?

Madman : Surely it is. Adipurana says, 'No virtuous man attains salvation that the man who chants the Name attains easily.'

Garudapurana states, 'In the Kaliyuga all sins are destroyed by the chanting. Hence chanting the Name of Sri Rama is the best way.'

One can be established in unattached witnessing, if one utters the name of Rama. Chant the name of Rama at all times. You will be freed from anxiety once for all.

Haridasa : Mad father, just sing the Name only once and teach me.

The madman begins to clap his hands and dance, saying 'Sri Rama, Jai Rama, Jai Jai Rama'. Haridasa also joins. Tears stream from the Madman's eyes. Madman's companions; the boys and girls also join the chanting. The sky up to the horizon resounds with the sound of the Name. The place becomes the Vaikuntha.

Jai Sitaram.

ಅ ಓಂ ಋ

21. An Imagined Affliction

Sri Chaitanyachandra was very sad; he was unable to speak. He was much distressed and very weak. At that time the merciful Sri Guru arrived and asked, 'Hello, Chaitanya! Why are you in such a state?' Chaitanya replied sadly, 'Well, I am very ill.'

(Throughout the dialogue, Pancha refers to the human body made of five elements)

Sri Guru : What ails you? You cannot be burnt by fire, drowned in water or dried up by air; why should you be in trouble?

Chaitanya : It does, it does. This Pancha, my body made of the five elements, knows. Speak Pancha, speak of my illness. Pancha said, 'Sometimes there is wheezing in the chest or bouts of cough or fits of asthma. On some days there is fever and on other days there is acidity. What else should I tell you?'

Sri Guru : This is Pancha's own illness! What is it to you? Why are you restless? The naughty Pancha has violated rules of hygiene and is suffering for it. What's that to you?

Chaitanya : I get troubled by Pancha's troubles.

Sri Guru : Can that ever happen? The naughty fellow Pancha is the house and the clothes. He may fall down or may get damaged; why should you be concerned? Let the Pancha die and become a ghost.

Chaitanya : What will happen to me if Pancha dies? Where will I live?

Sri Guru : Will you have to go with a begging bowl, from door to door? O silly Chaitanya, if Pancha dies you will get another Pancha. You have done nothing to get rid of Pancha forever. As a new house is built when the old one falls down or new apparel is worn when the old one get torn, so you will get a new Pancha.

Chaitanya : Alas! Will Pancha die?

Sri Guru : Pancha is not immortal, he is sure to die. Well, do what I say. Go up to the sixth floor. There the light of the Sun has entered through the crack of the door and the place illuminated. Inside that is the Pranava. Omkar is written there. Chant that Pranava and meditate on the God within the Pranava.

Chaitanya : What will happen then?

Sri Guru : Then you will be able to know yourself. The anxiety about Pancha will be set at rest. Obstacles like disease will not remain.

Diseases etc. are impediments to Yoga. They cannot be removed with medicine. They will have to be removed by Japa and meditation.

Chaitanya : But Pancha is sick!

Sri Guru : Again do you talk about Pancha! Foolish Chaitanya! Give Pancha the right medicine.

'All diseases are removed on uttering of the name of Govinda, Ananda and Achyuta. This is the truth and there is no doubt about it.'

Chant the name of Govinda, Anand and Achyuta. Then your pet Pancha will be cured.

Chaitanya : Then am I not Pancha? Then what am I?

Sri Guru : *You are Free, Intelligent, Absolute and Infinite,*

The Sun, the Moon and all the heavenly sparks of light

You only, the infinite universe surrounds

Eternities have passed; still it dances its rounds

O Great Light of Bliss, forgetting your true nature,

You play a billions of roles in this illusionary theatre.

269

Disown this dying body and know your nature true

Be established in the Self, and bid your pains adieu

Awake, sleeping creature, wake up and you will find

The great ocean of peace, that brings tranquility of mind.

So chant aloud 'Jai Guru Jai Guru', and sing it endlessly.

Your pains'll melt and disappear, in one touch of grace, you'll see!

ॐ

22. Surrendering the Mind

I felt sorry to hear Krishnachandra's tale of his imprisonment. There is so much toil in the prison; drawing the mill, grinding wheat, digging earth. Even a little slackness is punished by whipping. All he gets is burnt rice, burnt bread, clothes and blankets discarded by others; they have such a foul smell! How many such things one has to bear!

As I was mulling over these thoughts, I realized that I too have been jailed. I was confined within a decaying and ailing body. Filth was being incessantly discharged through nine outlets. I nearly died of fear. What is this! What is this? I seem to be forgetting myself. After entering the jail, I have begun taking this room to be myself. Though I know that this room and I are not the same, yet I am treating this wonderful room made of twenty-four elements, to be me. A guard keeps watch on me. I work day and night and still he keeps beating me.

I am going to die! Look at the numerous marks on my back. Please do not beat me anymore! I have undergone your beating, not once or twice, but eighty lakhs times. See! See! My back has become bloody due to the beatings and I have been crying for countless ages. What is it that you give me to eat? A rotting body! I have eaten this meal countless times. Take it away. Take this away from here! Now what else do you bring me to eat; sons, daughters, houses and relations! Take them away! I do not want to eat these things. You have kept me under an illusion by feeding me this burnt trash. Oh, what have you fed me that I have lost myself and become the jail! This is I. This prison is not me! What should I do? Who should I tell? Who will deliver me from this prison?

O, dark-hued boy! Flute in hand, you stand aloof and smile. Please deliver me from this. I cannot see anyone else. You only deliver me.

Look, I have been seeing for a long time that you are calling me. I too have been longing to come to you but there is a great barrier! Whenever I think of coming to you, the guard whips me and I forget everything. Both you and I seem to get lost. I remain confined to this prison, entangled with my relations, wife, son and possessions. Again, a few days later, I see you smiling and calling me. As soon as I try to come to you, the guard lashes me with the whip of diseases, and everything is destroyed. Both you and I get lost. Again I look; and I see you calling me. This time, my brother, come and take firm hold of my hand and take me away from here so that I can save myself. I do not have the strength to keep holding on to you. Please come near so that we can embrace.

Ah! My soul is calmed. Come, nearer still; enter the innermost recesses of my heart. See! How have the jailors beaten me; see the marks of the beating. Sometimes I turned into a goat on being lashed by the whip of lust. See it has left its mark here. Sometimes, I became a buffalo on being lashed by the whip of anger. Here is its impression. There are not one or two, but eighty lakh marks here; I have been beaten very soundly. Whenever I stepped on the path towards you, I

MADMAN'S JHOLI

was flogged with the whip of fame. Forgetting everything, I have blundered from one prison of praise to another. Struck by the whip of prestige, I have been misled and have accepted service of so many. After being deceived so many times I have now understood that in order to reach you one has to be blind and deaf, and as tranquil, steady and pure as you. On plunging into this great ocean, I have to forget 'my' and 'I'. Is it not so?

O the dark-hued one! O piper! Tell me; why don't you speak a word? Are you made of stone? If you are in fact stone, then what is the use of calling you? What is the good of worshipping you? Did you not learn to speak? Don't any words come out of your mouth? O naughty fellow! Seeing your naughty face it seems to me you are the master of the prison and the jailer is your mate. This drama has been created by you! For goodness sake, brother, please release me from this jail. I am ready to quietly bribe you as well. What more have I to give? I have a mind. Please take it and keep it with you. Then I will not have to undergo any more pain. The mind will no longer act as the prison. Take it! Take it! Please do not hesitate and delay. Here, take it; take my mind. Keep this mind carefully with you; I will not want it back. Do what you please with my mind.

What else can I give to you?

O Shyama, Supreme!

At your lotus-feet, I place

My mind and my worldly dream.

ॐ

23. In the Mother's Lap

Just as the Madman came out of the cottage, repeating 'Rama Rama', Harekrishna came up to him and said, 'O Mad Father. You are in great joy, calling the name of Rama and here I am suffering from disease, grief and scarcity. Tell me what I am to do.'

Madman   : Repeat 'Rama Rama'. Everything will be alright.

Hare   : I love the name of 'Mother'.

Madman   : That is the best! Just say 'Ma Ma' all the time. Jai Sitaram.

Hare   : I would like to know a single path of practice which can prevent the world from torturing me and can pacify the mind. Is there a simple way?

Madman   : There is. Jai Sitaram.

Hare   : Please show me a way that will quench the fire ignited by this material world and give joy in the next world.

Madman   : Do you sit down every day to do your mantra?

Hare	: Yes, I do.
Madman	: Next time when you sit down, imagine that you are sitting in the lap of the Mother and, she is clasping you with both hands to her bosom. Sitaram.
Hare	: Then?
Madman	: Repeat 'Ma Ma'. When the mind flits hither and thither, say 'Ma Ma'. If the mind presents some evil thought, say 'Ma Ma'. Whenever the mind starts focusing on something else, say 'Ma Ma'. Hold her soft and gentle hands with which she has embraced you and gently rock calling, 'Ma Ma'. Sitaram, Sitaram.
Hare	: What will happen then?
Madman	: She will hear you. Sitaram, the Mother will respond.
Hare	: Will she respond?
Madman	: She will surely respond. I do not ask you to go only by what I say. For the next two to five days, sit down two to three times. Believe for a while that you are sitting in the Mother's lap. She will surely respond to your call. She will.
Hare	: Then?
Madman	: Rising, sitting, eating, lying; say 'Ma Ma'. On being tormented by lust or on feeling anger,

say 'Ma Ma'. Being distressed by scarcity, call aloud 'Ma Ma'. Call her all the time. Let not a single breath go in vain. Call 'Ma Ma', repeat 'Ma Ma' and sing 'Ma Ma'. Blow away the citadel of lust which is more impenetrable than rock, with the cannon of the Name of Mother. O, can lust ever come near him who chants the name of Mother? Extinguish completely the blaze of poverty with the deluge of the name of Mother. O Mother's son, O beloved son of nectar! Go on chanting the Great Mantra of the name of Mother. You have no cause of anxiety. Sitaram, Sitaram, Sitaram.

Hare
: O Mad Baba, merely by hearing your words, my heart is filled with joy. Will I be able to do this?

Madman
: Surely you can. Just try a little and then you can feel the grace of Mother. Her grace alone will make everything happen and give you peace.

Hare
: I have now heard about Sadhana in this world. What is the path on the other side? Which womb of darkness will I fall into after death?

Madman
: Why do you call it darkness? Sitaram, it is the kingdom of Light. You have to meditate on it thrice every day. Jai Sitaram.

Hare
: Tell me, mad baba, how shall I meditate?

Madman : Sitting in the Mother's lap and closing your eyes, think of your heart and visualise that the extremely bright Sushumna Nadi goes into the Sun's zone. Think that you are at the point of death. Keeping your eyes fixed between the eyebrows and uttering OM, think that you have come out of the body through the door of the Brahmarandhra and the gross body is left behind. Imagine that as you come out of the Subtle body, the presiding deity of the day is carrying you to the presiding deity of the fortnight of the waxing Moon. He then carries you to deity ruling the six months of Uttarayan. Jai Sitaram.

Hare : I did not understand this clearly.

Madman : Just imagine what I have told you. Sitaram, by doing this, you will automatically understand everything. Now the deity ruling the Uttarayan takes you to the deity presiding over the Samvatsar.

Hare : Are Uttarayan and Samvatsar different from each other?

Madman : The Samvatsar is the owner of the body and the Uttarayan and Dakshinayan are its parts. After finding the Uttarayan, the presiding deity of the half-year, you reach the deity of Samvatsara. Then you advance into the Suryaloka, Chandraloka and Vidyutloka. As you pass through, the gods of that place

worship you. Within no time you cross the
zone of Prakriti. Sitaram, Sitaram.

Hare : How do I travel? I go up to the Suryaloka
through the Sushumna, but after that?

Madman : Sushumna in the form of Viraja-Brahma has
mingled with the Supreme Being. Mother's
mercy is carrying you. You are being
automatically drawn by the higher attraction.
Your subtle body goes away as soon as you
plunge in the Viraja River, which separates
the Prakriti Mandal (the zone of Nature)
from Tripad Vibhuti. Your body becomes
minute, full of purity and consciousness. You
go on advancing. You reach a land of light as
bright as a million Suns and cool as a million
Moons. A number of great Maharishis reside
there. Bowing to them, you advance slowly
and arrive at the throne of the One you
desire. He calls you. As you approach Him
and bow, He puts you on His lap. Sitaram,
Sitaram.

Hare : What then? What happens after that?

Madman : Putting you in His lap, He asks you. 'Who
are you?' You say, 'I am your servant. In
how many fires I have burned! How much
suffering have I endured to reach here! I
will not go there again.' He says, 'No, no,
you need not go again. I only am you, and
you are I. I am the Sun and you are the ray;
I am the Moon and you are the light; I am

the ocean and you are the wave. There is no difference between you and me. Live forever in this abode of consciousness, engaged in my service.' Jai Sitaram.

Hare : What then?

Madman : Then your God puts you on the lap of that very Mother whom you had been dreaming of for so long, and says. 'Here, take your son who has returned after a long sojourn.' The Mother clasps you to her bosom. You put your hands around Her neck and fall asleep with your head upon her shoulder. Mother Mother Mother!

Here you sit on the Mother's lap with your back turned to Her but there you are firmly embracing Her. Sitaram, Sitaram. Mother is everywhere. Spend the few days you have here in joy and go there to rest your head on Her bosom, belonging to Her forever. That's it! The citadel is conquered. There is no need for fear. Come, take my hand, and let us both dance, chanting the name of Mother.

Jai Ma, Jai Ma, Jai Ma, Jai.

Jai Ma, Jai Ma, Jai Ma, Jai.

ॐ

24. Found Him!

In the evening the Madman was dancing a wild dance with his hands raised, singing, 'Rama, Rama. I have found! I have found!' His dancing knew no respite! Haladhar saw him from a distance and asked, 'Why is there so much dancing? What have you found, mad baba?'

Madman   : Rama, Rama! I have found God.

Haladhar : Where did you find Him?

Madman   : Just here. Rama, Rama! I have found Him. I have found Him.

Haladhar : Where is God?

Madman   : You only are God. Rama, Rama!

Haladhar : Am I God? Then you have made a good discovery. I am God! Who has given you this good news?

Madman   : The hands and feet of all creatures are His hands and feet. The eyes, ears, heads and mouths of all are God's own. The hands, feet, eyes, ears, heads and mouths of every living being are all His own. Your hands, feet, eyes and ears all are God's. The hands, feet eyes and ears of all creatures, whether men or of cows or of dogs or of tigers, are His. Rama, Rama, Sitaram.

Haladhar : Who has told you this? You say whatever you feel like. The heads, hands and feet of men, cows and goats are of God himself? O Mad baba, are you intoxicated today? Where is this mentioned?

Madman : God says it in the Gita.

'The hands and feet of all living beings are His. The eyes, the ears, heads and mouths of all creatures are His. He pervades the whole universe.'

Is it contained only in the Gita? It occurs in the Swetashwatara Upanishad also. 'What eludes grasp has now been caught. He has dressed Himself in the garments of all.'

Rama, Rama. The elusive one has now been captured.

Haladhar : If these hands, feet, eyes, mouth and ears are not mine, then why do I call them mine?

Madman : Rama, Rama. This is root of all problems. Rama, Rama, do the Shastras say it only once?

'The heads and mouths of living beings are His. He resides in the hearts of all.' God is all-pervasive. He, who is the receptacle of all the wealth, heroism, fame, beauty, knowledge and weariness of the world, dwells in the heart and everywhere else. He is all benevolent. Rama, Rama, Sitaram.

Haladhar : God resides in my heart. My hands, feet, head and mouth are all His. Then who am the 'I', bereft of hands, feet, eyes and head? Where is that lame, blind, deaf and headless, human trunk?

Madman : Sitaram, there is a downward-facing lotus in the heart. Within that lotus, as tiny as an atom and full of energy, are you. Jai Sitaram.

Haladhar : I am in the heart! Then is this body not mine?

Madman : No, no Sitaram. Your body is His body; your soul also is His body. The way oil is present in a sesame seed or ghee in milk, the same way He resides in the soul within each creature's body. Rama, Rama, Sitaram.

Haladhar : Then, whosoever one looks at, one sees only Him. Well, this is very nice. The sight of the mouths, heads, eyes and ears will remind us of Him!

Madman : Jai Jai Sitaram. All the Sadhana and worship is done only to remind us of Him. Rama, Rama, Sitaram.

Haladhar : Please tell me, mad baba, how can one constantly remember the fact that all the hands, feet, heads, mouths and ears of all the creatures, are His?

Madman : Rama, Rama, Rama. This can be done by chanting the name of Rama incessantly.

Haladhar : O Mad Baba, please explain again, that thing about His hands and feet.

Madman : Rama, Rama. (Raising his hands) these hands of mine are His.

(Points to each body part as he speaks) These feet of mine are His, this head of mine is His head, this face of mine is His face, these ears of mine are His ears, this soul of mine…this soul of mine (places his hands on his breast and becomes silent).

Haladhar : O Mad baba, please speak. Please speak.

Madman had gone as stiff as a log. Haladhar could not wake the Madman up, even by shaking him. Giving up, Haladhar himself sits down and starts chanting, 'Rama, Rama.'

Rama, Rama, Sitaram.

ಇ ॐ ೩

25. The 'You Cannon'

One day the Madman was talking to himself: 'Rama Rama' 'The You Cannon' 'The You Cannon.'

Ramadas appeared and said, 'O mad father, what is this 'You Cannon'?

Madman   : When everything around me is blasted away by the fire of the 'You Cannon', I become You. Joy! What joy there is when all merges into one! Rama, Rama, Sitaram.

Rama   : What does 'You Cannon' mean?

Madman   : Jai Sitaram. Hit the sky with the 'You Cannon' and at once the sky is blown away and there remains only You. Fire at the river Ganga with the 'You Cannon', the river disappears, leaving only You. Fire at the ocean with the 'You Cannon', and instantly the ocean ceases to exist and only You remain. Fire at those trees and at once they are gone; there remains only You. Fire at the cow with the 'You Cannon' and the cow is gone, leaving only You. Hit a man, and only You remain. Fire at the mother and she disappears, leaving only

You. You! You! You! Everything is You.

Rama : The purpose is not bad. What is to be done after firing the 'You Cannon'?

Madman : Rama, Rama. Bow your head. Jai Sitaram.

With the 'You Cannon', blow away all that you see, hear and consume. Everything will lose its separate existence but will become 'You'. Joy, happiness, fearlessness and nectar, everything is 'You'. Having become one with joy, fearlessness and nectar you start to dance like this. (The madman begins to dance.)

Rama : Stop, stop, mad father. I may blow away every external thing by the 'You Cannon'. But what is to be done about the internal distractions and the hue and cry? I start thinking of buying shoes when I sit down to worship and of getting groceries while meditating on Rama! What is the solution for this?

Madman : Sitaram. All those things too are to be blown away by the 'You Cannon'. While you are meditating you remember that the farm worker will come today and you have to get up soon. Fire the 'You Cannon'. The peasant disappears and becomes 'You'. Carry on meditating. You now get reminded that Harekrishna had abused you. Fire the 'You Cannon' at Harekrishna and think that 'You have washed away my sins as Harekrishna.'

Go on with the meditation. The mind tells you that your son is disobedient. Fire the 'You Cannon' at the boy. The son and his disobedience are blown away! The daughter-in-law loves to gossip. Blow away the daughter-in-law with the 'You Cannon'. What will be left is 'You'. Dogs, cats, jackals; good and bad; lust and anger; hypocrisy or deception, whatever comes and stands in your way, Sitaram, blow it away with the 'You Cannon'. Being in the middle of the limitless kingdom of 'You' and seeing 'You' all around; in disease and grief, in want and praise, you will also become immersed in 'You'. Rama, Rama, Sitaram.

Rama : Provided I am able to remember this!

Madman : Say 'Rama Rama'; only 'Rama Rama' and you will remember everything. Ordinary gun-fire has limitations. The 'You Cannon' is limitless, infinite and inexhaustible. So long as the world exists this 'You Cannon' will not be exhausted, and no one can snatch it away. Blast away whatever is visible with the 'You Cannon', and enter into that great empire of fearlessness, joy and immortality.

The madman began to dance, saying, 'Rama, Rama, Sitaram'

Ramadas could not stop him anymore.

ॐ

26. That Hole

It was early morning when the madman started to dance wildly, crying, 'Rama, Rama, Sitaram, Sitaram, the hole, the hole.' Just then, Haladhar came and said, 'Many are the manners of a madman! Why are you shouting, 'Hole, Hole', in the early morning?

Madman : Sitaram, when the devotee, gives up the mortal coil while repeating, Rama, Rama, the air parts to create a hole that looks like a chariot wheel. The devotee rises through that hole and reaches close to the Sun. The Sun also quickly creates an opening in itself like the hole in a musical instrument. The peerless devotee passes through that passage to reach the Moon, which too, creates in itself, an opening similar to that in a kettle-drum, to let him pass. Jai Jai Sitaram. The devotee goes straight through that opening into the world of eternal joy, overflowing with waves of light and nectar, and remains in proximity to his revered deity, for eternity.

(The madman begins to dance chanting 'Sitaram Sitaram.')

Halada : You say whatever comes to your mind! Are

the ways of Archi etc. like this?

Madman   : Sitaram, Sitaram. Otherwise what are the paths like?

Halada   : Chhandogyasruti says, 'At first, the emancipated Purusha passes in sequence, Archi, the deity presiding over the day, then each of the deities ruling over the six months of Sun's northern course, and the worlds of the Sun, the Moon and Energy. Then a superhuman being arrives from the world of Brahma and takes him along. This is said in the Shastras. You have taken this somewhere else and for no reason, are shouting 'Hole Hole' since the morning.

Madman   : Sitaram, Sitaram. There is not just one Shruti or one kind of path. This is also described in the Koushitaki and Brihadaranyaka Upanishads. Understood? Sitaram.

Halada   : Well, can you tell me one thing?

Madman   : Please ask. Sitaram.

Halada   : When the ears are closed tightly, one hears a sound like that of a blazing fire, the bellowing of a bull or the wheels of a chariot. What are these sounds?

Madman   : Sitaram, these internal sounds are the signs of perception of the divine light which pervades the ultimate world situated above the heavens. This Fire is called Vaishwanara

288

Agni. If you can perceive that sound, then
your task is done.

Halada : How is it?

Madman : As you listen to these sounds, you get
immersed in the light and joy. You reach your
true home and clamber onto your mother's
lap. Jai Jai Sitaram.

Halada : Where does the mother's lap come into this?
You should say that the person becomes one
with the absolute Brahma. That is not the
state of instant emancipation but of gradual
emancipation.

Madman : Jai Jai Sitaram. Would you like to listen to
what Lord Shankaracharya says?

'There are one and a quarter lakh paths of
Laya Yoga. Of these, I consider the quest
of Nada the best. O quest of the Nada, I
bow to you. I know you as the Sadhana of
Tattvapada. By your Grace, my mind along
with life will merge with Vishnupada.'
Did you hear that? Sitaram, our rejecting
something that Shankaracharya himself
accepts, is it not laughable?

Halada : Well, has Nada anything to do with the path
you were speaking of?

Madman : The matter is not of this path or that! Sitaram,
there is only one path that merges with the
Bindu of light, Space and Nada.

MADMAN'S JHOLI

The madman begins to sing:

To the wondrous land of light, you'll go

A place awash with lustrous glow;

A mad delirious woman sings

And soothes your soul with honeyed hymns.

Look! Evening shadows are growing tall

There is no time, go out and call

'O Mother Divine! I beg your grace!'

She'll draw you into her embrace;

And douse your fire to set you free

From the shackles of mortality.

ॐ

27. Eaten Up!

The madman was shouting in the morning, 'Rama, Rama. It is eating up! It is eating up!' Haladhar came near and asked, 'O mad baba, who is eating up whom?'

Madman : 'You' is eating 'I'.

Halada : What is that?

Madman : With a mouth spreading from the heaven to the netherworld, 'You' has eaten up all the 'I's there were. Rama, Rama, Sitaram.

Halada : Has 'You' eaten up your 'I' as well?

Madman : Yes, Yes, Sitaram.

Halada : But your hands, feet, head and mouth are intact.

Madman : These have been eaten by 'You'.

Halada : The other day I heard that the hands, feet, mouth and ears of everyone belong to God.

Madman : Not only that, absolutely everything.

Halada : What do you mean by absolutely everything?

Madman   : Svetashwatar says that 'You' are the woman;
              'You' are the man and 'You' are the youth,
              the maiden and the old man with trembling
              limbs. 'You' only take birth as different things.

              Sitaram.

              These are no longer hands, feet and head.
              They have become everything; the whole.

Halada   : Then the woman, the man, the youth and the
              maiden, are all 'You'?

Madman   : Yes, Sitaram.

              'You' are also the blue insect and the large
              black-bee; 'You' are the red-eyed parrot;
              'You' are the cloud with the lightning in the
              belly and 'You' are all the seasons. 'You' are
              the seas that exist. 'You' have no beginning.
              'You' are all-pervading. The whole universe
              has been created by 'You'. Rama, Rama,
              Sitaram.

Halada   : It is so, mad father. 'You' are all, 'You' are all.
              Nice! It is very nice. 'You' are all; 'You' are all.

Madman   : *Rama, Rama, Sitaram.*

              The vast world is only 'You'

              There is no thing as 'I'

              'You' were; 'You' are; and 'You' will be

              Not 'I' or 'Me' or 'My'

Rama, Rama, Rama, Say Rama, Rama, Rama.

Haladhar : O mad father, why does the man cry and suffer on taking the 'I' out of this joyous kingdom of 'You'?

Madman : Sitaram, everything is an act! As there can be no game with just one player, it is 'You' which is also becoming 'I' and playing the game. Rama, Rama, Rama.

Halada : Mad father, the 'I' ties itself down to one place and keeps lamenting. How can this 'I' be uprooted?

Madman : Sitaram, finish your 'self'. Jai Sitaram.

Halada : Is there no way other than finishing one's self?

Madman : Sitaram, blast the false 'I' with the cannon of the Name. Blow away the 'I', its house, its belongings and its roots by firing 21,600 shots from the cannon, everyday. One day you will find that 'You' will appear smiling before you, like a deluge of joy; dressed in clothes whiter than moonlight and more brilliant than the Sun. Jai Jai Rama, Sitaram, Rama, Rama, Rama.

Come, running if thou wantest to see the death of 'I'

'You' alone is playing on this earth, devoid of 'I'.

ॐ

28. Give the Key

One day the madman was sitting in the cottage and saying 'Rama, Rama, give me the key; give me the key' when, Haladhar came in.

Halada : O madman! Who are you putting under lock and key?

Madman : All are camping together. They are all gathered there in that den! Give me, give me the key. Rama, Rama, Sitaram.

Halada : Who have gathered and where?

Madman : Sitaram.

'The object of knowledge of the absolute desireless Harihar Brahman, Yogi's object of realization, the destroyer of the fear of life and death, the embodiment of Being and consciousness, and the seed of the entire universe, have become manifest in the Brahma-conscious Heart Lotus. Guru is also seated on the throne in the centre of the Lotus.'

Sitaram Sitaram.

Halada   : So? What then?

Madman   : The cloud-complexioned and beautiful One says in the Gita, 'It is I and I alone, which enjoys cozy and permanent occupancy in each person's heart!' Jai Sitaram.

Halada   : So what of it?

Madman   : He not only lives in the heart but pervades it totally, in as perfect a manner as possible. Life exists as long as He lives in the body. Death comes as soon as He departs from the body, like a balloon deflating as soon as its air escapes. Sitaram, 'God exists in the hearts of all.' Not only does He live in this recess of the heart, but He also makes everyone dance like puppets, with his illusion or maya. Jai Sitaram.

Halada   : Rama, Rama, Sitaram. Oh, look! I too just uttered, 'Rama, Rama, Sitaram' with you, in a moment of absent-mindedness. Now what?

Madman   : Sitaram, this absent-mindedness is good absent-mindedness. After having placed Apana in the rectum, Samana in the navel, Vyana all over the body and Udana in the Sushumna, Prana himself is sitting in the heart. Sitaram Sitaram. This soul is in the heart. Atmarama is also there; comfortably leaning on the shoulders of that Prana. Shandilya Shruti says, 'In this body the living being rides on the Prana.' Dhyanabindu Shruti says, 'In the heart there is the Ashtadalapadma. Within it is a circle. In the centre of which, is the minute self-effulgent Jivatma'. Whatever there is, resides in this Jivatma. Rama, Rama, Sitaram.

Halada : This is extraordinary! Everything is right here; within the heart?

Madman : Sitaram, listen on. Yogatattvopanishad says, 'In the heart there is a downward-facing lotus, with its tube pointing upwards and the Bindu below; the mind resides within. '

Jai Sitaram.

Halada : Then the absolute attributeless Brahma, Gurudeva, Lord Krishna, God, Prana, the soul and the mind, are all in the heart!

Madman : Not only this, Sitaram. This is the lotus of the unstruck sound. This is where the flute plays on its own. The kingdom of Omkara is there. Dhyanbindu recommends that one must meditate on God in the form of the pure Omkara, located in the seed-vessel of the Heart-lotus; the size of one's thumb and as steady as a lamp.

Halada : Pranava is to be meditated on in the Heart-lotus. But that is not the home of the Omkara.

Madman : Rama, Rama, Sitaram. Does Shyama come to the house of Rama? This is their permanent

house! All have gathered in the same home.
Sitaram, Sitaram. One mad woman lay
sleeping below. She woke up and began
to dance wildly. Not only dancing but also
singing. With so many different notes, tones,
drums, bells and flutes as accompaniment.
That song is sung without rest; without
end. Is there only dancing, singing and
instrument-playing? No, she is also creating
at the same time. Dancing and giving birth.
In all four directions there is only glorious
effulgence! Jai Jai Rama, Sitaram.

Halada : What is she giving birth to?

Madman : Sitaram, Sitaram. She is creating one Bindu
after another. White and soft; tiny ones; tinier
than the grains of dust! She is giving birth to
masses of light and spreading sky. Dancing
all the while! Jai Sitaram.

Halada : Well, how?

Madman : Rama, Rama, Sitaram. Dancing in the heart-
lotus of yogis, the serpent; the all-consuming
Mother, has created an upheaval by all this
creation. This dancing has to be controlled.

Rama, Rama, Sitaram, now where is the
key? Let us lock them. Attributeless Brahma,
Brahma with form, the Soul, Prana, mind,
Omkara and this dancing Mother Kundalini;
all have gathered in the same place. Lock
them up together. That mad woman will

unite them all with her rhythm and music.
All quarrels and confusion will be settled.
Rama, Rama, Sitaram.

ఆ ఓం ఔ

29. The Master and the Mistress

One day, in the morning, the madman was sitting on the bank of the Ganga; looking at the sky and saying to himself, 'Rama, Rama, the Master of the Doer.' Ramadas Bhattacharya was returning after bathing. On hearing what the madman was saying, he said, 'O Mad Father, why are saying 'The master of the Doer?'

Madman : Sitaram. At first the Master was alone. Suddenly he felt a sensation in his self and felt afraid. Next moment he thought, 'there is none other than me, whom am I afraid of?' Fear was dispelled but he was no longer happy. He felt empty. Wishing to be two, he split his own body into two and became husband and wife.

Ramdas : What then?

Madman : Rama, Rama, Sitaram. He united with her and from that men were born. His mate thought, 'He created me out of him. How is he copulating with me? Let me flee.' Thinking thus, she became a cow. The Master at once became a bull and copulated with her. As a result, cattle were born. As soon as she became a mare, the Master became a horse. As a result, the horses were born. When the Mistress became a jenny-ass, the Master became a jack-ass; and beasts with uncleaven hooves were created. The Mistress became a female sheep and then the Master became a male sheep and copulated with her. Thus the sheep were created. In this way, all creatures were produced by that Mistress and the Master. All the living beings that are seen in the world came from that couple; the Mistress and the Master.

Ramada   : Of them which is the Mistress and which the Master?

Madman   : Sitaram, what is seen is the Mistress and what cannot be seen is the Master. Jai Jai Sitaram, Sitaram.

Ramada   : Then you cannot call everything the Doer or Purusha. Call it the Doer and the Prakriti.

Madman   : As the Doer lives in it, this body is called Brahmapura.

The Purusha resides in the right eye and the Prakriti resides in the left eye.

Once it happened that a petty thief called 'I' went to steal the authority of the Doer. When the Doer came to know, he began to whip the thief mercilessly with the whip of disease-grief-want-lust-anger-greed, which was fashioned like the tail of the Shankara fish. Dear me! What a whipping it was! The thief ran away and began to cry, 'Mother, Mother', shedding rivers of tears. The mother, being unable to stop herself, drew him into her bosom. At once, 'I' became a little child, laid his head on the mother's shoulders, clasped her neck with both hands and went to sleep. There was no knowing whether he is dead or alive. Jai Sitaram. Yes, from that point the Master and the Mistress lived happily in the world created by the two eyes.

Ramada : Is it so?

Madman : Yes, Sitaram. They live in the eyes. One day the master said, 'Mistress, let us go to Kashi.' The two together went to Kashi and lived in a two roomed house of light, resonant with music and melodies. Rama, Rama!

Ramada : Where is Kashi?

Madman : Kashi is just between the two eyebrows in line of the Sushumna. Sitaram Sitaram.

Ramada : What then?

Madman : Rama, Rama, Sitaram. One day the Master wished to be the sky. At once he became a vast sky. The Mistress became a very little point and went to measure the extent of the Master and was lost in him. There was

301

no trace of her. Nobody now knows her whereabouts. Rama, Rama!

There's no one but the Master,

He's the darkness and the light;

The Creator, the Sustainer, and

The one who brings the Night.

ॐ

30. Possessed by God

The madman was sitting in his cottage, chanting the name of Rama, when Haladhar came and said, 'O Mad baba, people say, 'I am He, I am Brahma'. What is this?'

Madman : Rama, Rama, Sitaram. As people are possessed by ghosts, so they are possessed by God or Brahma. The ghost speaks through the patient, 'I am so and so and I have possessed him.' Similarly, the man possessed by Brahma says, 'I am Brahma, I am He.' He who is possessed by God or an Avatara says, 'Whenever there is loss of Dharma...'

Halada : On the one side, there is Brahma; the Lord of an infinite number of worlds, and on the other, there is the tiniest worm. Are not such speeches as 'I am Brahma' and 'I am He' audacious utterances?

Madman : Rama, Rama, Sitaram. Of what are the untold billions of worlds made? It is said; 'I shall be born as many', 'Brahma is one and without a second', 'There is nothing else in the world' and 'Everything there is, is Brahma. Always was, is today and will remain.'

The fundamental Tattva is Brahma. Then what is the harm if someone says, 'I am Brahma, I am He'? Rama, Rama, Sitaram.

Halada : Are all Brahma?

Madman : Yes, Sitaram. Yoga Shikhopanishad says, 'As a golden necklace, a bangle, an ear-ring or a nose-ring remain gold, so the world arising from Brahma, remains Brahma.'

Rama, Rama, Sitaram.

Well, Sitaram, say if there is any difference between a bangle and gold.

Halada : No.

Madman : Rama, Rama. Similarly, there is no difference between Brahma and immoveable things and moving animals. Sitaram, God says in Srimadbhagavata, 'Like gold turned into ornaments such as ear-rings and used in many names, remains gold even afterwards and in the interim period, I am like that in relation to this universe. That is, I am the beginning, the end and in the middle.' Rama, Rama, Sitaram.

Halada : Then are all things of the world, God?

Madman : Rama, Rama, Sitaram. Just as a big vessel, a pitcher and a round earthen pot are made of earth, so whatever there is in the world is made of God. Rama, Rama, Sitaram.

Halada	:	Are all the various kinds of hills, mountains, water, air, fire, trees and plants, birds and animals and men; God?
Madman	:	Yes, Rama, Rama, Sitaram. Yes Sitaram, In Srimadbhagavata, Sridharaswami says, 'Like gold turned into crowns, ear-rings, tinkling ornaments, truly remain gold, so the great Tattvas, pride, sky, etc. are fundamentally Narahari and nothing else.' Rama, Rama, Sitaram.
Halada	:	It is a strange thing that I see a tree but call it God. How can I say that?
Madman	:	Rama, Rama, Sitaram. I see a bangle. Why shall I not call it gold? Is not a golden bangle gold? Rama, Rama, Sitaram.
		Mahopanishat says, 'Just as the meaning of the word bracelet is not different from that of gold, so gold is not different from a bracelet. In the same way, the world and Brahma are not different.' Rama, Rama, Sitaram.
Halada	:	Why does one Hari become so many?
Madman	:	Jai Jai Sitaram. To perform Leela, with the help of Yogamaya, not differentiated from his self, Hari alone is playing in many forms. Sitaram.
Halada	:	How can it be understood that Hari alone is all? What is the way of getting rid of the vision of multiplicity?

Madman : Rama, Rama, Sitaram. Through uttering the name of Rama, the One must be seen first, in the temple of the heart. After seeing the One, the belief that all are One will be established. Sitaram, Sitaram.

Halada : What will one find by chanting 'Rama Rama' and looking inwards?

Madman : Rama, Rama. You will see light and hear all kinds of melodies and sound of numerous musical instruments. Rama, Rama.

But getting enchanted by the music will not do. You will have to go forward following the music of the flute. There is no respite till you find the flautist. Once you find him, your aim is fulfilled. Jai Sitaram.

Halada : What happens on listening to the flute?

Madman : One is possessed. The mind melts and the sounds of 'I am Brahma', 'I am He' rise from within. Rama, Rama, Sitaram.

Halada : People say 'I am Brahma, I am He' when they are possessed by Brahma. What do they say when they are possessed by God?

Madman : Rama, Rama, Sitaram. They say, 'Whenever there is lassitude in religion and rise of irreligion, I create myself, O son of Bharata.' (Gita)

Halada : If a man is possessed by a ghost, the ghost

leaves him if an exorcist drives it away. Is there any exorciser in this case?

Madman : In this case, worldly distractions are the exorcisers. Jai Sitaram. The Mother wakes up when the mind turns inwards. If the man is allured by the worldly distractions, he starts identifying with the body and the upward movement of the mad woman is stopped. He remains stuck in 'I...I...my...my.' Rama, Rama, Sitaram.

Halada : Who can get to the state of 'I am He' and 'I am Brahma'?

Madman : Rama, Rama, Sitaram. Those, who eat pure food, associate with good company, and worship in time and always chant the name of Rama, can reach Brahma. The words 'I am He' and 'I am Brahma' rise within them and their bodies are thrilled. It happens when one is possessed by Brahma. When one is possessed by the Avatara, the words 'Whenever ....' start rising.

Halada : Should 'I am Brahma' and 'I am He', be practiced orally?

Madman : Rama, Rama, Sitaram. To say, 'I am He' orally, means expressing pride. This 'I am He' dances with the sound of soundlessness and resonates in the mind and Prana. Those who say 'I am He' and 'I am Brahma' orally, say so by standing aloof from the state of 'I am He'.

When the 'I am He' happens, speech ceases to exist. Sitaram, this is to be experienced and cannot be described. Brahma is one and without a second. If by saying 'I am Brahma' or 'I am He' I declare my self-glory, then it will no longer remain one. Only by diving inside, one will get to hear the Nada. Even an Avatar has to come down into this cage of three cubits and a half in length and has to accept worship and criticism. Rama, Rama, Sitaram.

Halada   : Has he to accept both worship and criticism?

Madman   : Worship and criticism live side by side like light and darkness. Those who are worshipping today are sure to denounce tomorrow. Those who decry today will surely worship tomorrow. This is the general law. There are exceptions only in special places. The mood-child that is born when the mind turns inward and the kundalini awakens, is to be nurtured carefully, out of the sight of the people; and the work carried on. One, who does so, reaches Brahma or Avatara. The misery of the person who proclaims his being Brahma or an Avatara, knows no bounds. These things are not to be spoken of but experienced. Rama, Rama, Sitaram.

Listen to this story. Lord Shankaracharya went to the Old Brahmananda in Kakadwip and said, 'I am a preacher of non-duality.

I would like to debate with you.' Old Brahmananda heard him and said, smiling, 'How will you preach non-duality? You are far from the knowledge of non-duality. For a knower of non-duality, where can there be arguments, for and against? When there is only one, where can there be another to debate with? Well, well. You go and preach non-duality.' Then Lord Shankaracharya went to holy Puridhama and founded the Govardhana Monastery. He founded no monastery in Bengal. Rama, Rama, Sitaram, Rama, Rama.

Halada : What should they do, who wish to reach Brahma?

Madman : Move away from worldly distractions, go to an isolated place and mediate with mind, body and soul. Whatever needs to happen next will be taken care of by their revered deity. Rama, Rama, Sitaram, Jai Jai Sitaram.

Halada : Look here, mad baba, I do not understand Brahma. Tell me how can I have peace and get rid of anxiety.

Madman : Rama, Rama, Sitaram, Jai Sitaram. Always chant the name of Rama. You will not need to worry. You will land right in the kingdom of joy.

Halada : Yes, another point. You say that on the appearance of the feeling of Avatara, the attitude 'Whenever...' awakens. What does 'Whenever...' mean?

Madman : Rama, Rama, Sitaram. 'Whenever religion is reproached and irreligion raises its head I create myself. For the rescue of the virtuous, destruction of the evil-doers and establishment of religion I appear in every age.' Rama, Rama.

Halada : Then God comes as an Avatar and destroys irreligion and establishes religion. What is religion?

Madman : Rama, Rama, Jai Jai Rama. What you bear and protect is religion. God protects the Vedas and so he came as the Fish-avatar and protected the Vedas from the deluge of destruction. For the nourishment of the Sattva-filled gods, He assumed the shape of the tortoise during the churning of the ocean for nectar. Similarly, He ascended as Varaha, Nrisinmha, Vamana, Parashurama, Rama, Balarama, Buddha and Kalki. Narada, Kapila, Vyasadeva, Rishabha etc. are all Avataras of God. Rama, Rama, Sitaram.

Those in whom the desire of 'Whenever...' arises, also reestablish order in this world. Lord Shankara, Lord Ramanujacharya and Gour; the embodiment of love, also established religion. Rama, Rama.

Halada : What are the attributes of religion?

Madman   : Rama, Rama, Sitaram, Jai Rama

            Patience, forgiveness, self-control, abstaining from theft, purity, suppression of the senses, wisdom, spiritual learning, truth and absence of anger are the ten indicators of religion. People in whom the impulse for 'Whenever…' rises, become established in these ten attributes and follow the religion throughout their life with single-pointedness. The dictionary meaning of Dharma is Karma as prescribed by the Shastras. Men with god-like characteristics consciously do only such actions. Rama, Rama, Sitaram, Jai Rama.

Halada   : Mad father, what does 'rescuing the virtuous' mean? The sadhus are delivered by dint of their own Sadhana. What does God do to deliver them?

Madman   : Jai Rama, Sitaram, Rama, Rama. The sadhus, who get delivered and sit silently, commit an offence. The duty of the sadhus is to preach true religion. So God says. 'Look, I am God. I need nothing. Still I perform actions. You too must do the same.' Setting an example and inspiring the sadhus to engage in the welfare of the world, is called the deliverance of the sadhus. Rama, Rama, Sitaram.

Halada   : Do the sadhus also have their duty?

Madman   : Rama, Rama, surely. Anusmriti says, 'the fruit of giving away of the whole earth is not comparable to that of giving knowledge to the ignorant.' Sitaram.

The Gods show favour to those who give knowledge to the ignorant.

Halada : Does the giving of knowledge bear so much fruit?

Madman : Rama, Rama. Narada Pancharatra says, 'Removing the fear of the living beings, protecting him who seeks shelter and giving knowledge to the ignorant are the greatest causes of Nirvana'. Rama, Rama, Sitaram.

Halada : What knowledge can an ignorant person impart?

Madman : The Shastras say that he who has no knowledge will acquire it from others and will give advice to those who are more ignorant than himself. Sitaram.

The establishment of religion is the main duty of the sadhus. Karmapurana says, 'No one in the world is greater than the person who establishes the highest religion and knowledge about God. He is the greatest Yogi. That Muni who despite having achieved Yoga and being capable, is deluded and does not establish Dharma, is not very dear to God.

Jai Jai Rama, Sitaram, Rama, Rama.

Halada   : Then the sadhus also establish religion.

Madman   : Jai Jai Rama, Sitaram. It is God who does so by using the sadhus as instruments. He appears before the sadhus. He begins to inspire and create a feeling of 'Whenever...' in those through whom He wishes to get Dharma established. Sitaram, Sitaram, Rama, Rama, Sitaram.

Sadhanasamar says, 'It is the Supreme Soul that reveals itself as an Avatara for the welfare of the living beings. The living beings gain their welfare if, instead of denying it, they try to believe in it. At the same time, they must be very careful. It should be understood that the image of the Avatara is not God. He appears by taking the help of the image. None should take the image itself for the Avatara.'

Chant the name of Rama; rising, sitting, eating or lying; delay no more! There the flute is calling. Chant the name of Rama.

> *Rama's name is the essence of the world.*
>
> *Rama's name is the nectar-like sound.*
>
> *Rama's name takes away crores of sins.*
>
> *I believe in Rama's name.*

313

The sadhu always remembers Rama's name.

The devotee takes the name of Rama.

With Rama's name gods face the struggle

And the wise man stands in the struggle.

Jai Rama, Sitaram, Jai Rama, Sitaram.

ॐ

31. Sadhu Beware!

The madman sits in the cremation ground on the bank of the Ganges, chanting the name of Rama. There is no man or even a living being in sight. The evening is about to fall. At that time he hears, 'Sadhu, beware.' Chanting the name of Rama, the madman looks around but sees no one. There's only a human skull showing its white teeth, which speaks again, 'Sadhu, beware.'

Madman : Rama, Rama! Is the skull speaking?

Skull : You can speak but why can't I speak?

Madman : I am alive and you are dead. Sitaram.

Skull : Who tells you that you are alive? You are dead. You have fallen into the mouth of Time and it is slowly swallowing you. You too are like the dead.

Madman : Rama, Rama! Why did you say 'Sadhu, beware'?

Skull : It is because you are making merry in the middle of the road.

Madman : In the middle of the road?

315

Skull   : Yes, in the middle of the road. Do you know where you have to go?

Madman   : Rama, Rama. Tell me.

Skull   : You will have to go to the kingdom of the One 'I', like the shining, densely forested and sky-scrapping Himalayas! Know that you are loitering on the way so long as you do not reach there.

Madman   : Rama, Rama. By what sign can I know that I have reached there.

Skull   : When the sense of duality will go and all will be reduced to one. Ganga water and drain water; a garland of flowers and a string of shoes; praise and blame; man and woman; friend and enemy; all will become the same. You will wear no clothes and will wander about like a dull mad man. You will be united for ever with the immovable One.

Madman   : It is only to reach there, friend, that I am clapping my hands and chanting the name of Rama!

Skull   : Do you know them who are dancing frantically around you and taking you away from your path?

Madman   : Whom are you talking about?

Skull   : Those who are saying, 'you are a great man, a high soul, you are doing the greatest good to the world.' Someone is worshipping you with clothes, ornaments and wraps of silk. Someone is offering you scented flowers, blossoms, incense and lamps. Someone is decorating you from head to foot with garlands. Someone is eager to besmear you with sandal. Someone is very eager to pour essence on your body. After being initiated by the Guru and with the desire to see God, disciples perform Sadhana and Bhajana. Leaving aside all this, some are beating the drum 'My preceptor is an Avatara'. Posing as the favourite disciple and accepting worship from simple innocent people. All these things are not your worship but only self-worship. They mesmerize simple and innocent people by presenting you as an Avatara and make you a subject of ridicule among Sadhus and good men. They are eager to keep your unbroken, infinite and boundless sky-like self, in a rotten, worn cage and are trying to rouse in you your pride in this cage. Some pose as your representative to mercilessly destroy the trust the simple householders repose and ruin them. Someone else is trying to trick you into forgetting your own true self. Someone is determinedly pouring heaps of money to destroy this knowledge that 'There is nothing but You; You alone permeate the entire world.' Some are fulfilling their own worldly desires and indulging in misdeeds by giving up Sadhana, Bhajan, Japa and Tapa, and pretending to be courtiers of Vishnu. They are always pushing you to identify with the physical world. Do you know who they are?

Madman   : Please tell me.

Skull   : They are the disturbances sent by gods. Srimadbhagavata says, 'The friends, relations, devotees and disciples who always create disturbances in the way of life and try to rouse materialism, are disturbances sent by gods.' The gods do not want you to bypass them and gain self-realization. So they come in the disguise of devotees and disciples with the intention of keeping you confined to the old cage. They want you to forget that temple is not God or the pot is not the sky. They want to make you forget that you are boundless, unexpressed, inexpressible, unstained, unbroken, that you alone exist, and want to put you in the cage and keep you there. So I say, 'Sadhu, beware.' Do you know who is able to acquire such knowledge?

Madman   : Please tell me.

Skull   : He alone who is afraid of the company of the people, thinks sweetmeat to be like poison etc., is capable of gaining knowledge about Brahma. So I am saying 'Sadhu, beware.'

Madman   : Rama, Rama, Sitaram.

Well, friend, what are you asking me to do?

Skull : Make yourself scarce. Let no one find any trace of you anymore. Let no one know that you are alive. Flee, flee.

Madman : Rama, Rama. You make me laugh, friend! Do you think that man can do anything he wants? Whatever is to happen has been already settled. No one is independent, my friend. I know that I am not shelterless. I have a protecting guide. He is always protecting me and guiding me. Rama, Rama, Sitaram.

Friend, as a band of people are raising a hue and cry calling me a great man, an Avatar, so there is another band of people who enjoy themselves by calling me a hypocrite, an impostor and an insincere man. Do you know this?

Skull : I know that.

Madman : Do you know what I think of these two bands of people?

Skull : Say.

Madman · : I mentally bow to them thinking all of them to be my tutelary deity. I practice to bow mentally to mothers as givers of birth. I am not free to live in the dwelling place of men or to go to the forest renouncing all company. He who has put me in human habitation will take me to the forest when he likes. In Srimadbhagavata, the last words He said to Uddhava, the best of devotees, were, 'Employing the mind, body and speech to find me in all creatures is the ideal way.' So I am practicing to bow mentally to all as God and utter the name of Rama. Friend, you are speaking of renouncing the company of people and going to the forest. Soubhari, the sage, left the human company, sat in water and meditated. But he saw a family of fish and the desire to lead a family life came to him. King Bharata renounced his wealth, people, kingdom and treasure and went to the forest. There he loved a deer and had to be born a deer. Even in the forest there live, crows, jackals, squirrels, peacocks and deer. Man can deviate from his aim not only due to company of humans, but also of deer, peacocks and trees. Rama, Rama.

Do you know what the matter is, friend? Dangers lie at every step for those who want to stand on their own feet and think themselves to be great. He always protects the one who goes on living as His refugee, slave and instrument.

Yes, people do give the title of 'Great Man or Avatar' but it is not that they do it only now. People have always called devotees; great men and Avatars and they will continue to do it till the world lasts. If iron lies in fire people start calling it fire. Similarly, one who holds on to God is called a devotee, a great man or even God by not only the people but also the Shastras. It is said, 'One who knows Brahma is himself Brahma.' The main aim of the Aryan Sadhana is to give up materialism and to stay in an 'I' which is one, without a second and unbroken. If anyone calls a knower of Brahma, an Avatara is it not as laughable as calling an emperor an attendant?

At that honour, the traveler of the real path, only smiles. Even after becoming an Avatara one has to undergo much suffering. I know very well that it is not desirable to become an Avatara. I utter the name of Rama, when called a hypocrite, impostor, lover of fame, as much as I do when I hear the words, 'high-souled', 'great man' or 'God'. What I know, friend, is that I have become quite fearless thinking that I am a naked shelter-seeking child on the lap of Mother.

However, as you have cautioned me and wished me well, I thank you my friend and I bow to you.

Saying this, as the madman prepared to offer his obeisance by prostrating, he found his preceptor standing in place of the skull. The madman bathed his Guru's feet with his tears.

Jai Jai Sitaram.

༅ ༀ ༅

32. Be Silent

The Madman was sitting in the cottage, saying, 'Rama Rama. Be Silent, Be Silent', when Ramakrishna came and asked, 'O, Mad Father, Why are you saying, 'Rama Rama. Be Silent. Be Silent'? Can you tell me how man can find God?

Madman : One can find God if one can be silent inside while taking the name of Rama.

Rama : Does being silent mean remaining quiet?

Madman : Yes, being quiet is a very great Sadhana.

Rama : What good is the quietude if one merely keeps his mouth shut while the mind is turbulent and goes on thinking of useless things?

Madman : That is why I say that if one can move inwards by chanting the name of Rama, the mind cannot think of useless things any more. Always chant the name of Rama, go on chanting the name of Rama at all times; move Vaikhari to Madhyama and then the task is done. Sit and listen to the *ragas* and *raginis* of 'Jai Guru, Jai Guru', drums, *khols* and cymbals, and start moving towards the land of light.

Rama : Do you know what Lord Shankaracharya says about silence?

Madman : What?

Rama : 'Silence of speech is for boys.'

Madman : He also says in Vivekachudamani, 'The first door to Yoga is silence, not taking anything, freedom from desire, refraining from making any effort and a constant love of solitude.' The first step of Yoga is silence. Nothing will happen if this is not achieved.

But the case of those who have become Siddhas is different. There are silent ones even among the Siddhas. It is heard that Tailanga Swami had a taken vow of silence.

Lord Shankaracharya also says, 'Restrain the speech by the mind, the mind by the intellect, the intellect by witnessing; and immerse them in the absolute, to enjoy the peace.'

'To the wise man who well knows his own self and enjoys the joy of the soul, there is nothing more pleasant than freedom from desire and silence.'

'The wise man who delights in his soul will stay as he wishes by always observing silence; while going, staying, sitting or in any other condition.'

Jai Jai Sitaram.

Do you see that Lord Shankara has said much more on this subject than merely 'silence of speech is for boys'?

Rama : I can see. There are some people who oppose silence.

Madman : Jai Jai Sitaram. If there are people against God, then I am not surprised that there are some who oppose silence. Would you like to hear more on silence?

Rama : Please tell me.

Madman : Swatmaprakashika says, 'I always seek as the shelter that silence which is truth and consciousness condensed, infinite, without a second, devoid of all visibility, hale, the incomparable state of purity and good.

I always seek as shelter that silence which is full, without a second, unbroken consciousness, devoid of all destinations, having knowledge of the supreme without a second.

I always seek as shelter that silence which is devoid of birth and death, happiness and sorrow, has no caste, family or clan, which is the cause of this world evolved out of consciousness.'

Do you see? Sitaram.

Rama : So I see! He has spoken highly of silence.

Madman : Jai Sitaram. Listen to what Prashnottaramalika says.

'Giving suffering to one's own people is the cause of the destruction of one's family. The speech of those, who are truthful and observe silence, is infallible.' Rama, Rama, Sitaram, Jai Jai Sitaram.

Rama : Well, is avowed silence also called Tapasya?

Madman : Rama, Rama, Sitaram. Celibacy, silence, abstinence from food, non-violence, and all forms of peace are called Tapasya. In the Patanjali philosophy and its commentary by Vyasa, Kastha-mauna and Akara-mauna are mentioned.

Rama : What is Kastha-mauna?

Madman : Sitaram, not expressing one's own intention even through signs is called Kashtha-mauna. And merely remaining silent is called Akara-mauna.

Rama : Well, Shashtras prescribe silence for the Yogis. Are even devotees to remain silent?

Madman : There is no devotee who is not a Yogi. There is no way other than Yoga. As soon as Vaikhari is crossed, the role of Yoga begins.

Well, listen. Lord Krishna says in the Gita, 'He

who can maintain his equanimity in praise and blame, is silent, is pleased even with very little, has no fixed place of residence, is determined and is a devotee, is dear to me.' Devotees of God need silence a great deal. Listen to this shloka from Gita, 'Pleasantness of mind, tranquility, avowed silence, control of the mind and purification of the feelings, are mental Tapasya.' Jai Jai Rama, Sitaram, Jai Jai Sitaram.

Rama   : What is there in the Bhagavata?

Madman   : There are many things there. I will tell you a few things.

'Kardama Muni for whom, his soul was the only refuge, took the vow of silence and traveled over the world without fire and residence.' This is an example of Siddhi of the highest order.

Bhagawan Kapila set down these attributes of Yoga, 'avowed silence, constant mental victory, calmness, control over Prana and withdrawal of the senses from the objects of enjoyment into the heart.'

'Destroy all the impediments to Yoga, violence, lust, inertia, etc. with the help of silence.'

Removal of the impediments to Yoga with the help of silence is also mentioned in the Shantiparva of the Mahabharata.

'The *dandas* of speech, body and mind are respectively silence, effort and pranayama. He, who does not possess these *dandas*, cannot be an ascetic merely by holding a stick of bamboo.'

'O Uddhava! Use speech, mind, prana, sense organs and Atma to control the Atma. One, who does this, does not return to this world. One who does not control his speech and mind through knowledge, his vows, practice and knowledge dissolve like an unbaked earthen pot coming in contact with water. Hence, supported by your devotion to me, use your intelligence to control your speech, mind and prana, and you will be delivered.'

Rama   : God has said so much about silence!

Madman : Sitaram, if you want to go along the path of sadhana, speech must first be brought under control. The mind must then be turned inward with the help of truthfulness, remembering God's name, Leela and qualities, and maintaining silence. Then you will reach the kingdom of music and melodies. Kundalini will rise and change everything. Also listen to what Shivapurana Vidyeshwar Samhita has to say.

'By all means and at all places, eat pure food, always remain silent and do not reveal the secret.'

Rama : Eating pure food is the problem.

Madman : Jai Sitaram.

One who eats by begging or abstains from food, whether a sadhu or not, gets to drink the nectar every day. Begging does not amount to acceptance. Jai Jai Rama, Sitaram.

Rama : Is not begging acceptance?

Madman : No, Sitaram. Listen to Sanatkumar's song in Shivapurana. 'Holy ascetics, those who live according to the Vedas, worshippers of various Lingas, householders devoted to the Vedas and the Shastras, those who worship the *tirthas* and carry one or three *dandas* and those who observe the Hansavrata, all worship me daily by observing the vow of silence.'

Jai Jai Sitaram. Whether a householder or an ascetic, no one has any way other than silence. Padmapurana Swargakhanda says, 'One who holds a vow of silence, is free from attachment and is balanced and non-violent; is forever away from desires.'

Rama : At the ultimate stage, is there no way other than holding a vow of silence?

Madman : It is for that reason that avowed silence should be practiced from the beginning. It gives you strength. Jai Jai Sitaram, Jai Jai Sitaram.

Srimadbhagavata says, 'A Sadhaka longing for emancipation adopts silence like a heron and practices yoga etc. with determination'.

Rama : Then silence is essential to Sadhana and worship, I see.

Madman : Jai Jai Sitaram. Listen to what is said about silence in Yogavashishtha. Adhyatmamuktavali says, 'Silence is of four kinds; Vang-mauna, Aksha-mauna, Kashtha-mauna and Sushupta-mauna. Some admit another kind of silence called Mana-mauna. Stoppage of speech is called Vang-mauna. Subduing the senses by will, is called Aksha-mauna. Giving up all kinds of effort is called Kashtha-mauna. The undistracted state of the mind and the senses, of living emancipated beings is called Sushupta-mauna. The first three kinds of silence are seen only in the Kashtha hermits. The state of Sushupta-mauna is the supreme state. That is beyond the three states of dream, waking and sound sleep. The temporary state of mind during a swoon or sound sleep is called Mana-mauna.'

It is said in Revakhanda, 'Of all the vows, silence is the highest which fulfils all purposes.'

'Through perfection of introspection by silence and meditation on the image of Brahma, one can see God.'

Rama	:	I see that even the Yogavashishtha mentions the vow of silence.
Madman	:	Rama, Rama, Sitaram. Jai Jai Rama Sitaram.

It is said in the Annapurna Stuti, 'Then established the fire in accordance with the rules and perform the rites of Yagna; and be desirous of taking up the vow of silence.'

It is said in Shantiparva, 'Eliminate talkativeness by adopting silence and abjure fear by means of bravery.'

'The seeker should adopt silence during critical introspection. This is the treatment for the troubles of the world.'

'The Gods look upon him as the best knower of Brahma, who has been freed from all attachment in the form of the vanity of 'I' in the gross, subtle and causal frames; who exists in silence as an attributeless unattached space and who resides in peace; alone and invisible to the world.'

Do you know now, Sitaram, that not only boys but also emancipated men observe silence?

In Mokshadharma Parva it is said, 'Man gets knowledge by adopting silence, great fame by giving and eloquence by truthfulness; he is worshipped even in the next world.'

Also listen on to what is also said in Shantiparva, 'O beautiful one! You will be freed from sin if you give up objects of enjoyment. Those who wish to reach the boundless must free themselves from attachments through devotion to practice, charity, silence and self-control.'

Narada Parivrajaka says, 'The religion of the mendicant consists of partaking of food obtained by begging, silence, Japadhyana, perfect knowledge and detachment.' 'The ascetic freed from sin, will wander everywhere, adopt silence, be unmoved by sorrow and happiness, be forgiving, and eat the food received.'

Muktikopanishad says, 'The supreme position cannot be gained without giving up desire by all means and without silence.'

'You will conquer all impediments to Yoga with silence.'

'That Lord of the devotees whose beauty Brahma, Shankara and other gods themselves cannot describe adequately, is pleased if He is worshipped with silence, devotion and abstinence.'

'Silence is an ingredient in worship.'

Rama : I have heard much of what is said in the Shastras. What do you say in respect of silence? I find you remain silent month after month.

Madman : Jai Sitaram. In the heart of man there is a lotus named Anahata. Jai Jai Rama, Sitaram…

Rama : Leave aside the talk about the lotus. Tell me, what you have achieved by observing silence.

Madman : Jai Sitaram. By observing silence a man can give up the company of men. Well, listen to a story about a man who used to continuously chant the name of Rama and the name of Hari. Then the preceptor took pity on him and in a dream, initiated him in the Brahmi mantra. He merged with the mantra. As he chanted the Brahma mantra, he slipped into silence. What else was left? Jai Jai Sitaram.

Rama : Please tell me what happens next.

Madman : Jai Jai Sitaram, Jai Jai Rama, Sitaram. Sounds of various kinds, such as kirtan, drums, bells, cymbals, flutes, roar of the ocean, the shouting etc, are perceived. Jai Sitaram.

Rama : Adoption of silence leads to the giving up of the company of men and the experience of Nada, isn't it?

Madman : Jai Sitaram. It is not enough to say that Nada is experienced. By means of silence, the beauty of Nada is realized. Ordinarily, the

Nada experienced by people is not distinct. If one adopts silence, the sounds of 'Jai Guru', 'Guru', thunder, rain, cascade, croaking of frogs, flutes, lyres etc. are perceived. In the Nada of thunderstorm, it seems, Jai Sitaram, that a great storm is blowing, but Hari... Hari, if you come out and see there will be no trace of rain. The Nada of thunder is very deep. While listening to it, the Sadhaka thinks that there has been a heavy downpour. Jai Sitaram. There is not even a single drop of water outside. There are so many kinds of Nada that they cannot be described. Is it possible to describe all the millions of sounds?

Rama : Does one experience joy at the time of listening to a Nada?

Madman : Jai Sitaram. There is joy but fear also comes when Nada is very loud. The intensity of sound can be maddening. Gradually, the other Nadas recede. Only the thunder, 'Jai Guru', 'Guru...Guru', 'I am He' and 'Bam Bam', remain. When the OM appears, all is over and the poor mind melts and disappears. Sitaram, mind and intellect unite and are mysteriously transformed. Sitaram, Sitaram, Sitaram, I feel like dancing.

Rama : You've grown old and you still feel like dancing?

Madman : I really feel like it, so what can I do?

(The Madman began to dance, singing, 'Sitaram, Sitaram, Sitaram)

Rama : Does one only hear sound?

Madman : One reaches the kingdom of light. There are various kinds of lights; Bindugarbh, Red light, Yellow light in shape of a lotus, white light, blue light; how many kinds of light there are, cannot be said. There is a wonderful, out of this world, light that pulls the mind. The milder the Nada is, the stronger is the flow of light. These lights keep changing but finally a steady light is reached. Jai Jai Sitaram.

Rama : Does it end with the light?

Madman : Then the sky is reached; then a sky above the sky, and another one above that. So many skies appear! Jai Jai Sitaram.

Rama : Oho, what shall I do with skies? Does your Nada bring me to God?

Madman : Surely, the lower Nada ends. There is the Nada like the jingling anklet on the right side of the head. While listening to that, the devotee gets the vision of God.

Rama : Does God speak?

Madman : Yes. He speaks and gives boons.

Rama : Then silence is essential in Sadhana and Bhajan.

Madman	: Nothing can be done without control over speech. The mind cannot turn inward.
Rama	: Well, mad baba, is the experience same for everyone?
Madman	: No, it is not. Someone's mind dissolves while listening to the Nada; someone else's ends while swinging between the Nada and the light. Others may end up merging with God.
Rama	: Merge? What is that?
Madman	: He merges into God with the sound of 'M...M...M'
Rama	: What then?
Madman	: Jai Jai Sitaram. Then, Sitaram, the poor self dissolves while trying to measure the ocean. In the end, only God remains. Jai Sitaram. Jai Jai Sitaram.
Rama	: Then?
Madman	: Then Sitaram, that man who has lost all, wanders for a few days in this world, lost in the glory of God and then goes away to the land of God.

O my confidant, friend, sit a while, I would speak to you

of the flute of Shyam.

Shyam's flute committed robbery in broad

daylight

And snatched all,

Inflaming the heart the scorcher of life

Why has he done so?

Eating or lying I have nothing in mind

The flute has made me deaf.

Robbing me of all He has made me mad

The work of the family patience is virtue

Shame is smothering the heart.

Chandidas says for this the reason

Is Kala's enchanting flute.

ॐ

33. Finish it!

How shall I gain peace?

Hari, Hari. Gurudeva has given you peace and you have gained peace. Then why do you lament?

Gurudeva has given a mantra but has not given peace.

O Sitaram. That mantra is peace. Finish the mantra. Then you will understand what a great jewel Gurudeva has given you. Finish it. Finish the mantra.

What does finishing the mantra mean?

Finishing the mantra means that the mantra will end and will be no more. The mantra will show you God, deliver you from birth, death, decrepitude and diseases, and will merge you with the ocean of the joy of the realization of self.

How shall I know that the mantra has gone?

You will no longer have the power to utter the mantra. Even if you try to remember the mantra you will become still inside. God will appear before you and then the mantra will end. You will not be able even think of the mantra, leave alone, utter it.

I do not understand it!

It is not a thing to understand but to do. You will not be able to understand this with your outward focused intelligence. Finish it. Chant the name of Rama at all times. Meditate on the mystical prayer and let the mantra be finished.

You have done so many things; you have read so many books, you have performed so many Sadhanas and Bhajans but your sufferings have not ended because you have not been able to finish the mantra. Despite being immersed in the ocean of peace, you are looking everywhere for peace? You suffer from poverty despite possessing the touchstone? I proclaim that you are sure to gain deliverance in your lifetime if you finish your mantra. There is no restriction on performing Japa at any time, at any place and in any situation. Utter the mantra ceaselessly and peace will dance in and around your heart. The feeling of restlessness will not remain. Give up all other efforts and means and concentrate on the mantra with all your might. There will be no disease, grief, sorrow, suffering and want. What will remain are everlasting happiness and unsurpassed supreme felicity.

Finish it! Finish it! Finish your mantra.

Delay no longer.

You have got a human life which is hard to obtain. The preceptor has mercifully taught you the mantra. You will get whatever you want from that wish-yielding tree of mantra. Your mantra will give you virtue, money, desire and final emancipation. Finish, finish, finish up your mantra. Let not your human life go in vain.

Oh, enjoyment! Enjoyment can be had even in the life of an animal. But the mantra is not easily obtainable. You have got the mantra. It delivers you if you contemplate on it. Finish it.

As soon as you finish the mantra, you will see that you are no more a bird in this cage of three and a half cubits, self-forgetful and troubled by disease, grief, sin, and suffering. You have become as solemn as the ocean and as vast as the sky. Joy is dancing all around you. Walls of joy have surrounded you from ten directions. You are immersed in the ocean of joy. Finish it, you traveller! Do not cry; finish it. Finish your mantra. Resolve that either you will fulfill your mantra or lay down your life. With this resolve try with all your might to finish your mantra. I promise that you will get supreme joy as soon as you end your mantra. You will surely get it.

ॐ

34. The Battleships

The madman was dancing while saying, 'Rama, Rama, A terrible war, a terrible war, Rama, Rama.' Haladhar came and said, 'O mad baba, what is up?'

Madman : Rama, Rama. A terrible war! Rama, Rama.

Halada : Where is the war?

Madman : Can't you see that a terrible war is going on? There are only unsuitable practices and unbridled eating and enjoyment! All are running after pleasure. Rama, Rama! All is lost! All is lost! If you want to live, come running, board that battleship, otherwise, there is no escape. You will have to go round and round as different creatures. Rama, Rama. Pleasure is the bait on a fish-hook! As soon as you swallow it, you are caught. Rama, Rama. Come away, come away. Rama, Rama. Board, board the battleship. Jai Sitaram.

Halada : Mad father, where is your battleship?

Madman : O Rama, Rama! Don't you see that God is calling us with two battleships? One is the Bhagavadgita and the other is the

Uddhavagita? On board! On board! Come on board, quickly. There listen, He is saying, 'Whoever it is. However great a sinner you may be; there is no fear! Pray to God and your sins and sufferings will end. You will be completely purified.' Listen, listen. He is calling, 'I will save you.' O Arjuna, go beat your drums, go to the meetings of the debaters and in a loud voice and with uplifted hands say, 'My devotee is never destroyed.'

'Give up all religion and irreligion and come only to me for shelter. I will give you emancipation.' On board! On board! Quickly board the battleship. Make the Gita your shelter. God is pleased with him who makes the Gita his refuge and reads the whole, a half, one fourth, even a single shloka, everyday. Make the Gita your refuge and the Gita will take you across the ocean of the world. Jai Rama, Sitaram.

Halada : Mad father. You have changed your opinion. You say that everything can be achieved simply by chanting the name of Rama. Now, you are speaking of reading the Gita!

Madman : Rama, Rama. Can you forever chant only 'Rama Rama'? Sitaram.

Halada : No, I cannot do so.

Madman : That is why, Sitaram, I am asking you to

make the Gita your refuge. Board the boat of the Gita and happily go across. If you can chant the name of Rama incessantly, and even a single breath does not go to waste, you will not have to do anything else. Rama, Rama, Sitaram, Jai Jai Rama, Sitaram.

Halada : When did God give the teaching of the Uddhava Gita to Uddhava?

Madman : Rama, Rama, Sitaram. At the time of His departure, seeing the state of things in Dwaraka, He sent the people of Yadu clan to Prabhasa and sat alone in an isolated place. That is when Uddhava came there. The nectar that He gave to Uddhava is incomparable. This is His last teaching.

After receiving the Gita, Arjuna had said, 'My illusion is destroyed and I will follow your orders.' Then he fought and won the war and the kingdom of virtue was established. Arjuna got ensnared in the illusion of the world and forgot the teachings of Gita. God again preached him the Gita. That Gita is called the Anugita. Following God's departure to his abode, Arjuna became extremely grief-stricken. However, due to teachings of Gita, he attained detachment.

Uddhava was fulfilled on receiving the Uddhavagita. He performed penance and reached the heavenly abode. Rama, Rama, Sitaram.

Halada   : What is contained in the Uddhavagita?

Madman   : God said to Uddhava, 'On reading the Uddhavagita, nothing remains unknown.' God has spoken of a very easy way of gaining the knowledge of Brahma in the Uddhavagita.

'Ignoring the ridicule of your kith and kin, sense of high and low and any shame on account of that, prostrate before all creatures and beings. By this you will have the knowledge of Brahma. Do this in thought, word and action, till you perceive me in all beings.' As you go on bowing in this way, everything becomes one with Brahma. After that, with the knowledge of omnipresence of God, the devotee becomes free of doubt and becomes detached from all objects.' Rama, Rama, Sitaram, Jai Jai Rama, Sitaram.

Halada   : Then, is bowing a Sadhana?

Madman   : There is no Sadhana comparable to bowing. In the end, God said to Arjuna, 'Bow down to me.' Here He asked Arjuna only to bow.

He says in the Uddhavagita, 'Looking upon all creatures in thought, word and deed as mine own or as God is better than all other ways.'

In the end, He said to Uddhava, 'As no inclination to have any other drink remains after the drinking the delicious nectar, so the seeker of knowledge has nothing left to know after he knows the doctrine of the Gita.' Rama, Rama, Sitaram, Sitaram. A terrible war it is! On board! On board! Board the battleship!

ॐ

35. Your act

The Madman stands at the crossroads. He is beating a hand drum, saying, 'Rama, Rama! Your act! Your act! Your act is running well.' A crowd gathers. There is no break in the madman's dance. 'Your act goes on splendidly.' A wise man from among the spectators, asks, 'What is the matter, madcap'?

Madman: Your act! Your act is going on.

Man   :   Where is this show going on?

Madman   : Rama, Rama. That sky is You, this air is You, that Sun is You, the water is You, the earth is You, the Ganga is You, the pond is You, the ocean is You. Your act goes on splendidly. Rama, Rama, Sitaram.

The man, the cow, the goat, the cat, the ant, the mosquito, the bug and the louse, all are You.

The Sadhu is You, the dishonest man is You, the thief is You, the dacoit is You, the minister is You, the soldier is You, the contemplating conqueror of the senses is You and even that dissolute person smoking a *bidi* and whirling a walking stick is You. The chaste woman devoted to her husband is You, the lustful, luxurious prostitute engaged with the husbands of other women, is also You. The boy, the old man, the young man, the young woman, the Brahmin and the others are all You. That one-eyed man with a stick in his hand is You. That leper crying at the street side is You. Your act goes on splendidly. Rama, Rama.

(The mad man sounds the *damaru* and begins to dance).

Man : Go on.

Madman : The bullock cart is You, the bullock is You, the driver is You, the motor-car and its driver are You, the railway carriage, the lines, the guard, the driver; all are You. The Vedas, the Vedanta, the Tantra, the mantras, poetry, drama and the novel; all are You. Life is You and death is You. You are the bone, marrow, flesh, fat, blood, hands, feet, mouth, nose, ears and the eyes. You are the entrails, brain, heart and whatever belongs to the body. Sin, religion and irreligion are You. Your act goes on splendidly. Ahead, behind, right, left, high, low; all are You. Your act goes on splendidly. You are the Muladhara, Swadhisthana, Manipura, Anahata, Vishuddha, Ajna and Sahasrara. You are the Ida, Pingala, Sushumna and the Seventy Two Crores Seventy Two Lakh Ten thousand Two

Hundred and One nadis. The seven notes are You. The twenty-two Shrutis are You. The six ragas and the thirty-six raginis are You. One Crore Thousand Nada are You. A Hundred Crore lights are You. The past, the future and the present are You. Rama! Rama! Rama!

Your act goes on splendidly. You are Indra, the Moon, Vayu, Varuna, the planets and the stars. The earth is You and the land of Bharata is You. The Vindhyas, Himalayas, Tibet, Nepal, Kanya Kumarika and the Malay mountains are You. Arabia, Tartar, Africa, England, America, Russia, China, Japan, the Andamans and all the islands are You. The seven continents, the seven Varshas, the seven seas, Bhuvah, Swah, Mahah, Janah, Tapah, Satya; the seven Lokas are You. Atala, Vitala, Sutala, Talatala, Mahatala, Rasatala and Patala; the seven lower worlds are You. Andhatamissa, Maharourava, Rourava, Ambarisha, Mahakasha and Avichi, are You. The waters, ten times in expanse and surrounding these fourteen worlds, are You. The Fire surrounding the waters is You. The air surrounding the Fire, the sky surrounding the Air, the Ether surrounding the Air are You. The 'I', ten times greater and surrounding the Ether are You. Mahat element, surrounding the 'I' and ten times greater in size, is You. Prakriti, ten times larger than the Mahat element and surrounding it, is You. This universe is You. Ananta holding the universe on his head is You. The Mahakurma under Ananta and on the head of Adhara Shakti is You. You are the innumerable universes. Everything above, below, before, behind and on the sides of these universes is You. There is nothing in this grand act that is not you. Rama, Rama. Your act goes on splendidly.

(The madman begins to dance again, sounds the Damaru).

Man : And what about yourself?

Madman : Sitaram. This you is such an insignificant part of You! It is only an atom from the quarter part of the manifestation. Still there are You; in the three Padas above, immortal and full of light. Light and nectar flowing from there sustain this act. Rama, Rama. Your act goes on splendidly! The eternal Kailash above the universe is You. Seated there, the three-eyed, five-headed Sadashiva playing the Damaru is You. The shining and cheerful Mother is You. Kartika, Ganesha, Lakshmi and Saraswati are You. Nandi, Bhringi, ghosts, spirits, peacocks, lions, rats, snakes, bulls and the wood-apple tree are You.

The Golok is You. Nanda, Yashoda, Rohini, Sridama, Sudama, Dama and Vasudama are You. The female friends, Lalita, Vishaka and others are You. Radharani, full of pique, is You. Muralimanohara is You. The flute is You. The song of the flute is You. The kadamb-tree

348

and the bank of the Jamuna are You. Rama,
Rama. Your act goes on splendidly.

Eternal Ayodhya is You and Dasharatha is
You. Kaushalya, Kaikeyi, Sumitra, Bharata,
Lakshmana and Shatrughna are You. Nala,
Nila, Gaya, Gavaksha, Gandhamadana,
Jamavanta, Sugriva and Hanuman are You.
You are Rama armed with the bow; You are
the merciful mother Janaki. Rama, Rama.
Your act goes on splendidly.

You are Vaikuntha. You are the Five Hundred
nymphs wearing heavenly garlands,
collyrium, scent and clothes. You are the
heavenly goddesses. You are Sunanda,
Nandakumuda, Garuda, Sudarshan and
Viswaksena. You are the bejeweled canopy
with a thousand columns built of great
jewels. Seated there, Vimala and seven
others with the eight-petalled Lotus, are You.
Above that, You are the Purushottamottama
wearing yellow clothes, holding the conch,
wheel and the mace; cheerful faced, having
beautiful eyes, smiling and dark-hued. You
are the joyful Mother on the left. You are
dispersed in the joy and light. Rama! Rama!
Your act goes on splendidly. Rama, Rama.

The madman started dancing while playing
the Damaru and singing, 'Your act goes on
splendidly.' Nobody could stop his dance.

ॐ ॐ ॐ

36. The Darshan of a Sadhu

The madman is chanting the name of Rama to himself. 'Rama, Rama, Sitaram, Jai Jai Rama, Sitaram.' There is no pause or interval in the chanting of the Name. He chants the name of Rama incessantly and also breaks into a dance. People call him mad because of this dancing and chanting the name of Rama. The madman does not pay heed to anybody and always goes on chanting the name of Rama.

Haladhara came and said to the madman, 'Well, mad father, why do people go to see Sadhus. Is it just a fad?'

Madman   : Rama, Rama, Sitaram, Jai Jai Rama. Visiting a sadhu is not like going to an entertainment show that people will follow the others. Only some will do that.

The fruit of visiting a billion places of pilgrimage can be had just by reading the *shlokas* of the Gita, by singing to the memory of Govinda and by having a *darshan* of a Sadhu. Man can be rid of his sins by touching or visiting those who read the name of Purushottama, meditate and bow to Him.

Kenopanishad says, 'That Brahma is well known as worthy of being worshipped by creatures as the Highest and worthy of best possible devotion. All creatures pray to the one who worships Brahma in this way.' Rama, Rama, Sitaram. All creatures will want him who makes God his sole stay. Rama, Rama, Jai Jai Rama, Sitaram.

Haladhara : These Sadhus gain such strength by worshipping God with undivided attention that all people run towards them, mesmerized?

Madman : Rama, Rama, Sitaram. People who are pious are more attracted than ones with base nature. But these still join in criticism. Rama, Rama, Sitaram, Jai Jai Sitaram.

Haladhara : Well, mad father, what comes of worshipping God?

Madman : Rama, Rama. What happens if iron is kept in fire?

Haladhara : The iron becomes like fire.

Madman : Rama, Rama, Sitaram. Similarly, it is said in Mundak Upanishad, 'He who knows that supreme Brahma becomes Brahma himself.' Taittiriya Upanishad says, 'He who knows that supreme Brahma, reaches eternal joy which is Brahma.' Rama, Rama, Sitaram, Jai Jai Rama, Sitaram.

Haladhara : What does knowing Brahma mean?

Madman : Knowing with the help of Shastras that Brahma exists, is called indirect knowledge. Knowing 'I am Brahma' is direct knowledge of Brahma. Rama, Rama, Sitaram.

Haladhara : Brahma himself is God. Can he be seen? In this Age, can a man see him?

Madman : Rama, Rama, Sitaram. Surely he can. When a devotee gives up everything, even his love for life, and calls out to Him, He cannot remain unmoved. He appears before the devotee and grants him boons. Rama, Rama, Sitaram.

Haladhara : Is seeing this God, seeing Brahma?

Madman : Rama, Rama, Sitaram, Jai Jai Sitaram. The Jnani calls this knowledge; 'Brahma', the yogi calls it the Highest Soul and the devotee calls it God. Rama, Rama, Sitaram.

Haladhara : Can a man get what he wants, from one who has found God?

Madman : Rama, Rama, Sitaram. With firm faith, one can get one's desires through from a knower of Brahma. Mundaka Upanishad says, 'Men with pure and untainted mind attain the worlds of their desire or whatever they aspire for.' Therefore, those who desire wealth should worship the one who has the knowledge of Atma.

Haladhara : What is the reason for going to see sadhus?

Madman : Rama, Rama, Sitaram, Rama, Rama. Jai
Rama. A Sannyasi devoted to the drinking of
the nectar of Brahma through his Samadhi, is
Paramahansa Avdhoot. It is said in Mandal
Upanishad that the sight of him purifies the
whole world. Even his mother, father, wife
and descendants are liberated.

Chhandogya Upanishad states, 'Then, that
light of Brahma that is blazing in the worlds
of Supreme Truth above that heaven and
earth, also burns in the centre of the body
of Purusha.' When this body can be touched
in such a way that warmth can be felt, then
it is a means of seeing that light of Brahma.
When, by covering the earholes the sound of
the wheels of a chariot, the sound like that
of the bellowing of an ox, or the sound like
that of the kindling of fire is heard, it is the
sign of hearing that Light of Brahma. That
Light should be worshipped as something
seen and heard. He who does that becomes
respected and famous in the world. Rama,
Rama, Sitaram, Jai Jai Rama, Sitaram.

Haladhara : How will people understand that he is a
worshipper of Light and Nada?

Madman : Rama, Rama, Sitaram. He himself is taking
the form of everything and putting on this
act. He will indicate, you don't have to worry.
When it is seen that people are automatically
attracted to any Sadhu it is to be understood

353

that that Sadhu has found light, Nada etc. and worships God with undivided attention. Rama, Rama, Sitaram, Jai Jai Rama, Sitaram.

Adwayatarakopanishat says, 'The inward-focused uninterrupted sight is called Shambhavi Mudra. The land is sanctified by the presence of a wise man that has attained this Mudra.' Everybody is purified by visiting him. He, who gets the fortune of worshipping such a great Yogi, becomes emancipated.

Haladhara : What good does it do to the people?

Madman : Rama, Rama, Sitaram, Jai Jai Rama, Sitaram. In Adwayatarokanishat, the disciple said, 'O Lord, what good it does to the people? O Lord, what good is done to the people?' Rama, Rama, Sitaram. The preceptor said, 'Good is of three kinds'. Rama, Rama, Sitaram. The disciple asked, 'What is that?' Rama, Rama, Jai Jai Rama. The preceptor replied, 'Seeing, worshipping and speaking. Seeing leads to the destruction of sin, worshipping leads to the gradual increase of welfare and speaking leads to final emancipation. One realizes 'I am ever pure, wise and true natured'. One becomes wise by the grace of the preceptor and thus becomes specially liberated.' Rama, Rama, Sitaram, Jai Jai Sitaram.

Haladhara : Then the fruits from visiting a Sadhu are not insignificant! What are the characteristics of a Sadhu?

Madman : Rama, Rama, Sitaram. In Mahabharata it is said that that Sadhus have three attributes of Sadhupadas; they do not cherish enmity towards anyone, they give and they speak the truth.

They are not gladdened by honour. And they are not angry at dishonour. If ever they pretend to be angry at something, they do not utter harsh and cruel words. Rama, Rama, Sitaram.

Haladhara : What is the symptom of the Siddha?

Madman : Rama, Rama, Sitaram, Jai Jai Rama, Sitaram.

According to Bodhayana, being the giver and the enjoyer of mantra Siddhi as per Tantra and being free from desire are the three attributes of a siddha. Rama, Rama, Jai Jai Rama, Sitaram, Jai Jai Rama. As per Mahopanishad, 'He, who enjoys the world without having hostility towards anyone and desire for anything, is emancipated during his life-time.'

Yogavashishtha says, 'He who considers decrepitude, death, danger, kingly enjoyment, poverty and such other things as the same and goes through each with equanimity, is emancipated in his life-time.'

'He, who is emancipated, does not ignore the sorrowful condition or hope for happiness.

He is neither elated at success nor regretful at failure.'

According to Garudapurana, a wise man approaches and controls a person, using the very emotions and feelings the person has.

Adhyatmopnishad states, 'He who treats alike, the honour by Sadhus and persecution by the wicked, is emancipated.'

Rama, Rama, Sitaram, Jai Jai Sitaram.

Haladhara : How is one liberated in this life-time?

Madman : Rama, Rama, Jai Jai Rama.

Ramarahasyopnishad says, 'A Sadhaka becomes liberated in his life-time if he has succeeded in fulfilling his mantra. He is liberated in life-time if he ceaselessly utters the name of Guru'. According to Mundamalatantra, 'He who always utters the name, 'Durga, Durga, Durga', gets liberated in this life-time. He, who performs the Japa always; audibly or mentally, is liberated.'

Rama, Rama, Sitaram, Jai Jai Rama, Sitaram.

Aditya Purana states, 'The man who always utters the name of Sri Rama becomes liberated as a wise man; with Rama in his soul.'

None of the men, who always chant the two letters 'Rama' day and night, has any fear and they become liberated while they live

Rama, Rama, Sitaram, Jai Jai Rama, Sitaram.

Haladhara : O mad father, is that why you always chant the name of Rama? I have finally come to know you after so long. Please find me a way, mad father.

Madman : Rama, Rama, Sitaram, Jai Jai Rama, Sitaram. Only chant the name of Rama. If you hear of the arrival of a Sadhu, go and visit him. You will not have to do anything else. If the Sadhu just turns to look at you with grace, you will be fulfilled. According to Varahopanishad, 'Those who come into the line of vision of a holy man will be rid of all sins. Simply by coming into the sight of a knower of Brahma, the birds flying in the sky, the men, women, animals, insects and such other creatures, are instantly absolved of their sins from billions of lives. Rama, Rama, Rama, Jai Jai Rama, Rama, Rama.

Haladhara : Jai Rama. Just a glance of grace from a Sadhu or an emancipated being, destroys the sins of billion lifetimes of not only men but also of animals and birds! What joyful tidings! Let me go running and relate this to all.

Listen! It does not matter if you are not able to follow a practice, just visit a Sadhu. Glory to the presence of Sadhus!

ॐ ॐ ॐ

37. Easy Sadhana

The mad man was walking on the bank of the Ganga chanting the name of Rama, when Ramadas came and said, 'O mad father, can you tell me how God can be found easily?

Madman   : Rama, Rama, Sitaram. Pranaam or obeisance; if only you can bow in reverential salutation, you need not do anything else. God says in the Gita, 'Bow to me'. Rama, Rama, Rama.

Rama   : Is bowing mentioned in the scriptures? God can be reached by bowing to Him? Do the scriptures say so?

Madman   : Rama, Rama, Sitaram. Sure. Pandavgita says, 'A performer of ten Ashwamedha sacrifices is no equal to him who prostrates before Krishna only once. The performer of ten Aswamedha-sacrifices is born again but he who bows to Krishna is not born again.' Rama, Rama, Sitaram.

Rama   : Is it not an exaggeration?

Madman   : No, Rama, Rama, Sitaram. Listen on. Not to speak of obeisance, even he who utters the word 'Namah' with reverence, gains the eternal world even though he is one steeped in bad practices. God has said this in Anusmriti.

Rama, Rama, Sitaram, Rama, Rama, Rama. Listen on. Nrisinmha Purana says, 'Respectful salutation is best Yajna of all Yajnas. Through offering salutation, man gets purified and goes to the world of Hari.' Rama, Rama, Sitaram.

Rama   : Mad father, I cannot believe that man gets purified by bowing down only once.

Madman   : Rama, Rama. The Rishis have said this in all the scriptures. It is your misfortune that you cannot believe it! Sitaram, Rama, Rama, Sitaram. Well, listen to what the Shastras say. Skanda Purana says, 'One who prostrates before Vishnu in devotion, lives in heaven for as many cycles of creation, as the number of dust particles that stick to him while prostrating.'

Rama   : What if someone prostrates only to show to the world?

Madman   : Skanda Purana also says, 'Even if someone pretends to bow before Vishnu, the accumulated sins of his hundred previous lives are wiped out.'

Rama   : What happens if a great sinner bows down?

Madman   : When a devotee falls upon the ground to

perform a Shashtanga Pranama, all his sins fall upon earth with him; while he gets up, the sins do not. Rama, Rama, Sitaram, Jai Jai Rama, Sitaram.

Rama : It is a very wonderful thing! If a sinner bows to God even hypocritically, his sins are washed away?

Madman : Rama, Rama, Sitaram. These are not said by you or me but the Shastras. It is said in Revakhanda, 'There is no doubt in this, that the sins acquired in seven lives are annulled even if a man prostrates in hypocrisy to the God holding the Chakra.' Rama, Rama, Sitaram. My Chakradhari is highly pleased.

Revakhanda also mentions, 'Rudra is pleased with worship, Divakara is satisfied by Japa and Homa, and my Thakur holding the conch, the chakra and the mace, is satisfied in the highest degree by prostration.' Rama, Rama, Sitaram, Jai Jai Rama. Would you like to hear more? Sitaram.

Rama : I will listen most willingly. Please do say.

Madman : Rama, Rama, Rama. In Revakhanda it is mentioned, 'By performing a Shashtanga Pranama to Hari, a man gets the result that he gets by worshipping other gods.' Rama, Rama.

'By prostrating on the ground, the man

who offers obeisance is worshipped in the Vishnuloka for as many thousand years as the particles of dust that stick to his body.' Rama, Rama, Sitaram.

Rama : Listening to the glory of obeisance, hope rises in my heart. Even if I can do nothing else I will be contented merely by bowing down.

Madman : Rama, Rama. Is there any doubt about it?

It is said in Brahmandapurana, 'Though a man blinded by illusion commits many sins, he does not go to dark hell if he bows before Hari, who takes away all the sins.' Rama, Rama, Sitaram. Rama, Rama.

Yamagita says, 'All the sins of man who respectfully prostrates to Hari (whose lotus-feet are worshipped by the immortals) are washed away. Hence, O messengers consider that man to be like Agni moistened with ghee and leave him alone.' Rama, Rama, Rama. Rama, Jai Jai Rama.

Rama : Well, Mad father, what comes of bowing down to superiors?

Madman : Rama, Rama, Sitaram, Jai Jai Rama. Manu says, 'When a youth comes before an elder person, his Prana leaps upwards. By rising to welcome the elder and by saluting him, the Prana returns to its place. By prostrating before elders, longevity, learning, fame and strength are increased. Rama, Rama, Sitaram.

Rama : Well, mad father, why does Prana leap upwards when an elder comes near?

Madman : Rama, Rama. Jai Jai Rama, Sitaram. This world is the embodiment of Prana. It is the Prana only, which takes a gross form and appears as the world. Again, it is the Prana in its subtle form that contains everything. The sense organs in the body are the spiritual forms of the Prana. The presiding deities of the senses are divine forms of the Prana. Sound, touch, complexion, juice and smell are material forms of the Prana. The Prana has assumed physical form and has become man, birds and animals, trees and creepers, worms and insects, rivers and streams, oceans, and mountains. Virat is the creation of the Prana. It is the cause of the universe. Prana endowed with the power of resolution, is called mind. Prana endowed with the power of perseverance is called Vijnana. Pranava is another name of this Prana. The first manifestation of the joyful, Supreme Soul is the Prana. Those who establish the truth knowing that 'God is in all in the form of Prana', are fulfilled. Seeing an elder come in, the Prana of the younger person is automatically attracted and leaps upwards. If he bows down, his Prana regains its place. Rama, Rama, Sitaram.

Rama   : Well, mad father, how many kinds of Pranama are there?

Madman   : Rama, Rama, Sitaram, Jai Jai Rama, Sitaram. Pranama is of three kinds; physical, oral, and mental. Of them the bodily Pranama is the highest.

Kalikapurana says, 'The gods are always satisfied by bodily Pranama. Rama, Rama, Sitaram. Bodily Pranama and oral Pranama are of different kinds. Rama, Rama.

Rama   : Is Pranama mentioned in the Upanishads?

Madman   : Rama, Rama. Yes, they are. There is no other sadhana like Pranama. Taittiriyopanishat states, 'Worship the embodiment of Joy; the Supreme Soul, by uttering the word Namah.'

All the objects of enjoyment come with bowed head to the devotee who offers salutations in this way. He, who bows down to God without any desire, has vision of God. Rama, Rama, Sitaram, Jai Jai Rama.

According to Ramottaratapinyupanishad, the word Namah is the only means of obtaining complete joy. All the gods and all the seekers bow to Him who resides in the innermost depths of the soul. Rama, Rama, Rama, Jai Jai Rama, Sitaram.

Rama   : How many bows are to be made every day?

Madman   : Rama, Rama, Sitaram. According to Shivapurana Vidyeshwar Samhita, the learned will bow millions of times. All deities are satisfied by the Atmayajna in the form of respectful salutation. Rama, Rama, Rama. It is further said, 'a mind dedicated to the Supreme Soul has no relish for lack of emptiness. The vanity that I have vanishes when I see you.'

'O Lord! You are great! I bow down to you with my whole being. My form is not emptiness (I am a part of you), now I am your servant.'

'Properly perform appropriate salutation, which is sacrifice of the soul.'

Rama, Rama, Jai Jai Rama, Sitaram.

Rama   : Do Jnanis also do pranaam?

Madman   : Rama, Rama, Jai Rama, Jai Jai Rama, Rama, Rama, Rama, Rama.

Sutasamhita says, 'Ancient rishis have described obeisance as a characteristic of knowing that the sense of separation from the blissful God exists because of illusion and not due to difference in nature. The connection created with God through *namaskara* overcomes this separation. It is a sign of being one with Him.' Vriddha Harita says, 'Ma signifies distinction and Na eliminates it. Hence, the separation from God is eliminated by uttering the word Namah. Offering a salutation with this mantra yields higher results.' Rama, Rama, Sitaram. It is said in Revakhanda, 'The result of a single salutation offered with a mantra, is equal to the fruits of doing respectful salutation for twelve years.'

The Gita, the Chandi, The Ramayana, the Bhagavata and other scriptures speak loudly of offering Pranaam. Arjuna, the friend of Krishna, started with a number of salutations to Him.

God speaks of the highest sadhana with the words 'Be mindful only of me, be devoted to me, offer sacrifices to me; if you can do nothing else respectfully bow before me, that will suffice.'

In Chandi, Sakra rishi and others offer respectful salutation to Devi. The first hymn in the Uttaracharita is full of salutations. Brahmarshi says that these two mantras contain the essence of the whole of the Chandi.'

'To the Devi who exists in all beings as the Mother, I bow to you repeatedly in salutation.'

'To the Devi who exists in all beings as delusion, I bow to you repeatedly in salutation.'

The hymn to Narayani, in the concluding part of Chandi, says, 'Salutations to you, O Narayani, who are the fair one, the three-eyed goddess, the giver of shelter, the source of good in the world, the auspiciousness in all that is auspiciousness and the provider of all worldly and spiritual desires.'

Rama, Rama. Not only that. All the Gods say, 'O Goddess, you take away the sufferings of all, be pleased with us. O, Goddess, the object of the worship of all who reside in the three worlds, give boons to those who bow at your feet.'

It is mentioned in the Ramayana that, Valmiki received the seed of Ramayana from Brahma. On seeing Brahma, Valmiki worshipped Him with Padya, Arhga and Asana and prostrated.'

What to say of my Mahavirji. He says, 'I bow to Rama, Lakshmana and to that Goddess, the daughter of Janaka. I bow down to Rudra, Indra, Yama, Anila, Chandra, Arka and the Maruts.'

In Sri Ramacharitmanasa Goswami Tulsidasa has devoted the entire opening chapter to obeisance.

'I bow to the object of Rama's love; Sita, who is the cause of creation, existence and destruction, the remover of pain and the doer of welfare.'

Srimad Bhagavatam says, 'Before commencing, I offer my respectful salutations to the personality of God-head, Narayana, Nara-Narayana, the supermost being, the goddess, the mistress of learning and Vyasadeva, the author.'

The first shloka of the Vishnupurana says, 'Victory to you, the one with lotus-eyes, the origin of the universe, the lord of the senses, the greatest being and the first born.'

In the Srimadbhagavata Sri Suta begins, 'My respectful obeisance's to that great sage. When he went away to take up the renounced order of life, leaving home without undergoing the sacred thread ceremony, his father Vyasadeva, cried, 'Oh, my son!' and the trees echoed in response.'

'When Narada arrived, Vyasadeva worshipped him. Narada gave him the seed of the Bhagavata and left.'

In the Bhagavata that Vyasadeva composed, having got guidance from the mouth of Narada, obeisance, praise and worship are spoken of almost in every chapter. Rama, Rama, Sitaram, Sitaram, Rama, Rama.

Rama : Do all the Shastras sing the praises of salutation?

Madman   : Rama, Rama, Sitaram. The Shastras are replete with obeisance.

The poet says in the Bhagavata, 'Being devoted to none else and knowing that the sky, the wind, fire, water, the earth, the Moon, the Sun, the planets, the stars, all the creatures, the ten directions, all the trees, the rivers and seas are all my body; the devotee should bow to me.

Bhagvan Kapila says, 'God is present in all the creatures as the internal being; knowing this, bow mentally to all the creatures in the creation.' Rama, Rama, Sitaram, Rama, Rama.

God said clearly to Uddhava, 'Let people laugh at you. Discard the worldly concept of 'I am this or that' and prostrate before all beings and creatures.' Rama, Rama, Sitaram, Jai Jai Rama.

Rama   : A complete prostration?

Madman   : Rama, Rama, Sitaram. One bow fulfils the task. Rama, Rama, Sitaram.

Sri Chaitanya Mahaprabhu says, 'Lie prostrate before all with full respect; Brahmins, Non-Brahmins and all creatures. Respectfully bowing to all is the Vaishnava faith.

He who is not thus inclined is a hypocrite.'

Rama   : Mad baba, do the Vedas and Upanishads enjoin Pranama as the Chandi and Gita do?

Madman   : Rama, Rama, Jai Jai Rama, Rama.

Rudradhyana begins with 'O Rudra, my salutations to your anger and your arrows. Salutations to your bow and to your hands.'

Thereafter almost everything is imbued with Pranama. Svetasvatara Upanishad says, 'Salutations to the blissful and radiant supreme soul who pervades the entire world and is present in Fire, Water, Herbs and Vegetation.' Rama, Rama, Rama.

This is found in the Atharva Siropanishad. 'Om, He is Rudra. He is surely the God that is Brahma. I bow to Him again and again.' Thus salutations through Namo Namah are offered in thirty-two verses.

It is said in Nrisimhapurvatapini, 'Om, salutations to Him, who is Nrisimha, who is God and Brahma.'

Rama, Rama, Sitaram. Similar praise and *namaskar* is offered in thirty-two mantras.

The Ramotaratapini Upanishad says, 'Om, He who is Sri Ramachandra is God without a second, the source of highest bliss and the supreme soul. I also bow to Him who is the Supreme Brahma, Bhu, Bhuva and Swa.' It offers further salutations of Namo Namah

369

in forty-seven verses. Rama, Rama, Jai Jai Rama, Sitaram.

Rama : Do the Upanishads also contain many things about Pranama?

Madman : Rama, Rama, Sitaram. There is no way other than Pranama. Listen to what Rudrahridayopanishad says. 'The wise man that says, 'Rudra, Rudra' and sings the glory of the Supreme Being, is rid of his sins. Rudra is Man and Uma is Woman, I bow down to Him and Her.'

The salutation is made in eight such mantras.

Rama, Rama, Sitaram, Jai Jai Rama, Sitaram.

In Tarasaropanishad, the salutation is performed in eight mantras, such as 'I bow to Him who is Sri Paramatma Narayana. God expressed by the letter 'h', who is Jambavan, Bhu, Bhuva and Swa.'

The salutation is performed in the Gopalottaratapini Upanishad with seventeen such mantras as 'Om, I bow to Prana-Atma who is Bhu, Bhuva and Swa. Om tat sat. I bow to Prana-Atma.' Rama, Rama, Sitaram.

How much more shall I say? The Vedas, Upanishads, Purana and all Shastras are replete with salutation Namo Namah. Rama, Rama.

Rama : Well, why do Shastras have so many prayers and salutations?

Madman : Rama, Rama, Sitaram, Jai Jai Rama, Sitaram. The main root of the problems of the world is; I and mine. The more one has 'I and mine' the unhappier he is. Lesser the feeling of 'I and mine', more is the happiness. To get hold of 'I' one is to do away with 'mine'. The root of the feeling, 'all is mine', is 'my body'. Namah means 'not mine'. In Namah one 'm' is eliminated indicating that this body is not mine. Namo Namah is uttered to lose the identification with the body. One can become carefree only by offering the body to Him. That is why the Shastras speak so much of salutation; to respectfully offer this body to God. Rama, Rama, Sitaram.

Chant 'Rama Rama' and offer obeisance. The root of the malady will be destroyed. The body truly belongs to God. Inert or conscious; all are His forms. Calling His body as yours and putting the stamp of 'mine' on it, only creates untold misery. Rama, Rama.

Hand over His wealth to Him and set off, free, uttering Namo Namah. Rama, Rama, Namah, Namah.

'He is coming! '

The madman begins to dance, chanting the name of Rama. Ramadas also begins to dance with him.

Jai Rama, Sitaram.

ಇ ಓಂ ಜು

38. The Ashrama of a Vaishnava

The madman was meditating and dancing to the chanting of 'Rama Rama Rama'. It was ceaseless. The chanting of the name of Rama was incessant. At that time Haladhara came and said, 'O Mad father!'

Madman   : Jai Jai Sitaram, Rama, Rama.

Haladhara : Well, mad father, how many life stages (Ashramas) are there?

Madman   : Rama, Rama. A man's life has four stages; celibate student, a householder, a forest dweller and a renunciate. Rama, Rama, Sitaram.

Haladhara : To which Ashrama do the Vaishnava of these days, belong? I have heard that Bhagwan Ramanujacharya was a sanyasi and Sriman Mahaprabhu, too, embraced Sanyasa. What is the Ashrama of the Vaishnavas who wear white cloth?

Madman   : Rama, Rama, Sitaram, Jai Rama.

               Narada Pancharatra says, 'Brahmachari, Grihastha, Vanaprastha and Yati are the four

Ashramas. Those who specially seek refuge in me belong to the fifth Ashrama or the Vaishnava Ashrama. Rama, Rama, Sitaram.

Ashtayama says, 'Vaishnava is the fifth genre; Vaishnava is the fifth Ashrama. Sri Vaishnava Ashrama is the best Ashrama of all Varnas and Ashramas.'

There are five types in this Ashrama of Gaudiya Vaishnava, namely, Namashraya, Gurupadashraya, Mantrashraya, Bhavashraya and Veshashraya.

Charitasudha says, 'On embracing these shelters, the characteristics of Rupashraya, Gunashraya, Dhamashraya, and Leelashraya etc. get established automatically. Rama, Rama, Sitaram.

Haladhara : Then the Vaishnava Ashrama is the fifth Ashrama. What should they do and what should they not do?

Madman : Yes it is. Rama, Rama, Sitaram. Assuming the garb of a Vaishnava is being in Veshashraya. The rules for those Vaishnava are; not indulging in or listening to any gossip, not being attached to worldly affairs, not amassing wealth, not looking at or talking to any woman with the intention of gratifying one's lust or senses, not leaving the focus from one's own belief and criticizing or hating others. A Vaishnava must conduct himself accordingly. He should perform worship in the prescribed nine-fold way and avoid the company of a woman; outward pomp, inexact speech; false behavior; scandal-mongering; slandering; envy; malice; mischief-mongering fault-finding; gluttony; addiction; luxury; eating food without offering it to gods and such other things. What more shall I say? One needs to keep following this and the merciful Lord will create the necessary impetus in the heart. Rama, Rama, Rama.

Haladhara : Is this Vaishnava Ashrama found in the Bhagavata etc.?

Madman : Rama, Rama, Sitaram. Srimadbhagavata says, 'He, who does not identify with his self on grounds of work, Varna, Ashrama and caste is dear to Hari.'

'A wise, non-attached man or a desireless devotee should discard symbols of Ashrama like Tridanda and should act impartially according to the rules of the Shastra.' Rama, Rama, Sitaram, Jai Jai Rama, Sitaram.

Haladhara : Will there be no offence in transgressing the Shastras?

Madman : Rama, Rama, Sitaram. God said to Uddhava in Srimadbhagavata, 'Therefore, O Uddhava, give up Shruti, Smriti, tendencies, abstention and all that is worth hearing or heard, and take shelter with me; the shelter for all beings. All your fears will be dispelled by me.' Rama, Rama, Sitaram.

By making God their sole refuge, Vaishnavas enter the fifth Ashrama and are above the tenets of all. Nothing on the subject of Sanyas is found in Bhagwan Ramanandaswami's 'Sri Vaishnava Matabjabhaskara'. The Vaishnava will be purified by the five sacraments. The normal rule is that they wear white outer garments, a shawl and a loin-cloth, build a cottage in a holy place and spend their time in worship, study, meditation and chanting. After reaching the ultimate state, they wear only a belt made of grass blades and a loin-cloth, and engage in worship of God. Rama, Rama, Sitaram.

Haladhara : What is the name of the detached Vaishnava of the Brahmananda sect?

Madman : Rama, Rama, Sitaram. He is a renunciate Vaishnava. Rama, Rama, Rama. Jnana Sannyasi, Veda Sannyasi and Karma Sannyasi are mentioned in the Kurmapurana. Among them 'The Yogi is the best of these three kinds of Sannyasis. He has no enjoined duty or sign of any Ashrama.' Rama, Rama, Sitaram, Jai Jai Rama, Sitaram.

Haladhara : Then has a Yogi no sign of any Ashrama?

Madman : Jai Jai Rama. No Sitaram. Only a few yogis

bear symbols of Ashramas.

Haladhara : The sacred thread is seen round the necks of these who are Brahmins among Vaishnavas. That also is the sign of the Brahmin Varna.

Madman : Sitaram, Rama, Rama. They have had their *upanayana* ceremony in their childhood and have since worn the thread; they do not understand the necessity of giving up the sacred thread. Jada Bharata also wore the sacred thread. Sitaram, Rama, Rama.

Haladhara : Is this mentioned in the Shrutis?

Madman : Rama, Rama, Rama, Sitaram, Rama, Rama.

Narada-Parivrajakopanishad says, 'He, who knows the Ultimate Element which is self-effulgent and blissful; is free of the bodily sense; is a witness to everything, is knower of the highest truth and is beyond Varnashrama.

He who knows by the help of the Vedanta that, Varnashrama etc. is projected by Maya and does not affect the Atma, are above the Varnashrama.

He, who has got rid of the practices of the Varnashrama, by virtue of his own perception of self, has transcended all Varnas and Ashramas and resides in his own soul, is proclaimed to be above the Varanashrama by the knowers of Vedas.'

No processes, prohibitions and distinctions of unacceptable and acceptable apply to those who know Brahma but they do apply to others. Rama, Rama, Rama, Sitaram, Sitaram.

Haladhara : It is said that the rules of Varna and Ashrama leave a man when he gains Atmadarshana. What does Atmadarshana mean?

Madman : Rama, Rama. It means seeing God. Rama, Rama, Sitaram.

Haladhara : Can man see God in this Age?

Madman : Rama, Rama. Surely he can. Rama, Rama, Sitaram, Jai Jai Rama, Sitaram. Some knowers of Brahma however pretend to practise Varnashrama to educate the people, while others do not.

Haladhara : What does Brahmavijnani mean?

Madman : Rama, Rama, Sitaram. Those who do not merely repeat 'I am Brahma' but experience this truth are called Brahmavijnanis. Rama, Rama, Rama. A Brahmavijnani or one who has seen God, has not to shed his karmas, they melt away automatically. Rama, Rama, Rama, Rama.

Haladhara : God appears once like a dream and vanishes, and Varanashrama goes away. Has a seer of God any other characteristics?

Madman   : Rama, Rama, Rama, Sitaram, Jai Jai Rama.
              On giving darshan, God takes away the
              mantra of the devotee. The luminous sound
              of Om reverberates within him. Numerous
              unheard melodies are experienced. The door
              of the Sushumna is opened. His power to do
              any activity goes away. Rama, Rama, Rama,
              Rama Jai, Rama.

Haladhara   : He is able to do other things but the power
              to perform daily religious duties leaves him!
              How can this be? Does he lose consciousness
              when he starts to worship?

Madman   : Rama, Rama, Sitaram. No. As soon as he
              utters, Bhurbhuvaswa his Prana sinks in the
              Sushumna. Swa...a...this goes on for up to
              two hours. The devotee then sits silently
              with closed eyes. Ordinary people say he
              has gone into Samadhi. But that is not the
              fact. Sometimes, with the Prana entering
              the Sushumna, the mind is absorbed and
              Samadhi takes place. Sometimes while
              listening to a story about the Lord, a tear-
              filled Samadhi is reached. Light begins
              to play outside and inside. Rama, Rama,
              Sitaram.

              Suryagita Says, 'At first, when knowledge
              dawns, all actions focused on fulfillment of
              desires, leave the seeker. With knowledge,
              he no longer does worship for wealth etc.
              In the second stage, with the attainment

of full wisdom, he becomes free from such rituals as his son's sacred thread ceremony and Shradh. In the third, on the attainment of full wisdom, daily prayers, etc. come to an end. Then after the rise of the knowledge of non-duality, the wise man rises above Varanashrama. Rama, Rama, Sitaram, Jai, Jai, Sitaram.

Haladhara : How are the four states of Jnana understood?

Madman : Rama, Rama, Sitaram.

Yogachudamani Upanishad says, 'Although the Pranava is enjoyable and resides in all beings, it remains concealed during all states of enjoyment. It becomes apparent when Brahma merges into 'A', Hari into 'U' and Rudra into 'M'.'

Pranava faces upwards in a wise man and downwards in the ignorant. He who knows these positions of the Pranava knows the Vedas. In its unstruck form, it rises within the wise. At it rises higher and higher, ability to perform actions, begins to fade. Prana itself is Pranava. After the Prana enters into Sushumna, karmas continue to be cast off.

Preceded by a sound like the tolling of a bell, which flows like a continuous and unbroken stream of oil, the light manifests where Pranava fades. His fore-part is light but it cannot be described in words. The great souls, who perceive it with their subtle vision, are said to be knowers of Vedas. Rama, Rama. The Pranava pushes upwards. The seeker places his soul on the bow of Pranava and aims it at Brahma. The soul, accompanied by a sound of 'm...m...m', rises in the forehead and, like an arrow, gets embedded in Brahma. It becomes identified with Brahma. Rama, Rama, Sitaram, Jai, Jai, Sitaram.

Haladhara : Can all these be clearly experienced?

Madman : Rama, Rama, Sitaram. The Sadhakas perceives the rise of Pranava like the self-revealed sun, its assumption of the form of Nada and its union with Brahma. He is then freed from all actions. Rama, Rama, Jai, Jai, Rama.

Haladhara : These things happen to Yogis. Do the devotees also get freedom from action?

Madman : Rama. Rama, Sitaram. All become Yogis when speech advances from Vaikhari to Madhyama, that is, as soon as the Anahata Nada commences. Who is not a Yogi? Shiva, Narada, Suka all are Yogis. Jai Sitaram.

Shiva says in Shivapurana Vayaviya Samhita, 'For those who are purified by devotion born of my grace, it is difficult to preserve Ashrama dharma. They are under no rules and regulations like me.' Jai Rama, Sitaram,

Sitaram.

If somehow the mantra can be fulfilled by the chanting of the name of Rama, the fortress is conquered just at the appearances of Pranava. Jai Sitaram.

Would you like to listen to some more? Jai Sitaram.

Jnana Sankalanitantra says, 'Spiritual knowledge gives eternal happiness and emancipation. If that is achieved, religion, work japa etc. drop off.' Rama, Rama, Sitaram.

Haladhara : What happens if anybody drops it by force?

Madman : Rama, Rama, Rama, Rama. The pretence does not last for long. Soon they are found running after worldly things. There is no limit to their sorrow and downfall. Their fate becomes worse than that of lowly creatures. There can be no place for enjoyment in sacrifice. Rama, Rama, Sitaram. But enjoyment does come automatically to them, who have enjoyment in their Prarabdha. They however live in the midst of it without being affected. No wave rises in their hearts.

Haladhara : Then has not any one to give up Karma?

Madman : Rama, Rama, Sitaram. Only go on earning; you need not try to give up. Sacrifice will come by itself. The Varanashrama will melt away automatically. The devotee will not even get an inkling of it.

It is said in Ramagita, 'As the flowers in the hands of a sleeping person fall automatically, the customs of Varanashrama leave the person who is free from his body and emancipated.' Rama, Rama, Sitaram. Jai Jai Rama, Sitaram.

Haladhara : Then by this, are most people today, free from their bodies and emancipated?

Madman : Rama, Rama, Sitaram. Over the period of time, the Varanashrama was not found agreeable by those who were focused on the external world. The misery of those who give up Varanashrama of the own accord to exhibit equality and liberality, will know no bounds. They are restless due to the mad dance of disease, grief, want, suffering, pain and family unrest in their lives. They are running hither and thither, seeking peace. Well, who can give peace to him who defies the Shastras? He cannot get peace. Rama, Rama, Sitaram.

Haladhara : Nowadays it is difficult to follow the rules of the Shastras.

Madman : Rama, Rama, Sitaram. It is very true. Rama, Rama. If one keeps taking pure food, keeps good company, performs the daily prayers, and meditates on the Gayatri, it will not be difficult to reach the goal. Celibacy is the essence of all Sadhana. Whole hearted efforts must be made to preserve it. Rama, Rama, Rama, Rama.

Haladhara : This rule is hard to observe even if one wishes to, mad father.

Madman : Rama, Rama, Sitaram. Just chant the name and Rama will see to it. Rama, Rama.

Haladhara : Well, mad father, do those who have transcended the Varanashrama and are free of all actions, live only in caves and not come home?

Madman : According to his Prarabdha someone lives in a cave and someone else puts on various kinds of dress and wanders about. They move in various guises, sometimes as a wicked person and other times as gentlemen. Many also preach religion. Rama, Rama, Rama.

Haladhara : Do they not suffer a downfall?

Madman : Rama, Rama, Sitaram, Rama, Rama, Jai Rama. No Sitaram. Their play-acting is for the benefit of others.

Yogavashishtha says, 'Some live in caves, some live in Punnyashrama, some are householders, some wander about, some observe silence, some are engaged in meditation, some earn their livelihood by art and some behave like wicked people.' Rama,

Rama, Sitaram. Jai Jai Rama, Sitaram.

Haladhara : O, father, this means that there is no way to recognize emancipated persons. Well, those who do meritorious work, have no bondage?

Madman : Rama, Rama, Sitaram. No, Sitaram.

Annapurnopanishad says, 'One who has given up all actions, is always contended, has no shelter and does not get affected by merit, sin or any such thing.'

A crystal does not get coloured when the shadow of a red flower falls on it. There is no trace once the flower is removed. Similarly, a Jnani's soul is not tainted by likes and dislikes. Even though he wanders about amongst people, chanting and worshipping God, he is not touched by joy and sorrow. They are like images in a mirror that can be seen but disappear. Rama, Rama, Rama, Sitaram, Rama, Rama.

Haladhara : Then, can a wise man live even in a crowd?

Madman : Rama, Rama, Sitaram. Once a man sees God, there is no fear of his downfall just as butter after being skimmed from milk no longer mixes with milk. Also like iron, which after being transformed into gold by the touchstone, does not become iron again but remains gold wherever you may keep it whether in the house of god, in a heap of refuse, in a heap of ashes, in a furnace or under water. It may get covered by dust but starts shining again as soon as the dirt is removed. God says, 'Even if he kills people, he really neither kills nor is killed.' He has no bondage from the action. Rama, Rama, Sitaram. Jai Jai Rama, Sitaram.

Haladhara : Alas! Mad father, I have wasted my life. I have not known what is knowledge or devotion. My whole life has passed one day at a time and now I have to go! What is the way left for me, mad father?

Madman : Rama, Rama, Jai Jai Rama. O Sitaram, what worry should there be in this Kaliyuga, if it is time to go?

'Bow down to the Kaliyuga which is the essence of all Yugas in which the chanting of the Name of Hari is preached.'

Simply go on chanting and make others chant. Chant His glory and you will land in the kingdom of bliss. My Lord of Love said, 'The chanting should go on at all times. The Lord with the flute will not be able to remain still. He will begin to play the flute.' Rama, Rama, Sitaram.

(Sings a song by Rabindranath)

'I will utter only your name on many pretexts, will utter it sitting along in the shade of my own mind, will utter it without speech and without hope, will utter it in minds and tears, will utter your name without any necessity, my desires will be automatically fulfilled by that call; just as child calls its mother only because of the charm of the name. It can say that it utters the name of its mother only for this happiness.' Rama, Rama, Sitaram, Sitaram.

39. The Headless Goblin

The madman is sitting under a Bel tree, silently chanting 'Rama Rama'. Just then Haridhan comes and says, 'O madman, have you heard?'

Madman : Rama, Rama. What, Sitaram?

Hari : I am speaking of the misdeeds of that sixty-five years old sadhu.

Madman : Rama, Rama, Sitaram. No Sitaram.

Hari : There is a hue and cry in the country about his character. Everybody is condemning him. What is this, mad father? He is such a great Sadhu and has twenty five thousand disciples; still he has such bad inclinations. What is it, mad father?

Madman : Rama, Rama, Sitaram. That is nothing. That is nothing. It is only the doing of the headless goblin. Rama, Rama, Sitaram.

Hari : Well, mad father, I cannot understand all this. I become very depressed when I hear such things about the character of the sadhus. What is this? Do people who are teachers and spend their time in the worship and service of God, also get detracted? I have heard such things about not only this sadhu but several others. You must listen as well.

Madman : Rama, Rama, Sitaram, Jai Jai Rama, Sitaram.

Hari : Long ago there was a famous sadhu. His lectures had taken the country by storm. Then he was tried for sexual offence and was imprisoned. Many years ago an old sadhu lived in a village near Vaidyabati near the Ganga. He sexually assaulted a disciple of his. There was a great hue and cry about it. People condemned him.

Madman : Rama, Rama, Sitaram, Jai Jai Sitaram.

Hari : Long ago I heard from a woman that one day an old disciple and a young Sadhu came to their house. The young sadhu told her, 'You are the mother of my previous birth' saying this he showed some signs in that very house and said, 'I did these things in my last birth.'

Listening to the events narrated by the Sadhu and the signs showed by him, the woman started to believe that he was her first dead son. At night the Sadhu asked the woman to breastfeed him. When she agreed, her husband came to know and attempted to kill them both with a sword. The woman left with her two sons for a monastery in Calcutta. The Head of that monastery said,

'Has such and such Bhattacharya killed such and such Sadhu?' The woman said, 'No'. He said, 'I had sent him to the mother of his previous birth to breastfeed. Did he escape? I am glad his desire is ended.' How many kinds of things are heard about Sadhus! It is one thing that such things are said about ordinary people but it is very painful that blame is imputed to the character of Sadhus. What are these things, mad father?

Madman   : Rama, Rama, Sitaram. Sadhus say that all these things are the atrocities of the headless goblin. Rama, Rama, Sitaram. As, in a battlefield, after the head is cut off, the headless trunk rises and dances, these things that happen to a Sadhu who has won over the world, are the atrocity of the headless goblin. Rama, Rama, Sitaram.

Hari   : Do not sadhus suffer from any loss on account of this?

Madman   : Rama, Rama, Sitaram, Jai Jai Sitaram. Man is born carrying the balance of many past actions. Demerits acquired in a previous birth purify the Sadhus by having them commit such offences and making them subjects of blame. Following these incidents, they go far away from the company of human beings. For Sadhus, the company of the people, honour, and fame are as dangerous as poison. The sufferings of the foolish Sadhu that cannot abjure the company of human beings, know no bounds. Rama, Rama, Sitaram. A magnet need not be told, 'Attract iron,' and the ghee near the fire need not be told, 'Melt away.' A magnet is sure to attract and ghee is sure to melt. So Sadhus need must be on their guard. If they are not cautions; Jai Jai Rama, Sitaram; they will be disgraced. Rama, Rama, Sitaram.

All aspiring Yogis need to be cautious about attraction to women. The same female power is also the invincible Vaishnavi. Even Brahma, Shiva and other Gods have been unsuccessful in winning over her.

Hari : Sadhus know this and remain alert, then why do they fall?

Madman : Rama, Rama, Sitaram. A Sadhu's desires from his past lives get eliminated by his fall. This is a trick played by Prarabdha. The foundation for ascent is strengthened by this fall. The notion 'I am the greatest' is shattered and if the Sadhu moves carefully from there on, due to the elimination of his past actions and desires, he can stay away from human company and progress on his path. Rama, Rama, Sitaram.

Hari : Baba, how do we know that this is an outcome of past actions or present ones?

Madman : Rama, Rama, Sitaram. Jai Jai Sitaram. If a

person sits down to eat and as he takes the
first bite, someone tells him not to eat the
food as it is poisonous, the man will spit out
the food immediately and not look at the
plate again. In the same way, if the misdeed
happens due to outcome of past actions, he
will never return to that path again and go a
different way. Rama, Rama, Sitaram. Like the
dance of the headless trunk, the past action
will be over. However, the people who do not
shun the misdeeds but repeat them will need
to pay for the actions of this birth in their
next. Rama, Rama, Sitaram, Jai Jai Sitaram.

Hari   : Cannot this Prarabdha be conquered?

Madman   : Rama, Rama, Sitaram. It can surely be
conquered. If one can utter the name of God,
the Prarabdha will not be able to exert its full
influence. Chant the Name, only chant the
Name. Chant it always; at all times. Rama,
Rama, Sitaram, Jai Jai Sitaram.

The Madman begins to sing aloud 'Sri Rama, Jai Rama, Jai
Jai Rama'.

ॐ

40. Service of God

Never should a moment pass without service.

When will this mind turn,

That only desire of serving Him remains?

A devotee does not want anything except being in the service of his dearest Thakur. He does not want virtue, wealth, desire or emancipation. His only object of desire is service. He is satisfied with the resolve that 'I will come and serve your feet'.

God Himself says, 'The Heaven, happiness, wealth, riches and the Kingdom of Heaven are trifles.'

'The devotees do not accept anything except my service.'

Srimadbhagavata mentions, 'Even if I offer Salokya, Samipya, and Sayujya emancipation; the devotee does not accept them.

The devotee's only prays:

Never should a moment pass without service.

When will this mind turn,

That only desire of serving Him remains?

The act of anointing the house,

Cleaning the temple,

Cleaning the remains of offering from the Holy Body,

Picking Tulsi, sandal, flowers,

Meditation on God

Thinking of the Self with the uttering of the mantra,

Reading Suktas, hymns, chanting the Name,

Study of the Vedas, Puranas and other Shastras,

Worship of God according to rules,

Performing these five kinds of worship

I will remain always engaged in speech, body and mind

And cool all my agonies,

'Service alone lifts upwards'.

It is service that takes us to the higher world. That service alone does away with self-identification and the feeling of 'mine' and gives us experience of the soul. Service alone gives us direct perception of the loving and the loved Lord. Service alone keeps Him bound in love. No other Sadhana, worship, Yoga, sacrifice and penance, is needed. Service; only service is needed. The devotee, rendering service through body and mind, does not even realise when and how he has been set free. He does not even notice his crossing this vast ocean infested with dangerous creatures like lust, anger, etc.

In the Upanishads we see that God wished to become many and take different forms. Then, in innumerable universes, He took form of everything from a tuft of grass to Brahma, and started this act.

He says to Brahma in Srimadbhagavata, 'Before Creation, I alone existed. There was nothing; existent, non-existent or unmanifested. On Creation, I become all the objects that are, gross or subtle, and on dissolution, I alone will remain. I only was, I am and I only will be.'

There is nothing else.

Vishnupurana says, 'Gods, human beings, birds, beasts, trees and reptiles, though they exist like dissimilar things, are all the manifestations of Vishnu. Knowing this the whole world should be looked upon as the one Soul since Vishnu assumes all forms.'

'All objects that exist at any place, with or without any form, are His body.'

'Vishnu alone is the Moon, the Sun, the stars, and all other heavenly bodies. Vishnu alone is the fourteen worlds. Vishnu alone is all forests, mountains, directions, rivers and the oceans. He is all. All objects that exist or not, are all Vishnu.'

'This is my teaching to you in brief; the knowledge that there is no difference between all objects and the Supreme Soul is the highest truth and essence.'

'All that exists in the world is Lord Vishnu. There is nothing except Him. You or I and all the objects that exist, are the Soul. Give up the delusion of distinction.'

Maitreya said, 'I have already received the knowledge from you that this world is the manifestation of Vishnu, it exists in Vishnu and there is nothing except that Vishnu.'

'That Supreme Being is the manifested and the unmanifest. That universal soul Lord Hari exists as the Universe.'

'O Shankara, know yourself as inseparable from me, you are who I am. Even this world full of gods and demons and men, is the manifestation of myself. It is the men deluded by ignorance, who make a distinction.'

That, God himself is in the guises of all and is performing His act, is gradually understood by the devotee.

The loving devotee with undivided devotion, bows to all things; the sky, the air, fire, water, the earth, the Moon, the Sun and other heavenly bodies, all material objects, all creatures, the ten directions, all trees, all rivers, all oceans and all other things, thinking them to be the body of Sri Hari.

The devotee loses his self doing the service of God and in chanting His name. He offers obeisance with the belief that all are His form. His belief that, gods, human beings, beasts, birds, trees, creepers, worms and insects are all the images of God in His Leela, and that all things beginning from the atom up to the Himalayas are His forms, becomes strengthened.

Vishnudharmottara states, 'Anyone related to me is Vishnu, anyone who is my enemy is Vishnu, the heaven, the sky, the earth and the directions are Vishnu. The whole universe consisting of objects both animate and inanimate, is Vishnu. The fourteen worlds are Vishnu. I have no friends, I have no enemies, there is no collection of elements and there is no one apart from me. You, he and I are only physically different bodies of God.

I belong to that God and that King of the Gods is mine. I am not invisible to him and he is not invisible to me. I bow to God, who pervades this whole universe. I take refuge in only Him, who is mine and to whom I belong.'

While serving God, the devotee sees everything as the body of God. He also comes to look upon his own body as the 'Leela-image' of God. He begins to consider taking care of it as service to God. On eating his meal, the devotee says, 'I offered food to God.' He remembers nothing except service. Since everything is the image of God, this body is also His. The devotee is then filled with joy. He is not afraid of hearing the praise of the body and accepts it as praise of God. 'What I had so far known to be my body is the form through which He performs His Leela. Oh, what joy! What joy! I am without a separate identity. This 'Leela-Vigraha' of God is serving all the 'Leela-Vigrahas' of Himself! Oh, what joy! That Supreme Being Sri Bhagwan is playing his Leela as the doer and receiver of service, as worship and the object of worship.'

Glory to God!

Glory to service!

Glory to service!

ॐ

41. Here comes the train

One day, the madman, after having discarded all his clothes, was dancing on the bank of the Ganga, and saying, 'Rama, Rama. Here comes the train.' Haladhara came there and said, 'O mad father! Why are you dancing saying, 'Here comes the train? It seems you that you have completely lost your senses. Put on your clothes, quickly.'

Madman : Rama, Rama, Sitaram. Here comes the train. I am standing waiting for the train with my bag and baggage. Jai Sitaram.

Haladhara : Why do you say, 'Here comes the train'? What does that mean?

Madman : Have you not seen that the passengers book their tickets and wait for the train? As soon as the bell announces the arrival of the train, they pick up their bag and baggage and keep looking in the direction from which the train is expected. They board the train as soon as it comes. Since my train is about to arrive, I too, am standing with my bag and baggage, ready to board. Rama, Rama, Sitaram, Jai Jai Rama, Sitaram.

Haladhara : People wait for the train with their luggage but you have taken off your clothes and are dancing and saying 'Rama Rama'. Where is your luggage?

Madman : Rama, Rama, Sitaram. Well, this cage made of the five elements is the bigggest baggage. I am dancing because I will board the train with it.

Haladhara : What you are calling the cage, is you!

Madman : Rama, Rama, Sitaram. As fish and water are not the same, as the water-pot and the sky in the waterpot are different, and as man and his cloth are not one, this cage and I are different. Rama, Rama, Sitaram, Jai Jai Rama, Sitaram.

Haladhara : How do you know that you and your cage are separate?

Madman : Rama, Rama, Sitaram. I know it well.

Haladhara : How do you know it?

Madman : Jai Jai Rama, Sitaram. The Mother of 'I' is singing inside day and night. She has overwhelmed the cage by singing tunes and songs that sometimes sound like the cloud, the storm, an engine, a fountain or the cricket. No effort by the cage could stop her singing. Sitaram, by dancing and singing she creates points of light. She dances freely, creating points of light or vast empty spaces. By the impact of her dancing this cage has been shattered and ruined. Through this incessant dancing and singing I have realised that I am not this cage. The cage and I are separate. Rama, Rama, Sitaram.

Haladhara : Well, father, can 'I' be seen?

Madman : Rama, Rama, Sitaram. It can certainly be seen. However, 'I' sometimes hides behind the sound of 'OM' produced while chanting 'Whenever...' or while saying 'Soham' or 'Sohamasmi' or 'Shivoham', and cannot be located. Rama, Rama, Sitaram. Jai Jai Sitaram.

Haladhara : How does 'I' look?

Madman : Rama, Rama, Sitaram. Does 'I' always come out in the same guise?

Sometimes 'I' assumes the form of a supreme light; bright, incomparable and charming. Sometimes it becomes a very little point. Sometimes it becomes bigger and bigger, and becomes a vast empty space and smiles softly. Sometimes it swallows up everything and cannot be fathomed. What it becomes and what it does cannot be understood, Sitaram. Rama, Rama, Sitaram, Jai Jai Rama, Sitaram.

Haladhara : What good comes of the realization of 'I'?

Madman : Rama, Rama, Sitaram. If one attains 'I', nothing else remains to be achieved.

Everything comes to an end. One can become self-contented and self-satisfied. Rama, Rama, Sitaram. Once the four-headed Master said, 'I is sinless, free from decrepitude, deathless, free from mourning, free from hunger and thirst, seeker of truth and true to his vows. He alone should be sought. It should be one's duty to specifically know the 'I'. Those who get to know and experience the 'I', receive all that is desirable.' Rama, Rama, Sitaram, Jai Jai Rama, Sitaram.

Haladhara : What happens after that?

Madman : Without knowing this, Indra, the king of the Gods and Virochana, the king of the demons, went to Brahma. After they had performed penance and observed the code of conduct for thirty-two years, Brahma said, 'This Purusha that is visible to the eyes is 'I'.' Though he tried to illustrate and explain to Indra and Virochana, they could not understand completely. They left thinking the body to be the 'I'. Virochana took the cage for 'I' and went away. While on his way back, Indra realized that the cage was not 'I'. He returned and performed penance for another thirty-two years. Still he did not understand the truth. He went back to do yet another penance for thirty-two years. He still did not get the desired knowledge. After another five years' penance, the swan-riding Brahma gave him the complete knowledge.

After a total of one hundred and one years' hard penance, Indra received the knowledge of 'I'. Rama, Rama, Sitaram. Jai Jai Rama, Sitaram.

Haladhara : Mad father, I did not follow what you said about 'I'.

Madman : Rama, Rama, Sitaram. Everything is 'I'. The eye within eye is 'I'; the ear within the ear is 'I'; the nose within the nose is 'I'; the skin within the skin is 'I' and the mind within the mind is 'I'.

Haladhara : Where does 'I' live?

Madman : Rama, Rama, Sitaram. It lives in the eyes. Within the black pupils of the eyes is the dwelling place of 'I'. The master lives in the right eye and the mistress lives in the left eye. He lives even in the point in the middle of the forehead. Rama, Rama, Sitaram.

The madman began to dance saying, 'Here comes the train, here comes the train.'

Haladhara : Well, stop, stop. I have not completed my queries about the 'I'. How many forms of 'I' are there?

Madman : Rama, Rama, Sitaram, Jai Jai Rama, Sitaram. The Great 'I' is one. When he likes to play, he assumes crores of tiny forms and thus arise innumerable universes. He plays with the various forms of himself. Rama, Rama,

Sitaram. Here comes the train. Those who had come have gone away. Rama, Rama.

Haladhara : If Indra, the King of the Gods, had to stay in the house of his Guru for one hundred and one years to know 'I', there is no hope for us.

Madman : Rama, Rama, Sitaram. Well, this is not heaven; it is the mortal world. It is not the Satyayuga; this is the Kaliyuga. You have only to chant the name of Rama. If you can chant the name of Rama always, know your voyage to be complete. The Big 'I' and the tiny 'I' will begin to dance freely. In the end, the Big 'I' will swallow the tiny 'I'. There will be no trace of the tiny 'I'. Rama, Rama, Sitaram. Jai Jai Rama, Sitaram.

Haladhara : Mad father, what is the name of the 'I'?

Madman : Rama, Rama, Sitaram. All names are the names of 'I'; all forms are the forms of 'I'. 'I' itself is taking form of everything and playing. Once the Big 'I' told Brahma, 'At the beginning of the creation I alone existed, after the creation I was whatever there was, and after the creation is destroyed, I alone will remain.' Rama, Rama, Sitaram, Jai Jai Rama, Sitaram.

Haladhara : I cannot understand that, please explain.

Madman : Yogis call Kundalini as 'I'. The Vaishnava fathers call it Radharani and Jnani call it

Omkara. In the Sharada Tilaka the five-faced God riding an ox says, 'The consciousness of all beings is Shabdha-Brahma which resides in the bodies of all creatures as Kundalini.' Rama, Rama, Sitaram. Jai Jai Rama, Sitaram.

Do you wish to listen to some more?

Prapanchasara, says, 'This Omkar which is the seed, resides within all creatures. It also extends over the universe consisting of fourteen worlds. It pervades everything, whether movable or immovable. It is called Nada, Prana, Jeeva, Ghosha, etc.' Rama, Rama, Sitaram, Jai Jai Rama Sitaram.

Haladhara : How shall I find 'I', mad father?

Madman : Ceaselessly go on chanting the Name.

> *Surely will you gain direct perception of your Dear,*
>
> *He who chants the Name always*
>
> *is soon emancipated.*
>
> *God Himself appears as the Name,*
>
> *Dedicate your mind and life*
>
> *to the chanting of the Name.*
>
> *Rama, Rama, Rama.*
>
> *Well, well, listen to an old song.*

*A sweet strain is rising, resonating in
the sky*

*Who is that singing the chant 'He is I,
He is 'I'?*

*The cloud roars again and again, not
a drop of rain falls.*

*Being possessed, the body, life and
mind are absorbed,*

The body is thrilled.

*The singer is singing far away in
heaven,*

The song in that empty space.

It is bringing a flood of joy,

Into this trembling body of mine.

The startled mind longs for you,

Loving Lord, do not remain away

Let me see You.

Singing 'Rama, Rama, Sitaram, Jai Jai Rama, Sitaram', the
madman begins to dance with abandon.

Haladhara watches the ceaseless dance of the madman,
becomes struck and begins to chant 'Rama, Rama, Sitaram,
Jai Jai Rama, Sitaram.'

Rama, Rama, Sitaram, Jai Jai Rama, Sitaram.

ಅ ॐ ಬ

42. An Emaciated Sadhu

Hari   : Well, Dada, where had you been?

Hara   : Well, brother, I had been to see a Sadhu.

Hari   : What kind of Sadhu was he?

Hara   : He was sitting in the middle of a small room with his head leaning on a wall, and women surrounded him from the other three sides.

Hari   : What sort of women were they?

Hara   : Children, elderly and young women. They were from six-year old children to sixty year old women. They had surrounded the Sadhu. The room was packed. Those who could not enter the room were unhappy. They were looking at the Sadhu through the windows.

Hari   : What was the sadhu saying?

Hara   : 'Come in, there is room for more.'

Hari   : Is the Sadhu beautiful to look at?

Hara   : No, no. He is very old, with grey beard and moustache. Even his eyebrows are grey. He seems to be about 70 or 72 years old. He is toothless, bony, sickly and emaciated.

Hari : Why are the women so eager to see such an emaciated Sadhu and sit near him? What is going on? Does he smoke hemp or such other drugs?

Hara : O, no, no. Leave alone being addicted, he does not even smoke a cigarette or chew betel leaves or tobacco.

Hari : Does he accept much service from women?

Hara : Not at all. He does not accept any kind of service from any one.

Hari : What do the women do?

Hara : They sit there; call him 'father' again and again, and chant the Name.

Hari : What does he do?

Hara : He narrates stories about God and reads to them from books. The women just do not want to leave his company.

Hari : Do the women surround him day and night?

Hara : No, no. Perhaps the women remain for two hours. Then the men come in for the next two. Then the women come in again, followed by the men. This way he remains surrounded by people, day and night. Only by mid-night does he get some respite. Then, he and his disciples go to sleep. The crowds return in the morning; alternating sessions of men and women. This has been going on day after day. Is it good for a Sadhu to remain in the midst of women always in that way? Many men are speaking ill of him.

Hara : He does not remain always with women. You say that men also surround him. Then why do people blame him?

Hari : They speak ill of the Sadhu but also go and prostrate before him, and remain standing with folded hands. The matter cannot at all be understood.

Hari : What does the Sadhu say when he hears of his dispraise?

Hara : The Sadhu says that Muni Sanatsujata gave King Dhritarashtra the advice that it was the nature of those who were honest, to praise and those dishonest, to blame. So one should be neither be elated on hearing one's praise nor deflated on being dispraised. The Sadhu loves his critics. He says 'A detractor is a great friend of mine. By speaking ill of me, my detractor frees me from the sins that none of my relations, sons, friends and disciples will take.' He is an interesting Sadhu. He himself bows three times a day to the critics and asks everyone to do so. To him his detractor is much dearer than his admirer. He loves the drunkards, thieves, impostors, rogues and the licentious more than the ordinary people. He says, 'Can a man who is good be made better? If a licentious man and a drunkard take to the good path, the world will be greatly benefited.'

Hari : A strange Sadhu indeed! Is he not afraid of disrepute?

Hara : He is afraid neither of disrepute nor of fame. The Shastras and the Sadhus say that a man should put his fingers into his ears and leave the place as soon as anybody praises him. But that withered Sadhu listens to his praise without the least uneasiness and with great delight.

Hari : What does the Sadhu say after listening to praise?

Hara : He says, 'This is the praise of God. Nobody praises me. God has given me His Name to sing and keeps me near Him. Hence, so many people say so many things. Nobody will look at my face if today I give up chanting His name and commit something unjust.

Hari : I see that he is a unique Sadhu. But what needs to be considered, is why do boys, girls, the elderly, the youth , the rich and the poor, love him? Why do they seek his company? Why do they look upon him as their own? What is the reason for this?

Hara : I do not find any reason, dada. I have fallen in love with him at first sight.

Hari : Does he know any hypnotizing mantra?

Hara : What will he gain by hypotising anybody? He does not want anything from anybody. Rather, he gives everybody what he wants, according to his ability.

Hari : Where does he get it?

Hara : The disciples supply it. He does not pay attention to anything.

(Outside the madman chants 'Rama, Rama, Sitaram, Jai Jai Rama, Sitaram.)

There comes the mad father. Let us ask him.

(The madman enters dancing and singing 'Jai Jai Rama, Sitaram')

Harihara : Mad father, we bow to you.

Madman : Jai Jai Rama, Sitaram. I too bow to you. Jai Jai Rama, Sitaram.

Hari : Mad father, tell us why do men and women of all ages surround a Sadhu day and night? Why do women and men take turns to sit around him? We cannot clearly understand what the matter is.

Madman : Rama, Rama, Sitaram. How does the sadhu look? Does he like singing and dancing?

Rama, Rama.

Hara	:	He is bony, old and toothless. All his hair looks like flax. There is no telling his age. It does not seem that anyone in his past seven generations knew how to sing.
Madman	:	What attraction makes men and women love him? Rama, Rama, Sitaram.
Hari	:	That is what we are asking you.
Madman	:	Rama, Rama, Sitaram. Jai Jai Rama, Sitaram. If there is no outward reason for their love, Rama, Rama, they love him for the root cause. Rama, Rama, Sitaram. Jai Jai Rama, Sitaram.
Hari	:	What is the root cause?
Madman	:	Rama, Rama, Sitaram. Bliss! Rama, Rama, Sitaram. All the creatures are born of joy. They live in joy and will re-enter joy in the end, Rama, Rama, Sitaram. Perhaps he has attained bliss.
Hari	:	What is the proof that he has attained bliss?
Madman	:	Rama, Rama, Sitaram. The proof of this is that young and old, men and women, rich and poor, love him. Rama, Rama, Sitaram. Is anything known of his previous life? Rama, Rama.
Hari	:	Yes, he has lived with the name of God since

his boyhood. His disciples also try to live always with the name of God.

Madman : Rama, Rama, Jai Rama, Jai Sitaram, we now know the cause. Rama, Rama, Sitaram. That God, who is bliss, appears in the gross form as Name. The Name and the one who has the Name are not different. That is why the men and women, hankering after happiness, always surround the Sadhu. Rama, Rama, Sitaram.

Hari : Does he who chants the Name, find the blissful Lord?

Madman : Jai Jai Rama, Sitaram. Yes Sitaram. The name of Hari is the purest essence. The place where the Name is chanted becomes filled with the purest essence. Therefore, men and women tormented by the Rajas and Tamas surround that Sadhu, to get rid of their suffering. Jai Jai Rama, Sitaram.

Hari : How does the place where the Name is chanted, get filled with purest essence?

Madman : Rama, Rama, Sitaram, Jai Jai Rama, Sitaram. If iron is kept in fire what becomes of iron? Rama, Rama, Sitaram.

Hari : Iron is transformed into fire. All the energy of fire enters the iron.

Madman : Similarly, the power of the Name enters into him who is always immersed in the Name.

Rama, Rama, Sitaram. This is a unique transaction. Great scholars and learned men also start proclaiming the person who has the Name, as God. Rama, Rama, Sitaram

Hari : I see that the Name has great power.

Madman : Rama, Rama. Chant the Name and see what happens. Jai Sitaram. People will bow down to you as God. Rama, Rama, Sitaram. Jai Jai Sitaram, Jai Jai Rama, Sitaram. In the end, you will have to flee the place, overwhelmed by people's attention. Rama, Rama, Sitaram.

Chant the Name, father, chant the Name. Sin and suffering, disease and grief, sorrow and poverty flee from him who chants the Name. Heaps of money is poured at his feet. Men and women, rich and poor, run frantically for the dust off his feet, a loving look or a moment's company. Rama, Rama, Sitaram.

Hari : O mad father, are you speaking of this Age?

Madman : Rama, Rama, Sitaram. I am not speaking of the Satya, Treta and Dwapar Yugas. I am speaking of this Age. Rama, Rama, Sitaram. Jai Jai Rama, Sitaram

Hari : Can you show Him to us?

Madman : Rama, Rama, Sitaram. Surely I can. Rama, Rama, Sitaram.

'The Name and Hari are indivisible

Hari appears there where the Name is chanted'.

(The madman begins to dance with abandon).

Hari : It will not do merely to dance like this. You must show Him to us.

Madman : Rama, Rama, Sitaram. Surely I will show you, come along with me.

(The madman goes out dancing and chanting 'Sri Rama, Jai Rama, Jai Jai Rama'. Along with him, Hari and Hara also go out dancing and singing 'Sri Rama, Jai Rama, Jai Jai Rama').

ಇ ॐ ೞ

43. The Rama Naam Charitable Dispensary

Rama, Rama, Sitaram. A devotee has given the Madman a room in the bazar. The Madman has put up a board in bold letters 'Raam Naam Charitable Dispensary'.

The name of Rama is written on all the walls. Tulsi is planted outside. The Madman is chanting the name of Rama.

A woman comes in and asks, 'O father, is it the dispensary of the Mad father'?

Madman   : Yes, Rama, Rama. What ails you?

Woman   : A bad headache.

Madman   : Only chant the name of Rama. At dawn, drink water through the nose. Bathe three times in the day. Eat less. Always chant the name of Rama. Your disease will be cured.

Woman   : Mad father, will I be cured?

Madman   : Rama, Rama, Rama, Rama. Surely it will be cured. Say, 'Rama, Rama, Rama'

(The woman bows and goes away chanting the name of Rama).

(An old man enters and bows).

Old man   : Save me father.

Madman   : What ails you? Rama, Rama.

Old man   : I am suffering from asthma.

Madman   : Rama, Rama. Make a garden of Tulsi plants and try to live in it as much as possible. Eat what is easily digestible. And always chant the name of Rama. Chant the name of Rama regularly in the morning, noon and evening.

Old man   : Baba, will I be cured?

Madman   : There is no ailment in this world which cannot be cured by chanting the name of Rama. Say, Rama, Rama.

(The old man goes away uttering the name of Rama)

(A Youngman enters and bows)

Madman   : Rama, Rama, Sitaram. What ails you? Rama, Rama.

Y. Man   : I am afflicted by phthisis.

Madman   : Rama, Rama. Is there any river near your house?

Y. Man   : Yes, I live just on the bank of the Ganga.

Madman   : Rama, Rama, Sitaram. Have you any garden? Rama, Rama.

Y. Man   : Yes.

Madman   : Rama, Rama, Rama, Rama. Create a garden
               of Tulsi plants on one or two grounds of
               land. Make a cottage in it and write the name
               of Rama on its walls. Live inside the cottage
               during sunshine and rain. Spend the rest of
               the time in the Tulsi garden, chanting the
               name of Rama.

Y. Man   : Will I be cured?

Madman   : I have seen people live as well as die chanting
               the name of Rama. Who can save the person,
               whose time of death has come? Chant the
               name of Rama. Regularly perform Japa in
               the morning, noon and evening. Write the
               name of Rama.

Y. Man   : What should be my diet?

Madman   : Rama, Rama, Sitaram. Eat sundried rice,
               plantain, *dal* made of peas, sugarcane jaggery,
               sea salt and cow's milk. Eat only as much as
               you can digest. And utter the name of Rama.
               He dwells in your heart. Beg his pardon for
               offences committed previously.

Y. Man   : What offence have I committed?

Madman   : Men are attacked with diseases because of
               indisciplined living. Rama, Rama. You have
               committed many irregularities and excess on
               your body. Rama, Rama.

Y. Man   : True, I did not observe discipline in my life.

Madman   : Rama, Rama. What has happened can't be helped. Only chant the name of Rama. He is within you. Till He responds and till He calls you, go on chanting His name.

Y. Man   : My mind is very restless.

Madman   : Rama, Rama. Let it be so. If you go on chanting the name of Rama, the mind will become steady. Rama, Rama. Phthisis is an infectious disease. Don't allow anybody to come near you. Bury your sputum and phlegm under the earth. Rama, Rama. Drink at least two and a half litres of water everyday. Light, water and air are good in the countryside. Always live in a ventilated place. Rama, Rama, Rama, Rama. You also say, 'Rama Rama Rama.'

(The Youngman bows and goes away uttering the name of Rama.)

(A boy enters).

Madman   : Rama, Rama. What ails you? Rama, Rama.

Boy   : I have the problem of bed-wetting and I am unable to commit my lessons to memory.

Madman   : Rama, Rama. Bow before your father, mother and other elders, daily in the morning, noon and evening. Drink the juice of Tulsi leaves. Always chant the name of Rama. Chant the name of Rama ten thousand times in the morning and in the evening. Do not eat rice at night. Do not drink water in the night. Lie on a hard bed. Sit on the bed and say the name of Rama, five thousand times. Rama, Rama, Rama, Rama. Say 'Rama Rama'.

Boy : How shall I keep count?

Madman : With the garland of Tulsi beads. Rama, Rama. Tell the beads this way (shows the method) and keep the count. Rama, Rama, Rama.

(The boy bows and goes away repeating the name of Rama)

(A Youngman enters)

Madman : Sitaram, what ails you?

Y. Man : I have a great pain in my stomach. I cannot digest anything.

Madman : Rama, Rama. Do you observe any rules about chanting? Do you eat anywhere and from the hands of everybody?

Y. man · : Yes.

Madman : Rama, Rama. You have invited pain. It is sure to cause you suffering. Everything depends on food. Those who eat pure food are not attacked by diseases. They always hear the call of God. Are you addicted to any intoxicating drug? How many cups of tea do you drink? Jai Sitaram.

Y. Man : I smoke twenty-five *bidis*, drink eight cups of tea and consume small quantities of opium.

Madman : Rama, Rama, Rama. Your disease is incurable. If you want to be cured, you must become peaceful. Drinking tea and smoking *bidis* is the same as taking poison. Rama, Rama, Rama. You must give up your addiction.

Y. Man : I try but I am not able to.

Madman : Only chant the name of Rama. You have been born as a man, you must find God. One addicted to intoxication cannot find God. He for whom the world has any fascination is far away from God. Day and night, utter the name of Rama at all times. Your addiction will go. Eat light food. Fill one-half of your stomach with food, one fourth with water and keep one-fourth empty for air. You must give up taking your meals from the hands of everyone and everywhere. Rama, Rama. Will you be able to do so?

Y. Man : I can do so.

Madman : Only chant the name of Rama. Your disease will be cured. Pray three times a day.

(The Youngman bows and goes away muttering the name of Rama.

Madman : Rama, Rama, Rama. Sitaram, Sitaram.

(A middle-aged man enters.)

Madman : Rama, Rama, what ails you?

Man : I cannot sleep at night.

Madman : Rama, Rama, Rama. Eat pure food. Utter the name of Rama in every breath. At dawn, drink at least a quart of water through your nose. In the afternoon sit on the bank of some river and watch the water for at least an hour. And utter the name of Rama. Drink the juice of Tulsi leaves. Rama, Rama, Rama.

Man : Will this disease be cured simply if I utter the name of Rama?

Madman : It is an ordinary disease! Sitaram, if one utters the name of Rama the disease of existence is cured. There remains nothing to see or hear except God. There is no cause of worry. Go on repeating the name of Rama.

(The middle-aged man goes away repeating the name of Rama).

Madman : Rama, Rama, Sitaram. Jai Jai Rama, Sitaram.

(A young man enters).

Madman : What is the matter with you?

Y. Man : There is a great want in the family. Diseases visit us often. I think of being good, of remaining restrained but I cannot. I commit wrong.

Madman : Rama, Rama, Sitaram. Always chant the name of Rama and everything will be set right. Pure food is the best medicine for the body and mind. The mind is purified only by the purification of body.

The person, who eats fish, meat, non-vegetarian things and drinks honey on Sunday, becomes a patient for seven lives and poor in every birth. He goes to the Suryaloka. Neem and ginger also are forbidden for Sunday. Those who want to keep their body healthy should follow the path shown by the scriptures. Do you know which kinds of food should not be eaten on certain *tithis*? Jai Sitaram.

Y. Man : No.

Madman : Know it and take care in the matter of food.

Y. Man : What have ailments to do with *tithis*?

Madman : Rama, Rama. Do you know that rheumatism, hydrocele etc give pain on the New Moon and Full Moon Tithis?

Y. Man : I know.

Madman : Whatever concerns man depends on the Sun. The Sun preserves every living being as life. The external life of everybody is the Sun. The blood is polluted on the New Moon and Full Moon. According to the movement of the Sun, rheumatism, and such other diseases get the upper hand on these days. On the Pratipada (the first lunar day), the movement of the Sun affects the gourd and it gets contaminated; eating it can cause illness. On the eighth lunar day, the movement of the Sun pollutes the coconut, which perverts the intellect. So if a man eats the coconut on the eighth lunar day, he becomes foolish. On the thirteenth lunar day, the movement of the Sun affects the brinjal and semen-polluting germs appear. So the eating brinjal on this Tithi prevents or causes loss of progeny. Rama, Rama, Sitaram.

Y. Man   : I do not understand these things.

Madman   : Rama, Rama. You have not done anything to help you understand them. You have only finished your body by unregulated diet. Judge Woodroff cut open a brinjal at the end of the twelth lunar day and examined it through the microscope. He said that as soon as the thirteenth day set in, the brinjal was filled with tiny germs. Again, on the fourteenth day, he said that there were no more germs. Rama, Rama, Sitaram. Everything depends on the Sun. Utter the name of Rama. Bow to the Sun. Eat pure food and chant the name of Rama.

Y. Man   : Will my poverty be removed if I chant the name of Rama?

Madman   : Rama, Rama, Sitaram. God will have mercy on

you. He says, 'I take away the poverty of that man whom I favour.' Only chant the name of Rama. He will take your entire burden and set your anxiety completely at rest. He has promised, 'I bring to them who meditates on me with undivided attention, what they do not have and I protect what they have.' Do not worry. Not a single Name will go in vain. There is hope for you however sinning, however feeble, however unrestrained you may be. Only go on chanting the name of Rama and the torture of disease, grief, want, lust and such other things will vanish.

(The Youngman goes away chanting the name of Rama.)

(A 'Babu' enters).

Madman : Rama, Rama, Sitaram.

Babu : Hello, Baba! What's your design here?

Madman : A charitable dispensary of the name of Rama.

Babu : Which diseases are cured by your name of Rama?

Madman : There is no disease in the world but is cured by the name of Rama. There is no problem but is solved by the name of Rama. This is said loudly in all the Shastras.

Babu : Mad father, it is the age of science. Nobody will now accept what is said in the rotten Shastras by all those Rishis.

Madman : Rama, Rama, Sitaram. Jai Jai Rama, Sitaram. It is because Shastric injunctions are not accepted that there are so many diseases, needing hospitals in every village. All are proclaiming the victory of science. Its noise is drowning out the cry of millions for food. Science has brought merely the message of enjoyment and has increased the suffering. Rama, Rama. Peace does not dwell outside; it dwells inside. The spell for entering inside is to chant the name of Rama.

Babu : I will listen neither to your rotten Shastras nor to a fraud! Can you tell me which educated respectable man in this age has spoken of your name of Rama and has said that diseases are cured by the name of Rama?

Madman : Rama, Rama, Sitaram. Have you heard of the name of Mahatma Gandhi?

Babu : Who is there in the world who has not heard his name?

Madman : Rama, Rama, Sitaram. Do you follow what he says?

Babu : I follow him a million times.

Madman : Rama, Rama. He says in Ramnama Ki Mahima, 'Today my sole physician is my Rama. As I go on singing hymns during prayer, Rama dispels all physical, mental and moral ailments. He who has the name of Rama in his heart stands in no need of any residence. The worshipper of Rama has no need of anything on the earth or water.'

Babu : Has Mahatmaji said these things?

Madman : He not only said them in the secret but also wrote them in books. He says, 'Similarly, he who seeks refuge in the name of Rama in unrest wins.'

It was not only Tulsidasji who sang the glory of the name of Rama. I also find it in the Bible. In the Romans 10.13 it is said that he who will take the name of God will be delivered. We are saved much trouble if we look upon the diseases in this manner and understand that Rama is the sole Vaidya, who can cure them all.

Babu : Which of his books contains these things?

Madman : Rama, Rama. Some devotee of his collected his messages from many of his books and from The Harijan and published them in a book called Ramanama Ki Mahima. Would you like to hear more on this?

Babu : Will I not listen? I will listen to Bapuji as long as I live.

Madman : There is nothing equal to the golden rule of saying the name of Rama in conquering matter. If there is any violation of the vow during sleep, the expiation for it is generally greater caution and the uttering of the name of Rama whenever one wakes up.

An unfailing way for being saved from perverted thinking is the name of Rama. If a man is attacked by a disease, it must be cured by taking name of Rama with sincerity.

The name of Rama is the same as Ishwar, Khuda, Allah and God.

Is not the name of Rama the central point in naturopathy?

Rama and I have nothing to do with the occult.

The real physician is Rama.

Man becomes well protected by the name of Rama. The only condition is that the name of Rama must come from within.

Did you hear, Sitaram, what Mahatmaji says?

Babu : He has laid emphasis on the words coming from the heart. Nothing will come of repeating the name orally like a parrot.

Madman : It is quite true that if the name of Rama is uttered with undivided attention by establishing harmony between the mind and the Prana, immediate result can be had. But for those who cannot do so, the Shastras say

'Whether by slighting or by reverence, with devotion or without devotion, if a man hears or utters the name of Rama by any means, he becomes successful.' A great man has said, 'If one is not able to involve one's body or mind, one can pray only by words. Bhajan has such powers that everything becomes divine.' Rama, Rama.

Babu : O Mad baba! I find your words very good. Let me ask you a question, 'A man in need may utter the name of Rama to get rid of illness and necessity; why will, he who does not suffer from any disease, has no need and unrest, labour in vain?'

Madman : Rama, Rama, Sitaram. There is no man without a physical or mental disease or need. So, all should utter the name of Rama. The name of Rama means God's name. If anybody utters the name given by his preceptor, he will be able to reach his destination.

Babu : Where is the destination? Man is born, lives for some time and then dies. He suffers from anxiety and troubles. What can give him peace? What can he do to live in peace in this world?

Madman : Man becomes successful if he discovers the 'I'. What men call the 'I' is not the real 'I' but the cage of 'I'.

Babu : Who is 'I'? Where is that 'I'?

Madman : 'I' is a part of God. 'I' is the Bindu, the light. 'I' resides in the heart. Pure food in a small quantity, good company, worship of God at all times, Japa and Dhyana lead to the Darshan of Pranava full of light, with Nada as its soul. Rama, Rama, Rama.

Babu : Then is light the Soul?

Madman : Rama, Rama, Sitaram. Yes.

It is said in the Annapurna and Rudrahridaya Upanishads, 'Paramarthikam is Pashupata Brahma. Those whose faults have worn away can see this Light in their own bodies. Those who are blind-folded by illusion cannot see it.'

Tattva Samagita says, 'Light is the Supreme Brahma. Light is the Supreme beatitude. Light is the highest peace. Light is the highest state.'

Babu : What is fault?

Madman : Rama, Rama. According to Mandala Brahmana Upanishad lust, anger, breath, fear, sleep; are faults.

Babu : How can they be removed?

Madman : By giving up, resolution, forgiveness, light meals, freedom from mistakes and wisdom.

Babu : What is he to do, who cannot do these things?

Madman   : All can be achieved by chanting the name of Rama. Man is sure to get what he wants by uttering the name of Rama. There is no medicine for diseases greater than pure meals, good company and the name of Rama in the world.

Babu   : I have become a slave to desires. It is not possible for me to have pure food and get good company. How am I to be saved?

Madman   : Chant the name of Rama at all times. By your calling, the mad woman will wake up. If she begins to sing, it is done. She herself will drag you to the very ocean of Joy and keep you immersed in it for ever. Rama, Rama, Sitaram. Jai Jai Rama, Sitaram.

Sing the name of Rama, say the name of Rama and meditate on Rama.

Rama, Rama, Rama.

ॐ

Glossary of Sanskrit and Indian Words

Ajamil: a character from Puranas, who with a single act of the utterance of a four-syllable word Narayana at the end of his life attained to God

Ana: one ana is equal to *six paisa*. *Ana* was in practice as a unit for buying and selling commodities in the early 50s

Arati: also spelled *arathi*, *aarthi* (from the Sanskrit word *aratrik* with the same meaning) is a Hindu religious ritual of worship, a part of *puja*, in which light from wicks soaked in ghee (purified butter) or camphor is offered to one or more deities

Asamprajnata Samadhi: highest superconscious state where the mind is completely annihilated and reality experienced

Ayodhya: also known as Saket is an ancient city of India, birthplace of the lord Vishnu's Hindu Avatar Rama, and setting of the epic Ramayana

Bazaar: Marketplace

Bhoga: Prasad, offerings for puja (prayer)

Bidi: hand-rolled leaf cigarette made in India

Bija: Seed

Burning-Ghat: Hindus "cremation" *ghats* where bodies are cremated waterside, allowing ashes to be washed away by rivers

Chakra: Vishnu's Discus

Charkha: spinning wheel, was the physical embodiment and symbol of Gandhi's constructive program. It represents localism (*swadeshi*) and self-sufficiency

Chaturmasya: the four months of the rainy season in India (approximately July, August, September, and October). During this period, there are certain rules and regulations which are strictly followed to decrease sense enjoyment and increase remembrance of the Lord.

Damaru: Tabour (of Shiva)

Danda: The word *danda* literally means stick or a staff and is also used in the sense of control and restraint, as in *vag-danda, karma-danda, mano-danda* etc.

Darshan: Vision, sight of, philosophy

Dhaks, Dhols, Kansar, Kamanagara, Drums, Khols, Cymbals: musical instruments used in singing hymns

Dhruva: in Hindu scriptures, Dhruva was an ardent young devotee of Vishnu, a prince blessed to eternal existence and glory

Diksha: Spiritual initiation from a Guru

Draupadi: In the epic Mahabharata, Draupadi is the "emerged" daughter of King Drupada of Panchala and the wife of the five Pandavas

Dravyashuddhi: All of the articles to be offered in worship must be physically pure according to scriptural standards. When physical purity is attained, the articles are then spiritualized with mantra and mudra.

Fifth Veda: Pancham Veda, text which lies outside the four canonical Vedas. This reference to *itihasa* was used by the Mahabharata, which belonged to the class of epic literature called *"itihasa"*, to refer to itself as the fifth Veda.

Gopikas:The name *gopi* (sometimes *gopika*) is used more commonly to refer to the group of cowherding girls famous within Vaishnava Theology for their unconditional devotion (*Bhakti*) to Krishna as described in the stories of Bhagavata Purana and other Puranic literatures

Hanuman, Sugriva, Guhaka, Jatayu, Vibhishana and Shabari: characters from Ramayana

Hari Om: 'Hari Om Tat Sat' is a very ancient mantra from the Vedas. 'Hari' represents the manifest universe and life. 'Om' represents the unmanifest and absolute reality. Together they laud the total Reality as God

Havishya: Sacrificial food

Jeevanmukta: liberation from *samsara*, the cycle of death and rebirth

Jholi: an Indian sling bag, generally made of rugged cotton

Kamandalu: Kamandalu or kamandal is an oblong water pot made of a dry gourd (pumpkin) or coconut shell, metal, wood of the Kamandalataru tree, or from clay, usually with a handle and sometimes with a spout. Hindu ascetics or yogis often use it for storing drinking water.

Karana Deha: *Karana Deha* or causal body or soul is formed by the combination of causal elements. The causal elements viz., the causal atoms of the above elements in the seed form are responsible for the formation of the causal body. All the three bodies are organised and systematised by the combination of atoms only. Therefore, the attributes, actions and habits or *Svabhava* are formed according to those atoms.

Kashi: Old Varanasi, a Hindu pilgrimage city

Khaddar: handspun and hand-woven cloth

Khol: a terracotta two-sided drum used in northern and eastern India for accompaniment with devotional music (*bhakti*). It originates from the Indian states of West Bengal, Assam and Manipur. The drum is played with palms and fingers of both hands.

King Ambarisha: Ambarisha was a great devotee of Vishnu and adhered firmly to the truth. He performed a Yagnya with such great devotional fervour that Lord Narayan was pleased to bless him with Sudarshana Chakra (Sudarshana meaning "good looking") and which manifested as a wheel of prosperity, peace and security to his kingdom.

Kumkum: a powder used for social and religious markings in Hinduism. It is either made from turmeric or saffron

Leela: Within non-dualism, Leela is a way of describing all reality, including the cosmos, as the outcome of creative play by the divine absolute (Brahman). In the dualistic schools of Vaishnavism, Leela more simply refers to the activities of God and his devotees, as distinct from the common activities of karma.

Madhyama: the intermediate unexpressed state of sound experienced in the heart

Markandeya, Narada, Vyasa, Vashistha and Vishwamitra: Hindu sages of highest order

Namaskar: salutation, prostration

Namavali: a lyrical string of names expressing divine attributes or the nature of the Divinity

Navadwip, Shantipur, Nilachal and Vrindavana: holy places especially graced by Sri Chaitanya Mahaprabhu

Nirmalya: floral decorations of worship of the previous evening.

Nirvikalp Samadhi: Samadhi in which there is no objective experience or experience of "qualities" whatsoever, and in which the triad of knower, knowledge and known does not exist; purely subjective experience of the formless and qualitiless and unconditioned Absolute. The highest state of samadhi, beyond all thought, attribute, and description.

Pinda: offerings of food to the deceased

Prahlada: a saintly boy from the Puranas known for his piety and bhakti to Vishnu

Prana: life force

Pranayama: control of the breath

Prasad: is a material substance of food that is a religious offering in Hinduism, which is consumed by worshippers. Literally, a gracious gift. Anything, usually an edible food, that is first offered to a deity, saint, Perfect Master or an Avatar and then distributed in His or Her name to their followers or others as a good sign

Purascharan: Purascharana means chanting of the mantra as many hundred thousand times as the number of letters in the mantra. Basically one Purascharana equals 100,000 times the number of syllables in the Mantra.

Ragas and *Raginis*: melodic modes used in Indian classical music

Ram Ram: A title of Brahman the Absolute. Though sometimes used as a contraction of the name of Rama, many yogis insist that it is properly applied to Brahman alone and employ it as a mantra in repetition and meditation to reveal the Absolute.

Ratnakar: bandit born in a Brahmin family who transformed into sage Valmiki, the author of Ramayana

Rishis: the scribes of the large body of nature hymns and spiritual science known as the Vedas

Sadhana: spiritual practice

Sadhu: Seeker for truth (sat); and person who is practicing spiritual disciplines

Sahasrara: the thousand-petalled lotus within the cerebral cavity

Sakalikarana: The universe has the support of Bindu. Both Bindu and Nada together support the entire universe. The unification of the Bindu and the Nada is called Sakalikarana and the universe takes its birth as a result of this Sakalikarana

Samadhi: a non-dualistic state of consciousness in which the consciousness of the experiencing subject becomes one with the experienced object

Samhitas, Purana, Tantras: *The Puranas* are a number of scriptures attributed to the sage Vyasa that teach spiritual principles and practices through stories about sacred historical personages which often include their teachings given in conversations

Tantras: A manual of or a particular path of sadhana laying great stress upon japa of a mantra and other esoteric practices relating to the powers latent in the human complex of physical, astral, and causal bodies in relation to the cosmic Power usually thought of as the Divine Feminine

Samprajnata Samadhi: is a state of concentration in which the meditator becomes fused with the object of meditation

Sanand Samadhi: also known as "supreme bliss", or "with ecstasy", is the third level of the four *samadhi* described in the Yoga Sutras by Patanjali

Sasmita Samadhi: fourth stage of Samadhi- the *samadhi* with self-consciousness

Sattva, *Rajas* and *Tama*: the three major *guṇas* that serve as the fundamental operating principles or 'tendencies' of *prakṛti* (universal nature) which are called: *sattvaguṇa*, *rajasguṇa*, and *tamasguṇ* and are accepted to be associated with creation (*sattva*), preservation (*rajas*), and destruction (*tamas*)

Satyakama: a character in Chandogya Upanishad, a young boy who is a Truth-seeker

Savitri: a name of the *Gayatri Mantra* dedicated to Savitar

Shabda Brahman: the transcendental sound of the Vedas

Shadanga Nyasa: placing the tips of the fingers and palm of the right hand on various parts of the body (six in particular), accompanied by particular mantra

Shalagrama: refers to the name of the village on the bank of Gandaki where the holy stones representing (Shila) Vishnu are picked up

Shashtanga Pranama: Prostrate obeisance

Shastras: scriptures

Shila: refers to a Vaishnava Hindu aniconic representation of Vishnu, in the form of a spherical, usually black-coloured fossil found in the sacred river Gandaki.

Shloka: a couplet, a verse of two lines in praise of the God; a category of verse developed from the Vedic Anustubh and is the basis for Indian epic verse

Shraddh: post death Hindu rite

Shrutis: the body of sacred texts comprising the central canon of Hinduism and is believed to be a direct revelation of the "cosmic sound of truth" heard by ancient Rishis who then translated what was heard into something understandable by humans.

Sthula Deha: the physical body (*sthula*- coarse or bulky), the vehicle of all the other principles during life and the means by which man is able to function on earth. The physical body, *sthulasharira* comprises *annamaya-kosha*, the material substance and *pranamaya-kosha*.

Sudama: a childhood friend of Hindu deity Krishna from Mathura. He was Narada born as a poor man in order to enjoy the transcendental pastimes of Lord Krishna

Sudarshan Disc: a spinning, disk-like super weapon with 108 serrated edges used by the Hindu god Vishnu

Sukshma Deha: The subtle body is the vehicle of consciousness with which one passes from life to life

Sushumna: the spinal cord

Tapasya: undergoing austerity or penance for the sake of spiritual realization

Thakur: God or Guru

Tilak: a mark created by the smearing of powder or paste on the forehead

Tirtha: places of pilgrimage associated with sacred water

Tolas: a Vedic measure, traditionally the weight of 100 *ratti* (ruttee) seeds

Tulsi: a sacred plant for Hindus and is worshipped by Hindus as the avatar of goddess Lakshmi

Upanayana: Upanayana is the initiation ritual by which initiates are invested with a sacred thread, to symbolize the transference of spiritual knowledge

Upanishads, Puranas: sacred texts of Hindus

Vaidya: doctor

Vaikhari: that form of speech which is uttered, expressed, or otherwise manifested as the vehicle of thought (Vak is the whole cosmos in its objective or manifested form)

Veena: a string instrument

Yojanas: a Vedic measure of distance used in ancient India

Yoni-Mudra: The Yoni mudra can be described as a gesture that allows a person to get detached from the chaos of the outer existing world. Yoni means uterus or womb and this gesture is named the Yoni Mudra, because the person who practices it regularly has no external contact with the world, pretty much like a baby in the uterus.

ॐ ॐ ॐ